BUFFETTOLOGY

The
Previously Unexplained
Techniques
That Have Made
WARREN BUFFETT
the World's
Most Famous
Investor

$

MARY BUFFETT & DAVID CLARK

Rawson Associates

"Absolutely the best book ever written on Warren Buffett's investment methods."

STEVIN HOOVER

Hoover Capital Management/Boston

RA

RAWSON ASSOCIATES
Scribner
Simon & Schuster Inc.
1230 Avenue of the Americas
New York, NY 10020

Designed by Jenny Dossin

Manufactured in the United States of America

1   3   5   7   9   10   8   6   4   2

Library of Congress Cataloging-in-Publication Data is available.

ISBN: 0-684-83713-7

To my children

ACKNOWLEDGMENTS

We wish to thank first and foremost our publisher, Eleanor Rawson. She is simply the most amazing person either of us has ever worked with. Every ship has a captain, and she was ours. We will be forever grateful to her.

We wish also to thank the staff at Scribner. They have a reputation for being the best. We can tell you that they far surpass their reputation.

We owe a very special thank you to Cindy Connolly, who suffered with us through our early drafts. She is a gifted journalist, who with just the simple stroke of her pen, solved many a literary conundrum that perplexed your authors.

We also wish to say thank you to Dan Mountain for being a dear friend and a rock of support in the most trying of moments. To Erica and Nicole for their wise and learned counsel. To Sam for being patient with both of us. To James Haygood, a beloved friend and wonderful father. To Valerie Schadt for running everything, including our lives. To Patti, who thirty-five years ago sat a small child down on the desk of a stockbroker and said, "You can either invest in the company where your father works or the company where Mickey Mouse works." (The child chose the mouse and the mouse paid for college.) To the late and great Benjamin Graham for being the most gifted of teachers. To the late Benjamin Franklin for teaching the Commodore about compounding sums of money. To Tim Zweiback for being a guiding light in a dark forest. To Brian Belefant for being infinitely the most creative and witty of our myriad manuscript readers. To Vincent Waldman and Alan Morelli at Manatt, Phelps & Phillips for always putting their clients' interests first. To Kitty O'Keefe for being a brilliant diamond in a world of junk jewelry. To our NYC research assistant, Andy Clark, who at times dug so deep into the stacks at NYU that we thought he'd end up in China. To our Omaha research assistant, Monte Lefholtz, who somehow managed to get government employees to find historical records they still maintain don't exist. To Richard Oshlo for taking the time to answer carefully all our questions about banking. To the brilliant British painter Helen Brough, whose stunning pastel drawings and paintings brought relief to tired eyes. To NYC artist Terry Rosenberg, who showed us how to get up every morning and attack an empty white canvas with gusto. To Beatrice Bonner, a dear friend from beginning to end. To John Johnson, our guardian angel. To Susie, who every day unselfishly and most graciously shares her heart with the rest of the world. And last but not least, to W.B. for his generosity and genius.

CONTENTS

Contents

PART II: ADVANCED BUFFETTOLOGY

DISCLAIMER

This publication contains the opinions and ideas of its authors. It is not a recommendation to purchase or sell the securities of any of the companies or investments herein discussed. It is sold with the understanding that the authors and publisher are not engaged in rendering legal, accounting, investment or other professional services. Laws vary from state to state and federal laws may apply to a particular transaction, and if the reader requires expert financial or other assistance or legal advice, a competent professional should be consulted. Neither the authors nor the publisher can guarantee the accuracy of the information contained herein.

The authors and publisher specifically disclaim any responsibility for any liability, loss or risk, personal or otherwise, which is incurred as a consequence, directly or indirectly, of the use and application of any of the contents of this book.

PART I

The Art of Basic Buffettology

1

Before You Begin This Book

This book is not another cut-and-paste of Warren Buffett's letters to Berkshire Hathaway shareholders, nor is it a biography filled with anecdotes about Buffett. It is, instead, the most comprehensive case study and detailed explanation ever written of Buffett's investment techniques.

The book is designed to teach you Buffett's extraordinarily successful system of business perspective investing, from the concepts and mathematical equations that assist him in making his investment decisions to the actual companies that have captured his interest.

Warren Buffett did not participate in the writing of this book, and I am sure he never envisioned that, of all people, his former daughter-in-law would write such a book. During the 1970s, I was a businesswoman working in the management of a music publishing company and the operation of a successful import-export business. But in 1981, after a very romantic courtship, I married Warren Buffett's son Peter and found myself a member of one of the world's wealthiest families.

F. Scott Fitzgerald wrote that the very rich are different from you and me. He was right. But they are different in the strangest of ways, the oddest being the code of silence that they demand of family and friends. While married to Peter, I was instructed more than once not to speak to anyone outside the family about Warren and his investment operations. Writing this book simply would have been out of the question.

But in 1993 Peter and I were divorced, which shattered my heart into a thousand tears. Shortly thereafter, I was set upon by a flock of hopeful literary agents, all beckoning me to write an exposé about Warren Buffett and his family. Very little had been written about Warren's personal life, and the deals I was offered, I admit, given my postdivorce state of mind, were very enticing. In the end I rejected them all.

I felt at the time, and still do, that people are really, truly interested only in learning how Warren, by investing in the stock market, turned an initial $105,000 into a $20 billion-plus fortune. I always found that aspect of Warren to be completely fascinating, which is why I wrote this book and not the other.

After deciding to undertake this project, I got in touch with David Clark, an investment analyst and longtime Buffett family friend in Omaha, whom I had met at Warren's home sixteen years ago. David once suggested to Peter that he write a book on his father's investment methods. (I know that many people assume Warren's children have little or no understanding of what their father does. This is not true. From the time the children were born, and throughout their teenage years, Warren ran part of his investment operations out of a small study in the family home. Though his oldest son, Howard, and his middle daughter, Susie, are probably better versed than Peter, all of them have an excellent grasp of how their father works his investment magic.)

I asked David if he would be interested in helping with a book on Warren's business perspective investment philosophy. David is considered by many in- and outside the Buffett camp to be one of the most gifted young Buffettologists practicing today. He is also something of a financial historian. Though I felt competent to present accurately the qualitative side of Warren's method of business perspective investing, I knew that I needed someone of David's caliber to fully explain the quantitative side. To my luck, David consented and soon became a major proponent in making this book the definitive work on Warren's investment methods.

Warren's interest in teaching his philosophy to his family ebbed and flowed. In the early years of my marriage, Warren celebrated Christmas morning by tossing out to each of his children and their spouses envelopes with a gift of $10,000. Like a jolly billionaire version of old Saint Nicholas, he would fling the envelopes across the living room, laughing "Merry Christmas" to each of the delighted recipients. Later he decided that we should be taking a stronger interest in the family business and replaced the $10,000 with $10,000 worth of stock in a business in which he had recently invested. The stock of Capital Cities, Americus Trust for Coca-Cola (a publicly traded trust, no longer in existence, that held Coca-Cola stock), Freddie Mac, and Service Master were some of the great companies I found in my Christmas stocking.

It didn't take long to figure out that as bountiful as Christmas was, it was even more profitable to add to our newly acquired stock positions. Without fail, these Christmas gifts would dramatically increase in value. They truly were the gifts that kept on giving. Eventually we began to refer to these gifts as the Christmas stock tip, with both stock and tip eagerly awaited as the holidays drew near.

But they were more than just Christmas gifts or stock tips. They were Warren's way of getting us to pay attention to the companies that these stocks represented. Walter Schloss, a great investor and longtime friend of Warren's, once said that you never really know a company until you own part of it. He was absolutely right. With each Christmas gift, annual reports and dividend checks would start appearing in the mail. The *Wall Street Journal* became a household fixture, and we all began carefully tracking our newly acquired interests in these wonderful businesses.

I realized Warren had little use for typical Wall Street banter. He didn't seem to care which way the Dow Jones Industrial Average went, and he certainly had no use for all the soothsayers and their predictions. In fact, he acted as if the entire stock market didn't exist. He never looked at a chart, and if anyone tried to give him a stock tip he would usually shut him or her off. He took particular delight in attacking the Efficient Market Theory, which he thought was absolute rubbish. He seemed to care only about the individual businesses he was interested in owning. He is an intensely focused individual.

As any good Buffettologist would, I began reading the old Berkshire Hathaway annual reports and Warren's original letters to his limited partners, all of which were fascinating. I was also fortunate to be on hand the few times that Warren lectured to graduate business students at Stanford University. Peter and I would sit in the back of the room with a video camera, recording Dad for posterity.

Eventually I perused copies of Benjamin Graham's two books, *The Intelligent Investor* and *Security Analysis*. As informative and insightful as Graham's books are, it seemed that his writings were very distant from where Warren now was. It was Graham who developed the concept of business perspective investing, which is the cornerstone of Warren's philosophy.

It was around this time that Warren began showing an interest in teaching the grandchildren. I'll always remember the day I discovered our eight-year-old twin girls curled up on the living room sofa with the *Wall Street Journal* spread out before them. They had just returned from visiting Grandpa's home in Omaha, and I couldn't help but be amused at what I found. Jokingly, I asked if they had any investment ideas. They looked up and replied, "Pillsbury," and then rattled off a list of consumer monopolies that Warren had taught them Pillsbury owned. The most fascinating to them were Burger King and Häagen-Dazs ice cream. As Warren says, invest in companies that make products you understand. (Pillsbury was bought out a few years later by Grand Metropolitan at about double the price it was trading at when the twins made their recommendation.)

I started to see Warren as a sort of collector. Instead of collecting expensive paintings, palatial mansions, million-dollar yachts, or the other clutter with which many superrich fill their lives, he collects excellent businesses. He has spent the majority of his life searching out a particular kind of business in which to invest. He calls it a consumer monopoly. It is a business entity that we'll discuss later on in great detail.

I noticed that Warren, like any sophisticated collector, was very careful about the price he was willing to pay for one of these trophy businesses. In fact, the price for the business absolutely determined whether he would buy it. I am not talking about whether he could afford it. That is a given. He was simply looking for the right deal. I discovered that Warren first identifies what he wants to buy and then lets the price of the security determine whether it should be bought.

These are two distinct thoughts: What to buy? At what price? That's what this book is about—how Warren determines what companies he wants to invest in and what price he is willing to pay. Sounds simple, doesn't it? It is and it isn't.

If you are at all interested in investing, I think that you are going to find this book immensely fascinating and very profitable. David and I wrote it in a manner that allows the reader to progress through the key concepts before diving into the more detailed stuff. The first half is the qualitative side of the equation. It covers the general theories for determining what sort of companies you should be interested in. The second half is the quantitative portion, and it is loaded with math. That's where you'll learn how to determine the right price to pay. Both parts are key to your understanding of Warren's investment philosophy. We think that you will find this book a complete revelation, for we cover an immense amount of never-before-seen material.

We have given you a list of fifty-four companies in which Warren has invested in the past and in which we believe he is still interested. Most of these companies are being identified as Buffett companies for the first time. But one word of caution. Don't fall into the trap of thinking that just because Warren might be interested in owning more of a certain company, you should buy it at any price. We will show you how to determine the right price. Please be patient.

We have incorporated into the book the use of a Texas Instruments BA-35 Solar financial calculator. Twenty-five years ago these little wonders didn't exist, but thanks to the brilliance of Texas Instruments, a world that once belonged only to Wall Street analysts is now accessible and understandable to anyone.

When planning the layout of the book we wanted it to be accessible to people who read on the run—in airports, on commuter trains, while waiting to pick up the children from school, or in that hour or so one has after the rest of the family has gone to bed. And so, the chapters have intentionally been kept short and focused. We also incorporate a teaching technique of reiterating key concepts throughout. So if you set the book down for a week or two, don't be afraid to pick it up and start reading where you left off.

I look to the future and see you truly understanding Warren Buffett's masterful manifestation of Benjamin Graham's brilliant insight: investment is most intelligent when it is most businesslike. In the process you will become, like Warren, an intelligent investor.

MARY BUFFETT
Los Angeles, 1997

2

How to Use This Book

Folly and discipline are the key elements of Warren Buffett's philosophy of investing—other people's follies and Warren's discipline. Warren commits capital to investment only when it makes sense from a business perspective. It is *business perspective investing* that gives him the discipline to exploit the stock market's folly. Business perspective investing is the theme of this book.

This discipline of investing from a business perspective has made Warren the second richest business person in the world. Currently Warren's net worth is in excess of $20 billion. *Warren is the only billionaire* who has made it to the Forbes list of the four hundred richest Americans *solely by investing in the stock market.* Over the last thirty-two years his investment portfolio has produced an average annual compounding rate of return of 23.8%.

As humans we are susceptible to the herd mentality, and so we often fall victim to the emotional vicissitudes that propel the stock market and feed enormous profits to those who are disciplined, like Warren. When the Dow Jones Industrial Average has just dropped 508 points and all the sheep are jumping ship, it is investing from a business perspective that gives Warren the confidence to step into that pit of fear and greed we call the stock market and start buying. When the stock market soars to the stratosphere, it is the discipline of investing from a business perspective that keeps Warren from foolishly allocating capital to business ventures that have neither hope nor prospects of giving him a decent return on his investment.

This book is about the discipline of *investing only from a business perspective.* Together we will explore the origin and evolution of this philosophy. We will delve into the early writings of Warren's mentor Benjamin Graham and the ideas of other financial luminaries of this century, and travel to the present to explore the substance of Warren's philosophy.

Warren made his fortune investing in the securities of many different types of businesses. His preference is to acquire *100% ownership* of an enterprise that has excellent business economics and management. When he is unable to do that, his next choice is to make *a long-term minority investment in the common stock* of a company that also has excellent business economics and management. What confuses people who are trying to decipher his philosophy is that he also makes investments in long-, medium-, and short-term income securities. And he is a big player in the field of arbitrage.

The characteristics of the businesses that he is investing in will vary according to the nature of his investment. A company that he is willing to invest in for arbitrage purposes may not be the kind of business in which he wants to make a long-term investment. But regardless of the type of business or the nature of the investment, Warren always uses the basics of business perspective investing as the foundation for his decision.

Most people have the intellectual capacity to understand Warren's philosophy of investing from a business perspective, but few have the dedication and willingness to work to learn the tools of his craft. The purpose of this book is to lay out, step by step, the foundation of Warren's philosophy *and the manner in which he applies it.* This book is a tool to facilitate the task of learning, and it is our intention to teach you Warren's philosophy so that you may acquire the skills to practice this discipline yourself.

Before we start, I would like to introduce a few concepts and terms that will be used throughout the book and give you an idea of where we will be heading as we voyage through the seas of high finance.

First of all, let's take the term "intrinsic value." Its definition has been debated for the last hundred years. It fits into our scheme because Warren will buy into a business only when it is selling at a price that makes business sense given the business's intrinsic value.

Determining a business's intrinsic value is a key to deciphering Warren's investment philosophy. To Warren the intrinsic value of an investment is the projected annual compounding rate of return the investment will produce.

It is this projected annual compounding rate of return that Warren uses to determine if the investment makes business sense. What Warren is doing is *projecting a future value* for the business, say, ten years out; then he compares the price he is going to pay for the business against the business's future, projected value, and the length of time required for the business to reach that projected value. By using an equation that we will show you later in the book, Warren is able to project the annual compounding rate of return that the investment will produce. The *annual compounding rate of return* the investment is projected to produce is *the value* he uses to determine if the investment makes *business sense* when compared to other investments.

In its simplest manifestation it works like this: If Warren can buy a share of stock in X Corporation for $10 and can project that in ten years the share will be worth $50, he can then calculate that his projected *annual* compounding rate of return will be approximately 17.46% for the ten-year period. It is this projected *annual* compounding return of 17.46% that he will then compare to other investments to determine whether the investment in X Corporation makes business sense.

You may be wondering: If Warren's intrinsic value model requires a projection of a business's future value, then how does he go about determining that future value?

That, my friends, is the crux of solving the enigma of Warren's investment philosophy. Just how does one determine the future earnings of a business in order to project its future value and, thus, its intrinsic value? This problem and Warren's method of solving it will be the focus of much of this book.

In short, Warren focuses on the predictability of future earnings; and he believes that without some predictability of future earnings, any calculation of a future value is mere speculation, and speculation is an invitation to folly.

Warren will make long-term investments only in businesses whose future earnings are predictable to a high degree of certainty. The certainty of future earnings removes the element of risk from the equation and allows for a sound determination of a business's future value.

After we have learned what Warren believes are the characteristics of a business with predictable earnings, we will learn how to apply the mathematical calculations he uses for determining the business's intrinsic value and what the return on his investment will be. The nature of the business enterprise and whether it can be bought at a price that will yield a sufficient return will determine the investment's worth and whether or not we are investing from a business perspective.

If I were to sum up Warren's great secrets for successful investing from a business perspective, I would offer up the following:

1

Warren will invest long-term only in companies whose future earnings he can reasonably predict. (You know that one already.)

2

Warren has found that the kind of company whose earnings he can reasonably predict generally has excellent business economics working in its favor. This allows the business to make lots of money that it is free to spend either by buying new businesses or by improving the profitability of the great business that generated all the cash to begin with.

3

These excellent business economics are usually made evident by consistently high returns on shareholders' equity, strong earnings, the presence of what Warren calls a *consumer monopoly,* and management that functions with the shareholders' economic interests in mind.

4

The price you pay for a security will determine the return you can expect on your investment. The lower the price, the greater your return. The greater the price, the lower your return. (We will explore this point in great detail in Chapter 7.)

5

Warren, unlike other investment professionals, chooses the kind of business he would like to be in and then lets the price of the security, and thus his expected rate of return, determine the buy decision. (This is like Warren in high school identifying a girl he wants to date and then waiting for her to break up with her boyfriend before beginning his pursuit.)

6

Warren has figured out that investing at the right prices in certain businesses with exceptional economics working in their favor will produce over the long term an annual compounding rate of return of 15% or better. How Warren determines what is the right business and the right price to pay for it is what this entire book is about.

7

Last but not least, Warren found a way to acquire other people's money to manage so that he could profit from his investing expertise. He did this by starting an investment partnership and later by acquiring insurance companies.

I'm going to teach what I have gleaned about how he does all the above, and if I have done my job, at the end of this book you will understand Warren and the craft of investing from a business perspective. But most important, you will see the secret to achieving an annual 15% or better compounding rate of return on your money.

Now, I know a lot of you think that in order to get rich you have to make tons of money overnight. That is not the case. You just have to earn consistently above-average annual rates of return over a long period of time. Just like Warren.

I'll also show you how to start an investment partnership, which is one of the keys to getting really wealthy, and a method Warren used with great skill. In short, it is my intention to take you from Step A all the way to Step $. So let us begin your education. Let's explore and learn the world of Buffettology.

3

Roots

The late Benjamin Graham, Wall Street's high priest of investment philosophy, stately author of four editions of the masterful treatise on investing *Security Analysis* (McGraw Hill, 1934, 1940, 1951, 1962), was Warren Buffett's professor at Columbia University, his employer at the New York investment firm of Graham-Newman, and his mentor and friend for nearly thirty years. It was Graham who taught Warren that "investment is most intelligent when it is most businesslike." If there is a single credo that Warren holds sacred and to which he attributes his success, it is this concept. It is upon the framework of this single idea that Warren has built his entire financial empire.

Warren's path to riches began in 1957, when friends and family invested $105,000 in his investment limited partnership. Warren's wealth today is valued in excess of $20 billion. Without Graham's tenet of "investing from a business perspective" guiding the way, Warren's performance as an investor might have been no better than the average. With it, he has created one of the great fortunes in contemporary history.

Although Warren readily espouses this philosophy—be it as the chief executive officer of Berkshire Hathaway, his publicly traded holding company, or in an occasional college lecture—its subtleties seem to have eluded the investment profession and public up until now. One would think that anyone whose profession is investing would make Warren a serious case study and analyze and dissect his philosophy. But the investment profession and its academic brethren seem to prefer to label him a four-star enigma, and pay essentially only lip service to his real gifts as an investment genius.

What few people realize is that Warren is first and foremost a thinker, a philosopher whose subject matter and realm of expertise are the world of business. He is a man who has taken the investment and business philosophies of some of the greatest minds that have addressed the subjects of commerce and capital and synthesized an absolutely new approach based on these old lessons. His approach is in many ways contrary to conventional Wall Street wisdom.

As we dissect Warren's investment philosophy you will see that he is really

+ part Benjamin Graham, from whom he took the concepts of investing from a business perspective and emphasizing price as a major motivating factor in selecting investments
+ part Philip Fisher, the legendary California money manager and author, from whom Warren took the idea that the only business worth investing in is one with excellent business economics and the theory that the time to sell an excellent business is never
+ part Lawrence N. Bloomberg, 1930s thinker and author, who introduced to both Graham and Warren the idea of the superior investment value of the consumer monopoly (Graham cites Bloomberg in his 1951 edition of *Security Analysis*)
+ part John Burr Williams, 1930s mathematician, financial philosopher, and author of *The Theory of Investment Value* (Harvard University Press, 1938), from whom Graham acquired the idea that a business's worth is related to what it will earn in the future
+ part Lord John Maynard Keynes, famed British economist and author, from whom Warren derived the concept of the concentrated portfolio and the emphasis of learning one area really well and not straying from it
+ part Edgar Smith, who in 1924 wrote the then much-heralded, but now long-forgotten *Common Stocks As Long-Term Investments* (Macmillan, 1924), which introduced to Graham the concept of *retained earnings adding value to the business* over a period of time
+ and most important, part Charlie Munger, legal pundit and financial impresario, who as Warren's friend and partner persuaded him to focus on the more sophisticated philosophy of purchasing excellent businesses at prices that made business sense, instead of seeking only Graham-type bargains.

This is an eclectic group, whose writings span nearly a hundred years of thought on the subject of investing in securities.

Graham was aware of all these philosophies, but it took Warren's extraordinary and unique turn of mind to synthesize them into a strategy that would *excel each of their individual efforts.* Warren is not afraid of anyone discovering his secret for success, for like any great chef he leaves out a thing or two when discussing the recipes for his best dishes.

Warren is an extremely intelligent and competitive individual. He is not about to give away the store. He has always maintained that great ideas in the realm of investing are few and far between and should be considered proprietary and guarded. He will discuss the details of his philosophy only with members of his family and inner circle. To the rest of the world he feeds tidbits, and then only enough to pique interest. He freely asserts that Graham's *Security Analysis* is the best book ever written on investing, but he may fail to tell you that Graham's philosophies are not the only ones he embraces today. Graham may have provided the foundation, but he is not the house.

Graham gave Warren the basics, and from there Warren went forward, borrowing and creating as all great geniuses do. But to say that Warren is Graham is to say that Oppenheimer is Einstein, or Balanchine is Diaghilev. One may have been influenced by the other, but in reality they are entirely different beasts.

Warren did not happen into investment genius overnight. His voyage began with Graham's 1934 edition of *Security Analysis* and has continued through a maze of financial thought to the present. Any strategy used in a highly competitive field requires the ability to adapt and change as the environment evolves. What worked for Graham in the 1930s and 1940s ceased to work for Warren in the 1970s and 1980s.

If one were to compare the relatively pure Grahamian investment style of, say, the legendary portfolio manager/investor Walter Schloss (who studied under and worked for Graham and now runs a very successful investment partnership with his son, in New York City) with Warren's current style, it would be apparent that they are as different as night and day.

Schloss runs an expansive and diversified portfolio, often holding more than a hundred different stocks. He lets price be the dominant force in the reasoning that goes into his buy decision. He searches for stocks selling at a price below their intrinsic value. Schloss, practicing a traditional Grahamian philosophy, then sells any investment that has reached its intrinsic value, thus ending the romance of the economic benefits of a great business and at the same time inviting the tax man to the party.

Warren, on the other hand, runs a far more concentrated portfolio, with the economic nature of the business weighing in just as heavily as price in his determination of what to buy. Warren is also willing to hold a stock forever as long as the economics of the business remain at least the same as when he bought it. This *ensures that he will benefit from the compounding effect of retained earnings.* It ensures also that he will avoid the profit-eroding taxes that would be imposed if he sold his investment.

Although pure Grahamian philosophy continues to have an exploitable niche in the investment world, its greatest value is as a foundation upon which to learn the investment process. Graham's *Security Analysis* is more than just a treatise on investing. It is a running historical commentary on the techniques used to evaluate securities for investment purposes. Between 1934 and 1962, Graham wrote four editions of *Security Analysis,* each deciphering and analyzing old and new methods of security analysis as applied to the present.

One learns through experience, and if not from experience, from those with experience. That is what Graham provides us with. While working for Graham, Warren made a vow that he would not make another investment until he had read Graham's book twelve times. To this day he keeps all four editions next to his desk, and he still finds subtleties that escaped his eye in past readings. As with the Bible, worldly experience enhances each reading of *Security Analysis,* sparking revelation upon revelation.

Truly, Graham was a man who planted trees so that others could sit underneath them and feast upon their fruit. Thus, it seems only appropriate that we begin your education in Buffettology with the basic tenet of Graham's philosophy and one that Warren holds as the foundation of his own thinking.

4

Investing from
a Business Perspective

Investing from a business perspective is the most challenging concept you will address in this book. This is not because it requires a fair amount of financial and accounting knowledge, which it does, but rather because it is so different from the prevailing wisdom peddled by the great investment houses of Wall Street.

As you read through this book you will come to see that having a business perspective on investing is more about discipline than philosophy, and once the concept is understood, it demands absolute devotion. Stray from it, and you will wander the financial lunar landscape, forever dancing to the folly called forth by fear and greed.

Adhere to its wisdom, and the foolishness of others becomes the field in which you reap your harvest. In short, other people's follies, brought on by fear and greed, will offer you, the investor, the opportunity to take advantage of their mistakes and benefit from the discipline of committing capital to investment only when it makes sense from a business perspective.

But be warned: it is not an all-encompassing discipline, on which the practitioner can rely in any situation in order to produce a profit. It is, rather, as Graham said in reference to bond selection, "a negative art." It is a discipline that tends to tell the investor as much if not more what *not* to buy as what *to* buy.

You will find that almost everything that relates to business perspective investing is alien to Wall Street folklore.

+ You will find yourself waiting for the market to go down instead of up, so that you can buy partial interests in publicly traded companies that you have been wanting to own.

+ You will adopt the wisdom of businesslike thinking and come to realize that the stupidest reason in the world for owning a common stock is that you think the per share price is going up next week.

+ You will change your perspective from one that leads you to buy a stock in hopes of a 25% move in the next six months to one that leads you to buy a partial interest in an ongoing business venture—a business venture that you anticipate will in five to ten years produce for you an annual compounding rate of return of 15% or better.

+ You will learn that diversification is something people do to protect themselves from their own stupidity, not because of investment savvy.

+ You will find yourself getting great investment ideas from shopping in the supermarket.

+ You will discover that Pollyanna and your stockbroker both may be wildly optimistic but neither is very intelligent in matters of finance.

+ You will learn that a $1,500 per share stock may be cheap and a $2 stock may be grossly expensive.

+ You will start thinking of stocks as bonds with variable interest rates.

And you will realize that though Warren adheres to the philosophical underpinnings of Graham, he has long since left the fold. Warren is seeking value, but not in the same mode or framework in which Graham did.

So let's begin by looking at the history of the thought process that Warren used to reach his revolutionary approach to investing. We will travel back in time to an earlier part of this century and look at the roots of Warren's strategy. We will discuss the financial philosophies of that time and how they influenced Graham and how Graham, in turn, influenced Warren. We will see the evolution of Warren's thinking as he digests not only his successes and losses but also wisdom bestowed upon him by two of the greatest thinkers of modern finance, Philip Fisher and Charles Munger.

We shall see where Warren breaks with Graham and has, as in the words of the poet Rainer Maria Rilke, a "conflagration of clarity," which gives birth to Warren's new synthesis of Graham's original idea that investment is most intelligent when it is most businesslike.

5

What Is Businesslike Investing?

What does "Investment is most intelligent when it is most businesslike" mean? It means that one stops thinking of the stock market as an end unto itself and begins thinking about the *economics of ownership of those businesses that the common stocks represent.*

What? Your stockbroker calls you up and says he thinks XYZ stock is a timely buy and that in the last week it has moved up three points! Stop right there. A common stock is a partial ownership interest in a business enterprise. That's right, a *business.* Your stockbroker is trying to entrap you in the enthusiasm of the horse race of numbers found every morning in the *Wall Street Journal.* But common stocks are in fact tangible representations of the equity owner's interest in a particular business. It was Graham who taught Warren, instead of asking *(a)* in what security? and *(b)* at what price? to ask *(a) in what enterprise?* and *(b) on what terms is the commitment proposed?* This puts the line of questioning into a more businesslike perspective.

Warren's chief idea is to buy excellent businesses at a price that makes business sense. So, what makes business sense? In Warren's world, making business sense means that the venture invested in will offer you, the investor, the highest predictable annual compounding rate of return possible with the least amount of risk. The reason Warren is able to do this better than other investment managers is that he is motivated by the long term—like a business owner—and not, like most Wall Street investment professionals, by the short term.

Think of it this way. If I offer to sell you the local corner drugstore, you would look at the accountant's books and determine how much money the business is making. If you see that it's profitable, you would then try to figure out whether the profits are consistent or they vary a great deal. If you determine that the profitability of the drugstore has been consistent, you would then ask yourself whether that could change materially. If the answer is no, you would ask what the store is selling for.

Once you know the asking price, you then compare it with the drugstore's yearly earnings and determine what kind of return you would get. A $100,000 asking price against earnings of $20,000 a year would afford you a yearly return of 20% on your money ($20,000 ÷ $100,000 = 20%).

Once you know the projected return, you can shop around to determine whether a 20% return on your money is a good investment. You would, in effect, be comparing rates of return. If it looks attractive, you make your purchase.

This is how Warren works. Whether he is buying an entire business or fractional portions, he asks himself: How much money can this business predictably earn, and what is the asking price? When he gets the answers to these questions, he can do some comparison shopping.

This is not how the prevailing Wall Street wisdom would have you operate. Warren and the buyer of the drugstore anticipate holding the business for a long period of time in order to get full advantage of ownership. A 20% return a year for, say, fifteen years is a nice ride.

Wall Street, on the other hand, looks at business from a short-term perspective. It wants the quick kill. A 20% return this year might not be enough to win an investor a spot on the top list of money managers. In the game of money management, a few bad quarters can mean the end of your career, so today outweighs tomorrow in importance.

If the drugstore was truly a good business with an attractive return, and you bought it, would you then sell it if someone were to offer you 35% more for it than what you paid? A fast 35%? Wall Street would take it in a heartbeat. Warren wouldn't. He'd say that it's a good business with a predictable 20% return, which is hard to find. And a fast 35% will cause even quicker IRS consequences, which would reduce my return to approximately 25%. If I cash out, I might be stuck reinvesting my money in lower-paying investments!

Warren, like any good businessman, likes to keep a good business. To Warren, ownership of the powers of production of the right businesses is of greater value over the long term than the short-term profits usually promoted by Wall Street.

6

Warren's View of Earnings

In order to understand Warren's view of investing from a business perspective, you must understand that he has a very unorthodox view of a corporation's earnings:

+ He considers them his, in proportion to his ownership in the company. So if a company earns $5 a share and Warren owns one hundred shares of the company, he is of the opinion that he has just earned $500 ($5 × 100 = $500).
+ Warren also believes that the company has the choice of either paying that $500 out to him via a dividend or retaining those earnings and reinvesting them for him, thus increasing the underlying value of the company. Warren believes that the stock market will, over a period of time, acknowledge this increase in the company's underlying value and cause the stock's price to increase.

This differs from the view most Wall Street professionals hold; they don't consider earnings theirs until the earnings are paid out via dividends. In the early eighties the stock of Warren's holding company, Berkshire Hathaway, traded at $500 a share. Today it trades at around $45,000 a share, and it still has never paid a dividend. The increase in the market price of the stock came from an increase in the underlying value of the company, caused by Warren's profitable reinvestment of Berkshire's retained earnings. (Please note: Berkshire Hathaway has two classes of stock, Class A and Class B. All Berkshire Hathaway examples in this book are in reference to Class A.)

+ Warren believes that a company should retain all its earnings if it can profitably employ them at a rate of return that is better than the investor could get by taking delivery of those earnings via a dividend. Warren believes also that since dividends are taxed as personal income, there is a tax incentive to letting the corporation retain all its earnings.

Wall Street has long been prejudiced against companies that retain all their earnings and don't pay dividends. This prejudice is rooted in the early part of this century, when the majority of people bought bonds instead of stocks for investment purposes. People felt more comfortable with bonds because they were secured with the assets of the businesses, which meant that bond-holders had first claim on the assets of the company if it went bankrupt. Bonds paid interest to investors on a quarterly basis, so investors knew there was trouble with the company if the interest check wasn't in the mail.

Common stocks at that time were considered dangerous for the financially naive, because of a lack of accounting regulations; majority owners and managements had enormous leeway to monkey with the books. (A good portion of Benjamin Graham's 1934 edition of *Security Analysis* explains how the security analyst can discover accounting fraud and such scams as pyramiding. But as Graham points out in later editions, the creation of the Securities Exchange Commission in 1940 caused this kind of abuse to all but vanish, which greatly improved the investment status of common stocks, which, in turn, gave birth to a new era for investing in common stocks as a whole.)

But even though the investment status of common stocks has greatly improved, people retain their prejudice for getting that check in the mail. Be it for bonds or for common stocks, Wall Street and its minions shy away from companies that don't pay a dividend. They see it as a sign of weakness.

To this day it is not uncommon for some security analysts to assign a higher value to companies that pay a dividend than to those that don't. This is true even when the company that is retaining all its earnings is an infinitely better enterprise. *(This strange form of prej-udice was one of the reasons why in the early eighties Warren's holding company, Berkshire Hathaway, traded at or below book value.)*

As we know, for Warren, common stocks have always represented ownership in the underlying business, and ownership means the company's earnings belong to you, the investor. The investors/owners of the company, through their elected board of directors, can instruct the company's management either to pay out the earnings as dividends or to retain the earnings for further development and expansion of the company's business.

This arrangement places a great deal of emphasis on the integrity of the company's management to do what is best for the shareholders of the company. Dishonest management can often manipulate a board of directors into fulfilling management's desire to build grandiose empires that enrich the management but do little or nothing for the financial benefit of the shareholders.

✦ Warren places a great amount of weight on the quality of a company's management when he makes his investment decisions. One way to determine the quality of management is to see what it does with its earnings. Does it pay out dividends, or retain them? If it retains them, does it *profitably employ* them, or does it squander them on dreams of grandeur?

✦ Warren believes that the test to which management should hold itself in determining whether or not to pay out a dividend is, *Would the investors/owners be better off removing the capital from the business and investing it in other enterprises?* For example, let's say company A has a great business that makes lots of money. Now, if the management can profitably put to work the money that the great business earns, then it would make sense to let management continue its course and improve the fortunes of the company. But if management makes foolish investment decisions with the company's earnings and ends up losing money, then the shareholders would have been better off taking earnings out of the company and investing them on their own.

With Berkshire Hathaway, Warren has managed to employ retained earnings at approxiamtely a 23% compounding annual after-corporate-income-tax rate of return. This means that each $1 of earnings that Berkshire retains, will annually produce a 23% return. If Berkshire chose to pay out the 23% to its owners, they would be taxed at personal income tax rates, which would thus reduce the return to approximately 15.9%. Additionally, the dividend payment would put the earnings in the hands of the investor, which would thus burden him with the problem of reallocating the capital to new investments.

For the Berkshire investor/owner, the question becomes, Does he want to take his share of the company's earnings as a dividend, or does he want Berkshire to retain the earnings and reinvest them for him? If Berkshire retains the investor's earnings, the investor can expect that those retained earnings will earn a 23% annual rate of return. And under Warren's theory, the underlying value of Berkshire would increase by 23% as well, which over time will cause the market price for Berkshire's stock to increase, which, in turn, benefits the shareholder/owner.

Following this line of thinking, Warren has come to the conclusion that common stocks bear a resemblance to bonds that have variable rates of return, depending on their earnings for a particular year. And he has realized that some common stocks have underlying businesses that create consistent enough earnings to allow him to project their future rate of return.

In Warren's world the common stock takes on the characteristics of a bond, with the payable interest being the net earnings of the business. He calculates his rate of return by dividing the price he pays for the stock by the company's annual net per share earnings. A $10 per share asking price for the company's stock against annual net per share earnings of $2 a share equates to a rate of return of 20%. Understand, though, that the integrity of this calculation is *wholly dependent* upon the *predictability* of the company's earnings.

In real life, if you were to buy a local business you would want to know how much it earned each year and how much it was selling for. With those two numbers you could calculate the annual rate of return on your prospective investment by simply dividing the business's yearly earnings by its asking price. Warren does this type of analysis whether he is buying an entire company or one share of a company. *The price he pays determines his rate of return.*

7

The Price You Pay Determines Your Rate of Return

The price you pay determines your rate of return. This is the key that you should wear around your neck at all times. It is the one tenet of Graham's that Warren lives by.

Before I go any further on the subject of price and the rate of return, I must warn you that I am going to simplify a few things for the sake of explanation. I know that a great many of you have some experience in the world of finance and will be biting to debate me on certain points. To those of you who fit this description, I can say that later in the book I will go into detail on the finer points. But for now I must get past a few of the basic concepts so that everyone can easily grasp the later chapters without getting the glazed look that comes from reading an accounting text.

So let's use a very oversimplified hypothetical case to start. (You of the experienced category should also pay attention to the following because some of the basic tenets are contrary to the conventional wisdom peddled by Wall Street.)

Let's start by asking a simple question: If I were willing to sell you the right to receive $1,100 at the end of one year, what is the maximum you would be willing to pay for this right on Day 1?

If you paid me $1,100 and I paid you back $1,100 at the end of the year, the return on your investment for the year would be zero.

However, if you paid me $1,000 for the right to receive $1,100 at the end of one year, your return would be $100 above the $1,000 that you paid me, which would give you a return of 10% on your money for the year.

Now, your next question is whether or not a return of 10% is a good rate of return when compared to other rates of return. To determine this you need to shop around a bit. You might find that the local bank is willing to pay you 7% on your money if you deposit it there for one year. This means that if you loaned the bank $1,000 for one year, it would at the end of that year give you back $1,070 which equates to a $70 profit, or a rate of return of 7%. Obviously, the 10% return on your money that I offered you is better than the bank's 7%.

If you looked around at a lot of different investments and still found that the 10% return was a higher rate of return than other investments were paying, you would conclude that I was offering you a better deal than the others.

Then, in answer to our question—what is the maximum you would be willing to pay today for the right to receive $1,100 in one year?—if you wanted at least a 10% return on your money, the maximum you would be willing to pay is $1,000. If you paid *more*—say, $1,050—your profit would be less, by $50, and your return would be less as well ($50 ÷ $1,050 = 4.7% return). If you paid *less*—say, $950—your profit would be $150, and your return would be greater ($150 ÷ $950 = 15.7% return). The higher the price, the lower the rate of return. The lower the price, the higher the rate of return. Pay more, get less. Pay less, get more.

Financial analysts use a mathematical equation called *discounting to present value* to solve problems like this. This equation allows them to plug in the future value (as in our example), the rate of interest desired, and the time period, and to come up with the present value. Using this equation is extremely time consuming, often involving a series of calculations and the use of tables. To fully understand its use one must usually take a college course in finance or business math.

Fortunately, as mentioned, the folks at Texas Instruments have programmed the equation into the BA-35 Solar calculator, so you and I have only to learn how to punch buttons to come up with the present value. Or, if we want, we can find out the future value of a sum growing at a rate of X for Y number of years. We can even figure out the annual compounding rate of return on an investment if we know (1) the present value, (2) the future value, and (3) the holding period of the investment.

And since projecting an annual compounding rate of return on an investment is the key to understanding Warren, I recommend that you acquire one of these useful and reasonably priced instruments now. Wal-Mart carries them, as well as most office supply stores and university bookstores. If you can't find one at a store near you, you can order one over the phone by calling Office Depot at 1-800-685-8800. *Please note:* Several other financial calculators out there will also perform similar calculations.

(In case you are wondering, Wall Street analysts long ago quit cranking out present and future value calculations by hand. They also use financial calculators today.)

When evaluating what a business is worth, Warren goes through a thought process much like the one we just went through. He takes the *yearly per share earnings* and treats them as the *return that he is getting* for his investment. So if a company is earning $5 a share and the shares are selling for $25 a share, Warren perceives this as getting a 20% return on his money for the year ($5 ÷ $25 = 20%). The $5 can either be paid out by the company by way of a dividend or be retained and utilized by the business to maintain or expand operations.

So if you paid $40 for a share of stock and it has yearly earnings of $5 a share, Warren would calculate the annual rate of return on this investment as being 12.5% ($5 ÷ $40 = 12.5%). In keeping with this line of thought, a price of $10 a share with yearly earnings of $5 a share would equate to a 50% return ($5 ÷ $10 = 50%). *The price you pay will determine the rate of return.*

One thing that should be readily apparent is that strength and predictability of earnings are an important consideration if you are considering holding a stock for any length of time. If you purchased a stock for $25 a share and it had earnings in the most recent year of $5 a share (which equates to a return of 20%), and the next year the company earns nothing, the annual rate of return on your investment goes to zero.

What Warren wants is companies with business economics and management that create *reasonably predictable earnings*. Only then is it possible for Warren to predict the future rate of return on his investment and the investment merit of a company.

Don't worry. We will go over all of this in greater detail later in the book. But for now it is imperative that you grasp two fundamentals of Warren's way of thinking:

✦ The *price you pay* will determine the *rate of return* you are going to get on your investment.
✦ In order to determine the rate of return, you must be able to reasonably *predict the company's future earnings.*

The three variables you will constantly address when using Warren's system of analysis are:

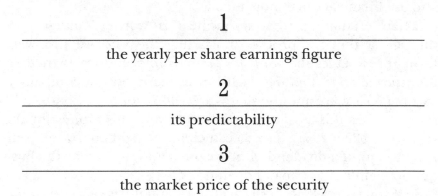

1

---

the yearly per share earnings figure

2

---

its predictability

3

---

the market price of the security

The higher the market price, the lower the rate of return, and the lower the market price, the greater the rate of return. The higher the per share earnings, the greater the return, given the market price for the security. All this may make perfect sense to you. Then again, it may not. Let's look at a real example of how this works.

WARREN'S METHODS AT WORK

In 1979 Warren started buying up the stock of a company called General Foods, paying an average price of $37 a share for approximately 4 million shares. What Warren saw in this company was strong earnings (in the prior year, 1978, of $4.65 per share) and that earnings had been growing at an average annual rate of 8.7%.

Since General Foods' earnings were growing at an average

annual rate of 8.7%, we, like Warren, could project that the company's earnings would grow from $4.65 a share in 1970, to $5.05 a share in 1979 ($4.65 × 1.087 = $5.05). Thus, we are *projecting* that 1979's earnings will be $5.05 a share.

So, if we paid $37 for a share of General Foods in 1979, we would be getting an initial rate of return of 13.6% for our first year ($5.05 ÷ $37 = 13.6%). (*Note:* actual per share earnings for General Foods in 1979 turned out to be $5.12, versus our projection of $5.05.)

If interest rates—the rates of return on, for example, long-term U.S. Treasury bonds (hereinafter referred to as "government bonds")—are around 10%, which they were back then, then a 13.6% rate of return on the General Foods investment looks pretty good.

And because we are projecting that General Foods' annual per share earnings are going to continue to grow at an annual rate of 8.7%, we can argue that we are getting an initial rate of return equal to 13.6% and that that rate of return is going to increase each year by 8.7%.

Thus, your share of General Foods stock, with its initial rate of return of 13.6%, which is going to grow at a rate of 8.7% a year, appears to be a better investment than the government bond paying a static rate of return of 10% a year. If you are making a strict business decision, based on projected performance, an investment in General Foods appears to be a much better investment than the government bond.

Now, if we paid more for our General Foods stock—say, $67 a share—then we could calculate that our initial rate of return would be less. On 1979 earnings of $5.05 a share, with a cost of $67 a share, our General Foods investment would produce an initial rate of return of 7.5% ($5.05 ÷ $67 = 7.5%). This is much lower than the initial rate of return of 13.6% we were projecting to earn at a purchase price of $37 a share. Likewise, a 7.5% rate of return is not nearly as competitive as the government bond that is paying a 10% rate of return. Choosing between the General Foods stock and government bonds becomes a tougher question.

If we paid less—say, $15 a share—then we could calculate that our initial rate of return would be 33.6% ($5.05 ÷ $15 = 33.6%). Pay less, get more. The price you pay determines your rate of return. The lower the price, the higher your rate of return.

Price determines everything. Once a price is quoted, it is possible to figure your expected rate of return and then compare it to other rates of return. They are simple comparisons to make. That is why Warren is famous for making extremely fast business decisions. He simply calculates the annual compounding rate of return he expects an investment to produce and then determines whether it's what he is looking for.

EPILOGUE

Warren believed that since General Foods was earning him an initial rate of return of 13.6%, which would increase at a rate of 8.7% a year, over a period of time the stock market would acknowledge this increase in value and adjust the stock's price upward. And from 1978 to 1984, General Foods' per share earnings rose at an average annual rate of approximately 7%, from $4.65 a share to $6.96 a share. During this period the stock market reappraised the stock's price upward, to approximately $54 a share in 1984.

Then, in 1985, the Philip Morris Company saw the value of General Foods' many brand-name products, which created a strong and expanding earnings base, and bought all of Warren's General Foods stock for $120 a share in a tender offer for the whole company. This gave Warren a pretax annual compounding rate of return on his investment of approximately 21%. That's right, a pretax annual compounding rate of return of 21%. A nice number in anybody's book.

Now, I know that some of you with advanced degrees in Buffettology are probably thinking that I have oversimplified things, which I have; but if I stormed off the deep end of financial esoterica, some of us would be forever lost when we get to the really heady stuff. Yes, it gets much more convoluted, and there are many subtleties to Buffettology, but for the moment we must concentrate on laying the foundation so that we can start building the house.

The Corporation, Stocks, Bonds— A Few Useful Explanations

I have found that a great many people have absolutely no idea what a bond is or, for that matter, what ownership in the common stock of a company represents. In fact, many people who own stocks would be hard pressed to explain what a corporation is. Not that you are in this group. It's just that you never know who is going to pick up this book. So I feel that a brief run-through on the corporate form of organization and its history is appropriate here. It is something that Warren has a good appreciation of, and it is something that will benefit any investor.

EARLY CAPITAL FORMATION

The beginning of commerce is lost in time; it was created before people were sufficiently civilized to leave a written record. The earliest commercial records now intact are found in the clay tablets of Babylonia. These include the correspondence of the great mercantile families as well as the records concerning property that belonged to the temples. The records show that in Babylonia under the great ruler Hammurabi (who lived around 1792–1750 B.C.), property was mortgaged and loans were made— all with the capital of dates, date wine, flour, oil, barley, and sometimes silver, with interest being paid in grain and silver.

Early commerce involved individuals or groups of people organized into partnerships. The Phoenicians (a people who occupied a strip of land on the coast of Syria and Palestine) and the Greeks give us some of our earliest examples of business partnership formation. A merchant wanting to engage in trade outside his town or country would gather together a group of merchants, who would in turn hire a captain and charter a ship to send their wares to another locale to trade for goods that were needed in their home port. Oil, figs, honey, wool, and marble were some of the things that early merchants traded.

The Greeks enjoyed many great trading opportunities that resulted from Alexander's conquests, which stretched from Greece to India. India long enjoyed a more developed textile industry, and Greek merchants saw the opportunity to profit from trading goods with their Indian counterparts. Indian silks and cottons became the textiles that clothed the rich and fashionable Greeks of the day. And a Greek merchant lacking in sufficient capital to hire his own caravan could organize a group of merchant partners who would combine their resources and employ a caravan for a trading venture to India.

As a rule, early forms of business organization were of the partnership/joint venture nature and therefore were somewhat limited in size. They usually lasted the duration of the journey to and from the foreign ports of call.

The earliest embodiment of the corporation concept can be found during the 1400s in Venice, which enjoyed great fortune and power by becoming a center for trade with the Middle East. It had a splendor that can still be seen in the magnificent palazzi that line its canals, palaces that were built by the great Venetian merchant and banking families.

Venice was known for early development of bookkeeping and banking, which added to its importance and gave new dimensions of financial power to the realm of the merchant. Often the sons of wealthy merchants in other parts of Europe were sent there to learn the art of commerce. In fact, double-entry bookkeeping was invented by Luca Pacioli, a friar who lived in Venice during this period. You can see how strong an influence Venice had when you think of all the words related to commerce and banking that are rooted in Italian words like: *conto, conto corrente, porto, disconto, netto, deposito,* and *folio.*

The corporate form of organization that developed in Venice during this time can be called a joint-stock company. Larger than the earlier partnerships and joint ventures, these joint-stock companies could gather large groupings of small merchants to form large, permanent capital bases to finance enterprises that, because of their size and financial power, enjoyed greater commercial opportunities. And greater commercial success meant a more secure political and financial position.

The joint-stock company took on many permutations as the great companies of old struggled with the church and with kings for power. The church and the kings needed the merchants for their financial advancement, while the merchants needed the church and the kings to protect their goods from thieves and their markets from competitors. The power of God and the armies of a king are important allies to have on your side. If you want a modern parallel, just look to the kingdom of Kuwait, which likely would have lost all its wealth to the kingdom of Iraq if the kingdom of America hadn't stepped in and pushed back the Iraqis. Kuwait businesses, that is, the oil empire, got American companies like Bechtel, which builds oil infrastructures, to lobby for armed intervention—a case of merchants pressuring their king to protect them from pirates and thieves.

As corporations became more and more powerful, they started to usurp the power of the kingdoms. Thus, kings soon realized that it was in their best interest to limit the power of organized capital; they created laws that forbade the organization of joint-stock companies without the approval of the crown. Early examples of crown-approved joint-stock companies are the East India Company and the Hudson's Bay Company, both with colorful and fascinating histories.

An interesting Dutch company that evolved around 1610 was the Dutch West Indies Company. It was an extraordinary business operation that paid high dividends for a time, but its earnings were necessarily precarious, for they came not from the ordinary operations of commerce and colonization but from armed attacks on the Spanish silver fleets. The character of the company is evident in its charter, which actually opposed peace between the Netherlands and Spain. In reality it was a corporation of pirates who gathered the capital of their investors to build and staff pirate ships to rob Spanish ships carrying gold and silver from the New World. (And those people on Wall Street think they know how to conduct a hostile takeover!)

THE FINANCIAL POWER OF THE MASSES

Long ago, before the development of banking and joint-stock companies, individual savings were hoarded, and thus made useless to society. The meager amounts of capital that the butcher, barmaid, cobbler, or day laborer saved were placed into hiding, and no one profited from their savings. This was due in part to the medieval religious doctrine that made it wrong to take interest on loans, but this doctrine lost its force when it appeared that loans were wanted by merchants, the pope, and kings. Thus the ruling class concluded that it was wise to encourage lending money by permitting the lender to take interest for it.

There is, however, a great difference between the lending of money by an ordinary individual who has more than he or she knows what to do with and the business of lending as practiced by a banker. The difference is this—the banker has made lending a profession. The banker steps in between the people who have capital but lack the ability or inclination to employ their savings profitably and the people who have the ability and inclination to conduct business enterprises but lack the desirable amount of capital. The banker is a specialist in this profession, and by his or her special knowledge can do more than anyone else to collect the surplus capital and place it where it can be used to the best advantage. Thus even the teenager working at a summer job can profitably employ his or her saved capital by entrusting it to the local banker, who will then loan out the money to a member of the community who is willing to commit legally to paying back the money *plus interest.* A banker spends a lifetime making money off the spread between the interest he pays the individual depositor and what he can lend the money for.

For most people, the first venture into the investment game comes when they open up a bank account and deposit their weekly paycheck. One person's paycheck may not seem like much, but multiply that by fifty thousand depositors and the numbers start to grow. So a bank is really a large pool of people who have loaned their money to the bank in exchange for a portion of what the bank can earn reloaning the money to other individuals and businesses.

When banks *loan* money, anyone who borrows that money is in debt. Businesspeople abhor debt because if things go bad and business gets slow the bank may foreclose and liquidate the business. Many businesspeople prefer to finance their operations by selling to the public partial ownership interests in their operations, called *equity* or *stock*. In the days of old, these transactions were done in what is called a market. A market back then was a specific place, designated by the local authorities, in which business transactions could take place. The reason for this was to create a public record of the transaction. It also ensured that the government could efficiently collect its taxes from the merchants doing business. Markets were designated for certain days at specific sites, and anyone caught trading outside these boundaries would have his goods confiscated.

One of the markets that developed was the stock market, a place in which partial ownership interests in different companies were traded between different investors. The New York Stock Exchange is the modern equivalent of the markets of old.

This is what Wall Street is about. Instead of a bank asking individuals to loan it money so that it can loan it to a business, a very special kind of bank called an investment bank, like Merrill Lynch or Salomon Brothers, acts as middleman for a business looking for wealthy individuals or institutions to invest in it. The investment may be in the form of a loan, which would manifest itself by the company selling a bond to an investor. Or the company may choose to sell an ownership interest—stock—to the investor.

The investment bank finds the individuals and institutions willing to buy the bonds or stocks of the company seeking to raise the money. The investment bank makes its money by charging a fee for the amount of capital it can raise for the business.

When General Motors wants to raise a large sum of money for plant expansion, it can go to one of the investment banks, like Salomon Brothers or Merrill Lynch, and have them sell to investors a GM bond (debt) or stock (ownership interest) in the company.

The first time that a business sells an ownership interest to the public, it is called an *initial public offering*, or IPO. The second time, it is called a secondary offering. Once stock is sold to the public, individual investors who own it may become enthusiastic or pessimistic about the future of the company and either buy more of the stock or sell it, depending on how they feel about the business's prospects. The New York Stock Exchange is a place where people gather to buy and sell ownership interests, or stocks, that were once sold to the public by a business through an investment bank. It is an auction market, where buyer and seller gather. The buyer bids a price and the seller asks a price, and when they meet, a transaction occurs and the ownership interest changes hands.

When your Merrill Lynch stockbroker calls you and says you should buy stock in General Motors, he is really doing one of two things. He is either trying to raise money for General Motors or he is acting as an intermediary between you and another investor, who wants to sell his General Motors stock. With one sale your Merrill Lynch broker is earning a commission by raising money for General Motors. With the other he is earning a commission for bringing a buyer and a seller together. Naturally, stockbrokers tend to be very enthusiastic people because if there isn't a transaction, they don't earn a commission.

STARTING A CORPORATION—ITS CAPITAL FORMATION

Let's say that you want to start a business, a corporation—not to rob Spanish silver fleets but to make cookies and cakes. Let's call it Katie's Baking Company. To get the money to start the business, you can either borrow from friends or a bank or you can sell stock to investors. Stock represents ownership in the business, and debt represents only a promise to pay.

In order to sell shares in a company, you must have incorporated the business. That means you file incorporation documents with the department of corporations in the state of incorporation. Every corporation that exists in America has filed incorporation documents in some state.

The great thing about being a corporation is a thing called limited liability. This means that if Katie's Baking Compay serves up a rotten cookie and is sued for poisoning one of its customers and damages are awarded, the shareholder owners of Katie's are protected from any judgments. True, the judgment may take all the *company's* capital, but the plaintiff can't come after the *shareholders*.

One other great thing about a corporation is that the ownership can be divided up and sold to raise capital to start or add to the business. Ownership, like Katie's pies, can be cut into as many pieces as one likes. And the more cuts in the pie, the smaller the pieces of pie. Likewise, the more shares issued, the smaller the portion of ownership the shares represent. Cut a pie into two equal pieces, and each slice represents half. If a company has only two shares outstanding, then each share represents a 50% ownership interest in the company.

But back to Katie's. After much investigation you find that your sister is willing to invest in your business venture if you are willing to put the same amount of money up. So each of you invests $5,000, and in return the company issues you each fifty shares of stock. These one hundred shares of stock represent all of the stock the bakery has outstanding. This means that you and your sister each own 50% of the bakery. Kind of like the pie.

Since you and your sister own the business, you must elect a board of directors to oversee the running of the company. As in most businesses that are owned by several large shareholders, you elect yourself and your sister to the board. The board of directors then hires management to run the company. In this case, since neither you nor your sister has any baking experience, you hire a local baker named Janet Sweetbreads to run Katie's. Ms. Sweetbreads is the chief executive officer (CEO) of the company and reports directly to the board. If the board doesn't like the way Ms. Sweetbreads is doing things, it can fire her and hire a new CEO.

If, in the first year of business, the company has net earnings (earnings after corporate income tax) of $100, then with one hundred shares outstanding, the baking company will have earned $1 a share. (Net earnings divided by the number of shares outstanding gives you the per share earnings figure.)

If Katie's Baking Company needs to raise additional money, it can either sell more shares or borrow the money from someone. If it sells more shares, there will be a dilution of the ownership interests in the company. If you sold fifty more shares, then there would be 150 shares outstanding and your fifty shares would represent a 33% ownership interest in the company. This doesn't sound very good to you as an owner. So at the next board of directors meeting you tell your CEO, Ms. Sweetbreads, that instead of selling stock she should sell bonds to raise any new capital the company needs.

A bond is a promise to pay. When you go to a bank for a loan, you are essentially selling it a bond. You give it a piece of paper saying that you borrowed X number of dollars and that you agree to pay it all back, plus interest. When the bank borrows money from you, it sells you a certificate of deposit, which is really a kind of bond. It contractually agrees that if you lend it money, it will pay it all back to you at a future date, plus a fixed rate of interest.

Large companies like General Motors not only borrow money from banks; they also issue bonds to the public. GM goes to an investment bank like Merrill Lynch and says it needs to raise $200 million. No small sum. Merrill Lynch, with thousands of stockbrokers all over the country, says it can raise that money by getting those thousands of stockbrokers to sell $200 million worth of GM bonds to its clients. Merrill Lynch in return charges GM a fee for providing this service. But the lender-lendee relationship is between GM and the thousands of people who buy the GM bonds.

One other way Merrill Lynch can raise money for a company is to sell that company's common stock to Merrill's customers. Let's say that when Katie's was starting up you had really big plans, and instead of needing $10,000 to start the business, you needed $10 million. Now, your sister just doesn't have that kind of money, so you put together a business plan and go see the investment bankers at Merrill Lynch. Merrill Lynch, liking your idea, says that it can convince its clients to invest in your company. You say, "Great," and agree to pay Merrill Lynch its fee for providing you this service. Merrill Lynch then calls its clients and sells them Katie's stock. This is called an IPO, or initial public offering.

With an IPO a large chunk of the ownership of Katie's stock ends up in the hands of thousands of people. Katie's has thousands of different individual owners, each owning a small portion of Katie's Baking Company.

An odd thing happens when you end up with a lot of owners. Some of them may want out of the business at some future date. Maybe they need the money or maybe they no longer think that the baking business is the place to have their money. Whatever the reason, they want to sell.

The shareholders who want to sell call their stockbrokers and tell them that they want to sell one hundred shares of Katie's Baking Company. Those who want to buy call their brokers and tell them they want to buy one hundred shares of Katie's Baking Company.

These two orders meet on the floor of the New York Stock Exchange, one of many stock exchanges found around the world. Buyers and sellers come together, one bidding to buy, the other asking to sell. When the bid and ask prices meet, a sale occurs. It is basically an auction pricing method. All of this is facilitated by people called specialists who sit on the exchange floor and act as market makers. These market makers have a fixed place on the floor where buyers and sellers of a particular stock meet. You want to buy some Katie's stock, and your stockbroker calls his agent on the floor of the exchange and tells him to buy one hundred shares of Katie's when someone offers to sell it at $10 a share. The agent goes over to the market maker for Katie's stock and puts in the order. Someone who wants to sell does the same thing. And the market maker acts as the matchmaker, bringing the two agents together for the sale. Sometimes when the market is slow for a particular stock the market maker will buy the stock for his own account. This stock becomes part of his inventory, which he will sell when a buyer finally shows up. The market maker always keeps a small inventory of the stocks he deals in so he can fill buy orders when there are no sellers.

For our purposes, any common stock that represents an ownership interest in a company is called equity. And bonds are called debt. The companies that we will be discussing in this book all went public years ago and have thousands of shareholders and are traded at various stock exchanges.

9

Valuing a Business

Now that we have laid some of the foundation, let us proceed to a more detailed analysis of Warren's philosophy of investing from a business perspective.

Let's start with a simple business and value it to determine at what price it would be an attractive acquisition. The business will be uncomplicated and straightforward, and we will forgo the effects of inflation and taxation on the valuation process. This will also give us a chance to explain balance sheets and income statements and the process of incorporation. The wise investor should have some understanding of these things, but many do not. Those of you with MBAs may be bored to death by this exercise, so I'll throw some Warren tidbits into the pot as we go along.

Let's say that young Warren develops a childhood dream of becoming the richest man in America and at the age of seventeen decides to start a business. Young Warren, forever commercially minded, has saved up the earnings from his *Washington Post* paper route, a whopping sum of $35. As with all young business tycoons, the money is burning a hole in his pocket. What should he do with it? Spend it on girls? No, he hasn't yet met Susie, his wife and the mother of his children. Maybe he should spend it on some candy and a soda. No, they rot your teeth, which will mean paying a dentist, which means capital expenditures with no return.

No, by golly, young Warren is going to go out and start a business and make some more money. If he wants to take full advantage of the wonders of compounding interest, he knows that the younger he starts, the better. As we all know, death is what stops the compounding of money and brings the tax collector to your door.

After searching, he finds an old working pinball machine and buys it for $35. Now that he has the first asset of his business, he realizes he needs to put it someplace where people will use it. The guy at the local pool hall says he's got four pinball machines of his own and he does not want Warren in there taking his customers away. Realizing that the pool hall has a sort of monopoly on pinball-playing types, young Warren becomes depressed at having been cut out of the action. As they say in the retail business, "Location, location, and location."

But wait. Young Warren suddenly realizes that all those pinball-playing pool-hall types have crew cuts, a type of haircut usually administered by a guy named Sarge. A trip to Sarge's barbershop indicates two things: (1) an absence of a pinball machine and (2) an abundance of pinball-playing pool-hall types waiting for their crew cuts to be administered by Sarge. At this very moment Warren has a "conflagration of clarity" and strikes his first joint venture, promising Sarge 20% of all revenues from the pinball machine if he will let young Warren put it in his shop. Sarge, always keen on making a dollar, says, "Yeah," and promptly goes into business with young Warren. The next day young Warren returns to the barbershop and finds $10 in the machine. Thinking that he just invented the wheel, he deposits 20% of the take ($2) with Sarge and pockets the other 80% ($8). Walking out of the barbershop, young Warren realizes that this is going to be a very profitable business venture.

All right, you MBA types, if young Warren's pinball business keeps making him $8 a day for the rest of the year, and Warren locks Sarge into a ten-year exclusive lease agreement for the space, and after ten years the building must be torn down, what is young Warren's business worth today?

Good question. But the answer isn't exactly clear. Let's look at some of the economics of the business. First, Warren's cash and property assets

ASSETS	
Cash	
(from one day of business)	$ 8.0
Property	$ 35.0
Total Assets	$ 43.0
LIABILITIES	
Debt	$
Paid-in Capital	
(the money he started the business with)	$ 35.0
Retained Earnings	
(the money he kept from operations)	$ 8.0
STOCKHOLDERS' EQUITY/BOOK VALUE	
(the sum of paid-in capital plus retained earnings)	$ 43.0
TOTAL STOCKHOLDERS' EQUITY & LIABILITIES	
	$ 43.0

are worth a total of $43 and he has no liabilities. So his balance sheet, a thing that accountants use to determine a business's financial position on a particular day, looks like this at the end of his first day of business:

Let's go through the balance sheet.

Assets of $8 in cash come from the first day of business; the property is the pinball machine, worth $35. There is no debt, so liabilities are $0. Paid-in capital is the money that was initially invested to start the business, which in this case is the value of the pinball machine, $35. Retained earnings are what was made by the business on its first day of operations, $8. Stockholders' equity is the sum of paid-in capital and the retained earnings ($35 + $8 = $43). Note that you can do a balance sheet for any day of the year, but most businesses only do it at the end of a fiscal quarter and the fiscal year.

The income statement is another document that shows how much money a business earned during a particular period of time. For Warren's pinball business the income statement for the first day would look like this:

Revenues	$ 10.00
Expenses	– 2.00
Income	$ 8.00

Revenues equal the amount of money that was taken in, $10. Expenses equal the amount paid to Sarge, $2. Income equals the amount young Warren can stick in his pocket.

VALUATION OF WARREN'S PINBALL BUSINESS

We can see from the balance sheet that the company's net worth is $43. Would you sell this business enterprise for $43, its net worth? No, I don't think so, because you believe, like young Warren, that it's going to make $8 a day for the next ten years. So what is Warren's business enterprise worth? Good question. We know that this is a business that can generate $8 a day in profits. We know also that Sarge keeps his business open seven days a week and takes particular pride in staying open on holidays, which means that he is open 365 days a year. (Okay, Sarge is a little weird.) Multiply the daily profit of $8 by 365 days and you get $2,920 a year in profits ($8 × 365 = $2,920). If you bought the business for its shareholders' equity/book value of $43 you would expect to pocket pretax profits of $2,920 in Year 1. Not a bad return on your investment. So, always looking for a great investment, you approach young Warren and make him an offer of $43 for his business. Young Warren, being nobody's fool, tells you that his pinball business is worth more than $43 and that you can go pound sand.

Feeling a bit miffed, you respond, "Well, if you're so smart, young Warren, just what is your pinball business worth?" And young Warren, being the intelligent business boy that he is, tells you what his business is worth.

He says that his pinball business makes $2,920 a year and he expects to be in business for the next ten years, so he will in effect be selling you an income stream of $2,920 a year for the next ten years. He also tells you that his business is worth the present value of that ten-year income stream of $2,920 a year. Present value? "What?" you say. And he says, "Present value." Standing there embarrassed by your business naïveté, young Warren launches into a dissertation on the theory of discounting to present value and comparing annual compounding rates of return.

He says, "Look, if you have an income stream of $2,920 a year for a period of ten years, at the end of that ten years you will have collected the sum of $29,200. That is, if you don't spend any of the money you take in, effectively retaining all the earnings.

"And get this," he says with glee. "If you save that money and make monthly deposits into a money market fund that pays 8%, at the end of ten years you will have approximately $44,516.86. So, Mr. Buyer, the question you have to ask is, What is that future $44,516.86 worth today, as we stand here?"

So you say to yourself (quietly, so young Warren can't hear you): If interest rates are at 8% how much money would I have to invest today to end up with $44,516.86 in ten years? You whip out your BA-35 Solar supercalculator, which can compute present and future values with the flick of a wrist. You punch in the number of years (N = 10), interest rate (%i = 8%), and the future value (FV = $44,516.86); push the calculate (CPT) button and the present value (PV) button; and voilà, $20,619.92.

What this means is that you, the buyer, would have to invest $20,619.92 at an annual compounding rate of 8% for a period of ten years if you want to collect and save, with interest, the sum of $44,516.86 by the end of Year 10.

You could pay young Warren $20,619.92 for the pinball business and expect the business to earn in total $44,516.86 after ten years of operations, which equates to earning a rate of return of 8% compounded annually for the ten-year period. This seems like a good return on your money, except for one thing. You can get a better return on your money by investing in ten-year 10% AAA corporate bonds.

What does this do to our evaluation? Do you want to invest your money and get an 8% return, or a 10% return? The 10% return would be your choice, given the same amount of risk for both investments.

Thus, if you pay young Warren $20,619.92, you can calculate that you will earn an annual 8% return. If you want to earn a 10% return, you would have to pay young Warren a lesser sum of money.

To learn what you could pay for Warren's pinball business and get an effective rate of return equal to 10%, you must adjust the interest rate input on the present value calculation to reflect a 10% annual compounding rate of return on your money.

The equation for the calculator goes like this: go to the financial mode, put in the number of years (10, N), then the interest rate of 10% (10, %i), the future value, $44,516.86 ($44,516.86, FV); then press the CPT button and the present value button (PV). The figure that comes up will be the amount of money that you can pay for Warren's pinball business and get a 10% return: $17,163.17.

This means that if you spent $17,163.17 for young Warren's business you could expect to earn your principal investment of $17,163.17 back, plus $27,353.69 in earnings, for a total of $44,516.86—which gives you an effective annual compounded rate of return of 10%. (Remember, it is this *annual compounding rate of return* that we are interested in.)

Thus, whatever your return requirements are, it is possible to calculate the amount you have to pay to get that return. Pay above that amount, and you are speculating that the business will do better than projected by past results. Pay less, and you will be getting a greater return on your money.

TAKING A BUSINESS PERSPECTIVE

What this means to you, the buyer, is that you know in advance what you can pay for young Warren's business to get the return you want. *You have taken a business perspective.* You realize the realities of the business and the return that is offered, and are willing only to pay a price that makes economic sense. (In Warren's world, economic sense means an annual rate of return of at least 15%. More on this later.)

You are not caught up predicting that young Warren is going to become the pinball baron of North America with a chain of barbershop pinball machines crisscrossing the United States. No, you will leave that one to the folks on Wall Street. What you are interested in is the *certainty* of the investment's annual rate of return.

Let's think about this from another perspective. Before he spends a dime, the cabdriver who buys a new cab figures out what the cab is going to cost versus what it is going to earn. But a guy who goes out and buys a '62 Corvette because he thinks that it will go up in price has no idea what the return on his investment will be.

The cabdriver has taken a business perspective to analyze the merits of his investment.

The Corvette buyer is speculating and letting greed and hopeful thinking dictate his actions. His ability to calculate his future return blows freely in the winds of fashion and greed.

Another real-life example is the individual who buys commercial real estate, such as an office building. Banks traditionally will not lend money to buy commercial property for more than 80% of what the property can support in rents.

Thus, if a commercial building that rents offices can net $100,000 a year and is debt free, and the banks are charging 10% for mortgage money, then a bank will more than likely be willing to loan the person buying the property up to $800,000.

Most banks will not lend money on a building for more than it will carry in the way of interest payments. Commercial property is almost always bought and sold on a business perspective basis.

Residential real estate, however, has a more speculative nature, with people buying apartment buildings and paying more for them than they can possibly carry with their rental earnings. Thus, any investor will have to put up a huge down payment to cover the excess speculative price in order to make the bank comfortable and give the bank a margin of safety. Banks try to lend money with a business perspective. They keep a sharp eye on what the property can earn, and care little about the rise in real estate values. What banks care about is the property's ability to *generate income* to cover the interest charges.

The speculator, on the other hand, is hoping that real estate values will increase and that in the future he will be able to sell the building at a higher price than he paid. He is not unlike the Corvette buyer, caring little about what the property can realistically earn compared to what it might sell for in the future.

And such is the stock market, where fractional interests in individual businesses are auctioned daily on the motivation of both business perspective investment and greedy speculation. On the business perspective side are the large corporations seeking to buy whole companies so that they can add to their earnings base. On the speculative side are the individual investors and many mutual funds buying not on the basis of sound business reasoning but on the basis of hope and greed.

Understand that the price at which a security is being sold is not always indicative of what the company is worth. Sometimes the true value of the company is more and sometimes it is less. The stock market is made up of people and entities, like corporations and mutual funds, that are motivated by two contrary strategies. Described in their polar extremes, these two strategies encompass investment from a strictly business perspective and rank speculation motivated by fear and greed.

It is this speculation that can send securities to spectacular heights and then to depressingly fear-motivated lows. It is the business perspective that calls them to a medium, down from the greedy heights and up from the fear-motivated lows. Case in point—RJR Nabisco in 1988 was selling for $45 a share. It was earning $5.92 a share and was carrying very little debt. It had a long history of spectacular earnings growth, which was made possible by the profits generated by the tobacco business. However, the public had labeled the company a pariah because of the lawsuits against it by people who claimed they had cancer, caused by smoking. The stock market saw this and responded by keeping the price of the stock low.

The management of RJR Nabisco saw the low price and realized that they could borrow the billions of dollars they needed to buy out the existing shareholders, thus taking total control of the company, and then use the *company's* free cash flow to pay off the billions they had borrowed. Seeing this opportunity, the management formed a group of investors that arranged for billions of dollars of financing from a Wall Street investment bank. With financing lined up, the management/investor group offered to buy all the outstanding stock from the existing shareholders for $75 a share, which equated to paying $17 billion for the entire company. This is somewhat like buying a commercial piece of real estate, paying the seller out of the proceeds from the new mortgage you obtained from the bank, and then paying off the bank with the proceeds from the rents.

In RJR's case, the management/investor group, acting as buyers, sought to buy the company, then mortgage it to pay the owners (the shareholders), and then use the free cash flow to pay off the banks. It was a very clever game, made possible because the speculative public, motivated by fear, oversold the stock and forced the stock's price downward. The management/investor group, knowing what the company was worth from a business perspective, saw an opportunity and jumped on it, moving the stock price from its fear-generated, depressed low of $45 a share to a business perspective valuation of $75 a share.

All would have gone smoothly for the management/investor group except that some guys at a leverage-buyout firm, KKR, thought the company was worth a bit more and found some banks that agreed with them. KKR ended up buying the entire company for roughly $28 billion and change. After the buyout, KKR used RJR's free cash flow, along with the proceeds from the sale of several of its subsidiaries, to pay down the debt, and as of the writing of this book, the company is profitable and has paid off a large portion of the debt incurred from the buyout. (Think of leverage-buyout firms such as KKR as a group of investors who go out and buy a building that doesn't have a mortgage on it, then use the rents the building generates to pay off the bank. But instead of buildings, groups like KKR do it with companies that don't have much debt and that the stock market has undervalued.)

Graham wrote in his 1951 edition of *Security Analysis* that "in general, the market undervalues *a litigated claim* as an asset and overvalues it as a liability. Hence the students of these situations often have an opportunity to buy into them at less than their true value, and to realize attractive profits—on the average—when the litigation is disposed of."

RJR is a perfect case of a fear-motivated public overestimating a liability, which caused the overselling of RJR's stock. Then the business world, motivated by a business perspective, saw the value and was willing to pay a price far in excess of that at which the stock market had been valuing it.

Please note, this is not to say that the business world is not capable of being caught up in speculative greed and then spending too much for an acquisition. It is something that usually happens when management's ego gets wrapped up in the game and the greed of increasing its empire goes to its head, replacing the sound business logic that investing from a business perspective dictates.

10

The Only Two Things You Need to Know About Business Perspective Investing: What to Buy—and at What Price

That's right. If you can answer these two questions, you've got it made. What to buy, and at what price? Seems simple, doesn't it?

The problem is that Wall Street, with its investment bankers and brokers, functions basically as salesmen working for a commission. Obviously they want to get the highest price possible for the goods they are selling. The buyer is almost ensured of never getting a bargain. New issues are priced at their maximum to allow the issuing company to receive the most money for its shares and the investment bank to receive the biggest commission. The stockbroker who calls you on the phone is a commission broker, and like all commission brokers, he is interested only in selling the priciest items that he can.

If the stockbroker is selling you a new issue, then you know immediately that it has been fully priced by the investment bank and you are not getting any bargain. If the stockbroker is selling you an issue that his research department is backing, then you know that you are following the herd mentality. For, as the stock price rises, the enthusiasm of the stockbroker will increase as well. "It's up two points today!" "The sky is the limit on this one!" "Better hurry up, the train is pulling out of the station!"

Warren, on the other hand, loses enthusiasm for any investment as the price rises. Interesting, isn't it, that the man who has made the most money in this game has a strategy opposite to that of the guy who calls you on the phone and is trying to sell you something!

For the oddest of reasons, Wall Street and the individual investor have jumbled the questions of what to buy and at what price into a myriad of financial pyrotechnics that befuddle the imagination. They screw it up by focusing entirely on the question of what to buy and totally ignoring the *question of price*. Like jewelry or art salesmen, they let the aesthetics of the form take precedence over the question of function. The Wall Street broker treats the financial economics of an enterprise as though they were aesthetic qualities and, almost without fail, separates the price entirely from the picture. They never call up and say, "XYZ is an excellent company but its price is too high," because, the truth be known, they probably think XYZ stock is an excellent buy at any price, which is about as dumb as you can get in this game.

Remember, the stockbroker is trying to sell you on the prospects of the stock rising in price, and this is where the aesthetic qualities of the economics of the business come into play. The broker creates the excitement with the economics, and you, the investor, salivating like Pavlov's dog, give him your money. In all that time no one ever said boo about whether or not you have received any true value for your money. But what does value have to do with aesthetics? After all, you have just been sold a painting for $1 million, and the cost of making it was probably less than $500.

However, if function had been your first question, you would view any investment as Warren does—from a business perspective. The nagging question should not be about the rising price of the stock but about whether or not the underlying business is going to make any money. And if so, how much? Once that figure has been determined, the return given for the price asked can be calculated.

It never ceases to amaze me that Wall Street can sell to investors, at wildly ridiculous prices, companies that are just starting out and won't have any earnings for some time. This happens while companies that show a long history of earnings and growth go for a fraction of the price of their speculative cousins.

For Graham the questions of what to buy and at what price were mutually dependent. However, Graham placed a greater emphasis on letting price dictate the what-to-buy decision than does Warren. As long as the company had stable earnings, the per share asking price would determine what could be bought, and Graham had little concern about the nature of the business. Graham didn't care if it manufactured or sold cars, batteries, airplanes, rail cars, or insurance, as long as the price of the company's stock was comfortably below what he thought it was worth. For Graham a low enough price compensated for poor inherent business economics.

Graham developed an arsenal of different techniques to determine the worth of the business in question. Everything from asset values to earning power found its way into his calculation of intrinsic value. Graham calculated the value of a company and then determined if the asking price was low enough for him to make a sufficient profit. Sufficient profit potential afforded him what he called the "margin of safety."

WARREN'S WINNING WAY

(This is a key concept, so pay attention!)

✦ Warren's approach, on the other hand, is to separate the two questions. As we know, first he discovers what to buy and then he decides if the price is right. A real-life analogy would be if Graham went to the discount store to shop for a bargain, any bargain, as long as it's a bargain. You have to know the feeling. You are walking through the store and there before you are snowblowers marked down from $259 to $25. Even though you live in Florida and will probably never use a snowblower, the price is so low that you can't pass it up. That is the essence of who Graham was and how he chose his investments.

✦ Warren's approach is to determine what he wants to buy in advance and then wait for it to go on sale. Thus, the only time he can be found in a discount store is when he's checking it out to see if anything *he needs* is selling cheap. Warren functions in the securities market the same way. He already knows what companies he would like to own. All he is waiting for is the right price. With Warren the what-to-buy question is separate from the at-what-price question. He answers the what-to-buy question first, then determines if it is selling at the right price.

✦ Warren believes that you should first decide what business you want to be in and buy into it only when it is selling at a price that affords you a return on your investment that makes business sense.

Now go back and read it one more time!

How Warren determines which are the right businesses to own at what price will be the focus of the rest of this book.

11

What We Can Learn from Warren's Secret Weapon: The Magic of Compounding

Understanding both the power of compound return and the difficulty of getting it is the heart and soul of understanding a lot of things.

CHARLIE MUNGER
Forbes, January 22, 1996

Before I take you any further, I would like to explain how the magic of compounding sums of money fits into Warren's philosophy and is often overlooked by those who are trying to understand his strategies.

Maybe as a child you were told that if you had one penny and doubled it in a year, you would have two pennies. Now, if you had two pennies in Year 2 and you doubled that amount, you would have four pennies. If you kept this process up for a period of twenty-seven years—.01, .02, .04, .08, .16, .32, .64, 1.28—you would increase your $.01 from Year 1 to $1.3 million in the twenty-seventh year. Sounds financially magical, doesn't it? You are seeing money compounding at a rate of 100% a year.

In the early days of Warren's investment partnership, he was fanatical in his letters and memos to his limited partners about explaining the virtues of compounding sums of money. The reason for this is that compounding is one of the wonders of the world and Warren has used it to dramatic effect in getting the value of his investments to grow at spectacular rates. *But his real trick is getting a high annual compounding rate of return that is not subject to personal income taxes.* It is probably his greatest secret and the one that eludes the majority of students of Buffettology. We will address this brilliant bit of Buffettology later in this chapter, but for right now let's focus on the basics of compounding.

COMPOUNDING

What Warren is seeking from an investment is the largest annual compounding after-tax rate of return possible. Warren believes that compounding is the secret to getting really rich. Let me show you why. Here's how compounding can make you rich.

Shown below is what $100,000 would be worth in ten, twenty, and thirty years if allowed to compound tax-free at an annual rate of 5, 10, 15, and 20%.

	5%	10%	15%	20%
10 years	$ 162,889	$ 259,374	$ 404,555	$ 619,173
20 years	265,329	672,749	1,636,653	3,833,759
30 years	432,194	1,744,940	6,621,177	23,737,631

It's amazing, isn't it? A difference of just 5 to 10 percentage points can have a tremendous effect on your total gains. Your $100,000 compounding annually, tax-free, at a rate of return of 10% would be worth $259,374 at the end of ten years. Increase the rate of return to 20%, and $100,000 compounding, tax-free, at the end of ten years has grown to be worth $619,173; after twenty years, $3,833,759. But $100,000 compounding, tax-free, at an annual rate of return of 20%, held for thirty years, will grow to be worth $23,737,631—a much more profitable number.

The difference that just a few percentage points can make over a *long period of time* is astonishing. Your $100,000 compounding, tax-free, at an annual rate of return of 5% will in thirty years be worth $432,194. But jump to 10%, and in thirty years $100,000 will be worth $1,744,940. Add 5 more percentage points, to compound at 15% a year for thirty years, and $100,000 will grow to $6,621,177. Go from 15% to 20% and you will find that $100,000 compounding annually at 20% will grow in thirty years to $23,737,631.

Here is what $100,000 will be worth in thirty years compounding annually at 5%, 10%, 15%, and 20%:

	5%	10%	15%	20%
30 years	$432,194	1,744,940	6,621,177	23,737,631

Warren is seeking to get the highest annual compounding rate of return possible for the longest period of time possible. At Berkshire Hathaway, Warren has been able to increase the underlying net worth of his company at an *average annual compounding rate of 23.8% for the last thirty-two years.* Which is phenomenal.

I cannot stress enough that the concept of compounding is a key to understanding Warren. It is simple and easy to understand, but for some strange reason its importance in investment theory is grossly understated. For Warren the theory of compounding reigns supreme. Lets look closer at why.

COMPOUNDING AND PERSONAL TAXATION

The objective is to buy a non-dividend-paying stock that compounds for 30 years at 15% a year and pay only a single tax of 35% at the end of the period. After taxes this works out to a 13.4% annual rate of return.

CHARLIE MUNGER
Forbes, January 22, 1996.

The first thing you must understand is that a compounding return is different from what is normally paid on passive investments, such as your basic corporate bond. Normally, the bond investor puts up a fixed amount, usually $1,000, and he loans it to the bond issuer, say, General Motors, for a fixed period of time, say, five years, at a fixed interest rate, like 8%. The investor receives $80 a year for five years, and at the end of the fifth year General Motors will give the investor his $1,000 back. The investor will have earned a total of $400 in interest (5 × $80 = $400).

From a tax standpoint, every time the investor receives his $80 from General Motors, the IRS considers this as income and taxes the investor at the appropriate personal income tax rate. If the investor is a person with high income, his tax rate on that $80 will be around 31%, which means the investor's after-tax yearly return will be $55.20 ($80 − 31% = $55.20). The investor will have earned after taxes a total of *$276* in interest ($55.20 × 5 years = $276) for the five-year period.

But think how great it would be if General Motors, instead of paying out the 8% to the investor and subjecting it to personal income taxes, automatically added it to the principal amount the investor originally loaned the company. This would increase the principal amount the investor loaned to GM and thus increase the principal amount on which the investor is earning 8%. This means that your investment in General Motors bonds would be compounding at an annual rate of 8%. It also allows the investor to skip the personal income tax levy until the very end, when bonds come due and General Motors pays him back the principal plus interest.

So, in our General Motors case the investor loans GM $1,000 and earns 8%, or $80, his first year. Instead of paying the money out, GM keeps it and buys more bonds for the investor. This brings the investor's loan to GM on the first day of the second year up to $1,080. During the second year GM will pay the investor 8% on $1,080, or $86. And that $86 will then be added to the increased principal amount of $1,080, which will thus bring up the amount of the principal invested to $1,166 on the first day of the third year. This process continues through to the end of the fifth year.

The following table shows the results of compounding tax free:

YEAR	AMOUNT INVESTED	INTEREST EARNED AND RETAINED
1	$1,000.00	$ 80.00
2	1,080.00	86.40
3	1,166.40	93.31
4	1,259.71	100.77
5	1,360.48	108.83
		$469.31

At the end of five years, when the bonds come due, the investor will get a check for $1,469.31. This means the General Motors compounding bond gives the investor back his principal investment of $1,000 plus total interest for the five-year period of $469.31. The investor would pay personal income taxes on the $469.31, which would reduce his earnings by 31%, to *$323.82* ($469.31 – 31% = $323.82). This means that his investment is compounding at an annual rate of 8% for five years before the IRS shows up.

Sounds great, doesn't it? Too bad the IRS won't let the investor get away with this. They long ago figured this trick out and will send him a tax bill in the year the interest is earned, even though he won't see a check until the end of year 5.

But for Warren the IRS missed one very important point. In Warren's world, buying a company's equity (common stock) is the same as buying its debt. Warren thinks of a stock as a kind of equity/bond. The only difference between it and a normal bond is that the rate of return on the equity/bond is not fixed, but will vary year to year in relationship to the earnings of the company. *What the IRS missed is that the return on Warren's equity/bond is not subject to personal income tax unless it is paid out as a dividend to the investor.*

Understand that the net earnings reported by a company in its annual report or by the investment surveys, such as *Standard and Poor's* or *Value Line,* are an after-corporate-income-tax figure. This means that those earnings will be subject to no further taxation unless the company pays out the earnings to you as a dividend. If the company pays out the earnings as a dividend, then you have to pay personal income taxes on the dividends received.

For example, if Company A has after-corporate-income-tax earnings of $10 a share and it pays that $10 a share out to its shareholders, then those shareholders have to pay personal income taxes on that $10, which gives them an after-personal-income-tax return of approximately $7. But if Company A chose to retain that $10 and not pay it out as a dividend, then the shareholders' money would sit inside the company, free from the punitive effects of personal income taxes and free to compound.

Warren saw that the income earned on corporate and government bonds was being taxed at personal-income-tax rates. This meant that if he bought a corporate or government bond that was paying 8%, his after-personal-income-tax rate of return would be approximately 5.5% (8% rate of return – a 31% tax rate = 5.5%).

Warren is interested in companies that have per share earnings that are strong and show an upward trend. This means that he can buy his equity/bond and get an expanding rate of return. Think of it: the rate of return, instead of being fixed, is growing. And if the company doesn't pay the earnings out to Warren as a dividend, but instead chooses to retain them, Warren is protected from personal income taxes until he sells his investment, which could be never.

The earnings that are retained by the company will compound at the effective rate of return at which the company can profitably reinvest them. Compounding earnings and no personal income taxation. Sounds great to me. (Remember, Warren's investment objective is to get the highest compounding rate of return possible for the longest period of time possible.)

As we said earlier, over the last thirty-two years Berkshire Hathaway has been able to earn an average annual *compounded* rate of return on invested capital of approximately 23%. So, if you paid book value for Berkshire, which you could do in the early eighties, you would in effect have been buying an equity/bond paying you an after-tax compounded return of approximately 23% a year. Of course, Berkshire can't send you the 23% that you earned on your investment, because to do so would bring the IRS to your door. Then again, you probably couldn't allocate capital as well as Warren does and would not be able to get a 23% return on your money. So it is better that you leave your money in Berkshire and let the increase Berkshire's net worth be reflected by an increase in the price of its stock. In Berkshire's case the stock price rose from $500 a share in 1982 to a high of $48,600 a share in 1997.

Of course, when you sell your investment in Berkshire the tax collector demands a cut of your capital gain. But when that happens is up to you, and in the meantime you are collecting your 23% free from personal income taxes.

$

So let's say that you invest $1,000 in a ten-year Warren-type equity/bond and you expect to earn a compounding annual rate of return of 23% a year. In Year 10 you should have an investment that is worth $7,925, for a profit of $6,925. If you subtract the 20% capital gains tax from that profit of $6,925, you will end up with an after-capital-gains-tax profit of $5,540. This gives you a compounding after-capital-gains-tax annual rate of return of 20.65% for the ten-year period. (In case you're wondering, a $100,000 investment that is compounding at 20.65% for ten years is worth $653,541 in Year 10. Stretch the time period out for thirty years, and the $100,000 will have compounded to $27,913,853.)

To get an after-personal-income-tax compounding annual rate of return of 20.65% out of a normal corporate bond, which pays a taxable fixed rate of return, the bond would have to earn an annual rate of return of approximately 29.94%. (A return of 29.94% – personal income taxes of 31% = 20.65%.)

If I offered you a ten-year bond paying a yearly rate of return of 29.94% in an AAA-rated company, would you take it? You bet you would. In fact, you would take all of it you could, and then set up a partnership to get your friends' money into it. You could have done the equivalent by investing in Berkshire Hathaway in the early eighties. In fact, all of Wall Street could have—but did they? Only a few, like Mario Gabelli, Sequoia Fund, and T. Rowe Price, but that's about it. And people wonder why the majority of Wall Street customers aren't the ones who own the yachts.

COMPOUNDING AND THE PRICE YOU PAY

Many investment analysts believe that if you are buying an excellent business you anticipate holding for a number of years, you needn't be all that concerned about the price you pay. *Nothing could be more wrong.* Consider this: In 1987 the tobacco and food giant Philip Morris traded in a price range of between $6.07 and $10.36 a share (adjusted for splits). Ten years later, in 1997, it traded at $44 a share. If you paid $6.07 for a share back in 1987 and sold it for $44 a share in 1997, your pretax annual compounding rate of return would be approximately *21.9%*. But if you paid $10.36 a share back in 1987 and sold it for $44 a share in 1997, your pretax annual compounding rate of return would equate to approximately *15.56%*.

If you had invested $100,000 in Philip Morris at $6.07 a share back in 1987, it would have compounded annually at 21.9% and grown to be worth approximately $724,497.77 by 1997. But if you had invested $100,000 in Philip Morris at $10.36 a share back in 1987, it would have compounded annually at 15.56% and grown to be worth approximately $424,693.22 by 1997. That's a difference of $299,804.55. Which is a lot of money!

To perform the above equation on your BA-35 Solar financial calculator, first make sure the calculator is in its financial mode (hit the MODE key until you see a small FIN on the screen). Punch in Philip Morris's 1987 per share market price of $6.07 as the present value (the PV key), then punch in the number of years, 10 (the N key). Punch in the per share price you sold the stock at in 1997, which was $44, as the future value (the FV key). Then hit the calculation key (CPT) and the interest key (%i). The calculator will tell you that your compounding annual rate of return for the ten-year period on your original investment of $6.07 a share is 21.9%.

A final thought on the wonders of compounding. Warren is famous for driving older-model cars. In the early days of his partnership he drove a VW Beetle. People observing this attribute it to a general lack of interest in acquiring material items. What they fail to see is how his compounding influences his spending habits. An automobile that costs $20,000 today will be worth little or nothing in ten years. But Warren knows that he can get a 23% annual compounding rate of return on his investments. This means that $20,000 invested today will be worth $158,518 in ten years. In twenty years it will be worth $1,256,412, and in thirty years it will be worth $9,958,257. To Warren, $9,958,257 is just way too much money to throw away on a new car.

12

Determining What Kind of Business You Want to Own

What are the characteristics of the business that you would want to own? In Warren's world this is the key question that sets the stage. You have to know what you want to buy before you look at the price.

Warren has always maintained that identifying what to invest in is a mind-challenging event. In Warren's case, after spending his early years following Graham's philosophy, which often led to his buying mediocre businesses, he rebelled against his mentor and embraced the philosophies of Philip Fisher and Charles Munger.

Fisher and Munger, through experience, developed an investment philosophy that advocated investing only in *businesses that have superior economics* working in their favor and are selling for the right price. Fisher and Munger agreed with Graham that the price you pay determines the return on your investment. But they differed from Graham on what was a *desirable purchase.*

Graham believed that most businesses were possible candidates for investment as long as he perceived them to be selling at a bargain price. For Graham, the possibilities were endless, and his investment portfolio reflected this thinking. On any given day he might own positions in a hundred or more different stocks. He thought that most businesses had an intrinsic value and that when they sold well below that value they were candidates for acquisition. The investor merely had to determine the intrinsic value of the business, which Graham said was more of a "range of value" than a single price. He liked to say that if a man was fat you didn't have to know his exact weight to know he was fat.

The problem with this approach is determining what is fat. Think of it this way. To most British people, the Germans seem fat, while most Germans think the British skinny. The same is true in business. What appears to be skinny may be fat, and what may appear fat may be really skinny. Graham wasn't all that concerned with the nature of the business he was buying. He couldn't be. He was involved in too many businesses.

What Graham did to try and solve this problem was set up standards for determining if a business was fat or not. One method he used over the thirty-odd years he was managing money was to purchase a group of common stocks at less than their working-capital value, or net-current-assets value, giving no weight to plant and other fixed assets, and deducting all liabilities in full from the current assets. Another method he used was to buy a group of stocks at less than seven times reported earnings for the past twelve months.

Graham warned that these methods were to be used for the purchase of a group of companies and not single stocks. Graham calculated that, as a group they would afford the investor an average annual return of between 15% and 20% over a long period of time, say, ten years.

Graham's philosophy failed, however, with the central problem of buying below intrinsic value. That is, in order for the investor to profit from the transaction, the price of the business he bought below its intrinsic value must someday rise *to* or *above* the stock's intrinsic value. Thus we have the *realization of-value-problem* of intrinsic-value-oriented investing.

To put it more bluntly, what do you do with those companies you bought at a price below their intrinsic value if they continue to sell below their intrinsic value?

Let's play with an example. Say Graham found a company that he believed was worth $62.50 a share but that was selling for $50 a share. In Graham's world this company's stock was undervalued by $12.50. If Graham invested in the company at $50 a share and the stock's price rose the first year to $62.50 a share, then he would have made a 25% return on his money. But here is the problem: If the company doesn't realize its $62.50 value in the first year, the return on his investment drops dramatically. If the company reaches full intrinsic value, $62.50, in the second year, Graham's return drops to 11.8% compounded annually. If the company doesn't become fully priced until the third year, Graham's return drops to 7.7% compounded annually. In the fourth year it drops to 5.7% and in the fifth year to 4.5%. If the company continues to sell at $50 a share, his return is a *big zero*.

Thus, the realization-of-value problem. If the realization of value doesn't occur, every year that you wait, your projected annual compounding rate of return *substantially diminishes*. And if it takes longer than a few years, you end up with an annual compounding rate of return that may be less than what you would have received if you had put your money into a savings account at the local bank.

Graham's solution to this problem was to require what he called a *margin of safety* (a concept he adapted from bond analysis). Thus, Graham would invest only in companies whose projected return was approximately 25% or better, which gave him a sufficient margin of safety to weather a number of years. (The projected return is the difference between the stock market price and Graham's determination of the stock's intrinsic value.) This way Graham ensured himself an adequate return even if he had to wait several years for the company to reach its full intrinsic value.

To protect against those companies that never reached full price he diversified his holdings, sometimes—as noted—owning up to one hundred or more different companies. He also instigated a program that called for selling any holding that had not reached its full value within two to three years. Graham was not a real long-term player. He couldn't be. For Graham, the longer the investment took to reach full intrinsic value, the lower his annual compounding rate of return would be.

Graham eventually concluded that many companies were incapable of being analyzed and their intrinsic value could not be determined. He developed a standard that required the company to have stable earnings before a security analyst should venture in and determine its intrinsic value. Stable earnings for Graham equated to predictable earnings, which would allow for a more exact calculation of intrinsic value. Thus, the requirement of stable earnings started Graham in a direction that allowed for exclusion of some businesses that didn't have stable earnings from the evaluation process.

Graham, by using this limited point of view, began to restrict his field of possible investments. Quantitative reasoning, though reflective of the qualitative side of a business, does not fully articulate *what is happening in a business.* Stable earnings may allow one to place an intrinsic value on a business, but they will not always indicate the nature of the business's underlying economics. Stable earnings merely allow for a perceived sound base from which to perform mathematical calculations.

Warren found that, effective as Graham's methods were, they lacked certainty and often left him holding on to investments that never performed. Warren's investments in such businesses as Vornado, Sperry & Hutchinson, Dempster Mill Manufacturing, and Hochschild-Kohn were made on a Grahamian basis, but their value continued a southward journey along with the economics of their businesses.

In addition, Grahamian philosophy dictated that an investment be sold when it reached its intrinsic value or after holding it for two to three years. But Warren found that every time he sold a Grahamian-type investment and it worked positively, taxes would erode his profit.

Warren discovered the solution to this problem in the philosophies of Charlie Munger and Philip Fisher, who advocated investing only in excellent businesses that have an *expanding value.*

13

The Theory of an Expanding Intrinsic Value

Philip Fisher and Charlie Munger realized that certain companies with particular economics had a sort of expanding value and that even though a company sold continuously below its intrinsic value, if the profitability of the company kept improving, *eventually the price of the stock would rise to reflect the improved economics of the business.*

A perfect example of this is the General Foods play, which we discussed in Chapter 7. General Foods' per share earnings continued to rise from the year 1979, when Warren started buying the stock, through 1985, when Philip Morris bought out the company. As the earnings of General Foods rose, the intrinsic value of the company rose as well. And with this increase in intrinsic value, the company's stock price also rose. But even with this increase in stock price the market continued to value the company just at or below its intrinsic value relative to the return on government bonds. Let me show you.

Year	Earnings	Selling Price	I.V.*	Govt. Yd.†
79	$5.12	$28–37	$51	10.0%
80	5.14	24–35	43	11.9%
81	4.47	28–35	34	13.1%
82	5.73	29–48	54	10.6%
83	6.10	37–54	51	11.9%
84	6.96	45–60	60	11.6%
85	Philip Morris buyout for $120.00 a share.			

*I.V. = Intrinsic value relative to government bonds. This is the amount you would have to invest in government bonds in a given year to earn the equivalent rate of return that a share of General Foods was earning. This method of valuation is fully explained in Chapter 34.

†Govt. Yd. = The average yield on government bonds in the given year.

We can see in the table we just looked at that in 1979 General Foods was earning $5.12 a share and the market price for the stock was between $28 and $37 a share. Earnings of $5.12 a share against a stock price of between $28 and $37 a share equates to a rate of return of between 13 and 18% ($5.12 ÷ $28 = 18%). We can see also that the rate of return for government bonds in 1979 was 10%, which gives a share of General Foods stock a relative value to government bonds of $51.20 ($5.12 ÷ .10 = $51.20). This means you would have to purchase $51.20 worth of government bonds yielding 10% annually to earn $5.12 a year ($51.20 × .10 = $5.12).

Using classical Graham, Warren might have sold the General Foods position in 1981 as the market price started to reflect the intrinsic value of the company relative to the return on government bonds. He might have done so again in 1984, when the stock price had risen to $60 a share, reflecting the increase in per share earnings. And again using Graham, Warren might have sold the stock after holding it for two or three years because there had been no significant increase in the stock's price.

But because General Foods *is the kind of business that has an expanding value,* Warren held on to the position. Even though the company continued at times to sell below its intrinsic value, the market price continued to rise. Warren knew that the market price would rise eventually because the economics of the business would allow the company to experience long-term economic growth, which would be reflected by increasing per share earnings. And the *stock market would eventually increase the market price of the stock to reflect the increase in per share earnings.*

Warren, using the rationale of Fisher and Munger, realized that eventually the stock market would fully value General Foods stock, and if it didn't, the stock would still rise in price as the market value of the stock followed up the increasing intrinsic value of the company. To paraphrase Graham: *Short term, the market is a voting machine, letting whim, fear, and greed dictate how it votes. But long term, the market is a weighing machine that values a company according to the weight of its intrinsic value.*

Regardless of where the winds of finance blew from 1979 to 1985, Warren could buy General Foods stock at a market price that in relationship to its earnings would allow him a return of at least

13%, and often near 20%. (Remember, Warren considers the per share earnings *retained by the company* to be his return.) Warren's only concern was whether the business nature of General Foods was such that *the earnings of the company would continue to grow, thus protecting and expanding his estimated rate of return.*

Thus, during the seventies, Warren began to realize that the Grahamian approach to investing—purchasing anything and everything that was defined as a bargain—was not the ideal strategy. Warren found that mediocre businesses really didn't have predictable earnings. An enterprise with poor inherent economics more often than not would remain that way. And though the company may have a period of hopeful results, the extreme competitiveness of commerce would in the end rule out any long-term profitability that would increase the value of the company.

He also found that the average or mediocre business would, in effect, forever tread water and the stock market, seeing lackluster results, would never become enthusiastic about the enterprise. The end result: a business with a stock price that did nothing. Warren also found that even when the market did close the gap between market price and the projected intrinsic value, his return was lackluster because the gain was limited to the difference between the spread of the intrinsic value and the market price. In addition, capital gains taxes would eat into his return. But because the inherent economics of the business were so poor, staying in it was like taking a boat that went nowhere.

Warren has defined Grahamian investment strategy as buying something at a low enough price with the hope that sometime in the near future there will be an event that increases the fortunes of the business and enables the investor to sell his holdings at a decent profit. With the low price providing the margin of safety, the investor was ensured against permanent capital loss.

But he discovered that the event that would cause the company's fortunes to increase often never occurred, and just as often the reverse would happen. Some event would occur that caused the company's fortunes to decrease, which left him scrambling either to dump the position or shore up a crumbling foundation.

Additionally, if the event did occur and Warren sold the position, the profits would be subject to the punitive effects of the capital gains tax, which would eat away a considerable chunk of his return.

His great revelation regarding this method of investing was that a mediocre business more than likely will remain a mediocre business and that the investor's results will probably be mediocre as well. Any advantage that the bargain purchase had originally given the investor would be eroded away by the low return the mediocre business earned.

Warren learned that time is the friend of the great business enterprise and a curse to the mediocre.

He discovered also that the economics of an excellent business were entirely different from those of a mediocre business. He found that if he could buy an excellent business, the business, in effect, would have an *expanding value* as opposed to the mediocre business's *static value*. He realized that the excellent business's expanding value would eventually cause the stock market to lift the price of the stock.

Thus the added kicker to the excellent-business expanding-value phenomenon: If the business continued to grow, it made more sense to hold the investment indefinitely than to get out of it. This would enable Warren to put off the capital gains tax to some far-off date and to enjoy the fruits of compounding retained earnings.

Warren loves to use two examples to drive this point home. The *Washington Post* is the first. With the *Post*, Warren bought roughly 1,727,765 shares in 1973 for $9,731,000. He has held that investment to this day, and it is currently worth in the neighborhood of $600 million. That gives Warren a compounded yearly return on his *Washington Post* investment, over a twenty-four-year period, of approximately 18.7%.

Imagine being able to invest in a bond that paid an interest rate of 18.7%. Now imagine that all the interest payments that were paid out would also earn 18.7%. Sounds sweet to me. And that is what Warren effectively got when he bought his interest in the *Washington Post* stock—an annual rate of return of 18.7%, compounding annually for twenty-four years.

Even though Warren has admitted that at times during the last twenty-four years the *Washington Post* has traded at market prices in excess of its intrinsic value, he has continued to hold the investment because it is an excellent business and because he knew that to take full advantage of the wonders of compounding he needed to hold the investment for a long time.

His investment in GEICO, an insurance company, was made under similar circumstances. Warren acquired $45,713,000 worth of GEICO stock around 1972. In 1995 it was worth approximately $1,759,594,000, giving him an annual compounding rate of return of approximately 17.2%. GEICO is another company Warren identifies as an excellent business. (In fact he liked owning GEICO stock so much that he bought the rest of the company in 1996. More of a good thing—is a good thing.)

He also is fond of the Coca-Cola example. Coca-Cola went public in 1919 at $40 a share. If you had bought one share for $40 then and held it until 1993, reinvesting all the dividends, your one share of stock would have grown to be worth more than $2.1 million. That equates to approximately a 15.8% annual compounding rate of return on your investment.

Warren, confronted with the realization-of-value problem, started to regard the Grahamian philosophy of buying any and all companies regardless of their nature as foolish and, as noted, started integrating into his philosophy the Fisher/Munger theory of the expanding value of the excellent business.

14

The Mediocre Business

One of the great keys to Warren's success is that he figured out a method for determining whether he was dealing with one of those rare excellent businesses that would allow him to reap a bountiful harvest year after year or with a mediocre business whose inherent economics would cement him to mediocre results.

To facilitate his thinking, Warren divided the business world into two separate categories:

1

the basic *commodity-type business,* which he found consistently produced inferior results

2

the *excellent business,* which possesses what Warren calls a *consumer monopoly*

He discovered that the underlying economics of consumer monopolies were the most profitable for their owners and that as a group they tended to outperform the market as a whole.

But first things first. Let us look at the commodity-type business and the subtleties that make it an undesirable investment when compared to the enterprise that has a consumer monopoly working in its favor.

THE COMMODITY-TYPE BUSINESS

When we say commodity-type business we mean a business that sells a product whose price is the single most important motivating factor in the consumer's buy decision. The most simple and obvious commodity-type businesses that we deal with in our daily lives are

+ textile manufacturers
+ producers of raw foodstuffs such as corn and rice
+ steel producers
+ gas and oil companies
+ the lumber industry
+ paper manufacturers

All these companies sell a commodity for which there is considerable competition in the marketplace. The price is the single most important motivating factor for the consumer making a buy decision.

One buys gasoline on the basis of price, not on the basis of brand, even though the oil companies would like us to believe that one brand is better than the other. Price is the dictating factor. The same goes for such goods as concrete, lumber, bricks, and memory and processing chips for your computer (though Intel is trying to change this by giving its processing chips brandname recognition).

Let's face it. It really doesn't matter where the corn you buy in the store comes from, as long as it is corn and it tastes like corn. The intense level of competition leads to very competitive markets and, in the process, very low profit margins.

In commodity-type businesses the low-cost provider wins. This is because the low-cost provider has a greater freedom to set prices. Costs are lower, therefore profits margins are higher. It's a simple concept but it has complicated implications, because to be the low-cost producer usually means that the company must constantly make manufacturing improvements to keep the business competitive. This requires additional capital expenditures, which tend to eat up retained earnings, which could have been spent on new-product development or acquiring new enterprises, which would increase the value of the company.

The scenario usually works like this: Company A makes improvements in its manufacturing process, which lowers its cost of production, which increases its profit margins. Company A then lowers the price of its product in an attempt to take a greater market share from Companies B, C, and D.

Companies B, C, and D start to lose business to Company A and respond by making the same improvements to the manufacturing process as Company A. Companies B, C, and D then lower their prices to compete with Company A and in the process destroy any increase in Company A's profit margins that the improvements in the manufacturing process created. And then the vicious cycle repeats itself.

There are occasions on which demand for a service or product outstrips supply. When Hurricane Andrew smashed into Florida and destroyed thousands of homes, the cost of sheet plywood shot through the roof. At times like this, all the producers and sellers make substantial profits. But increase in demand is usually met with increase in supply. And when demand slackens, the excess increase in supply drives prices and profit margins down again.

Additionally, a commodity-type business is entirely dependent upon the quality and intelligence of management to create a profitable enterprise. If management lacks foresight or engages in wasting the company's precious assets by allocating resources unwisely, the business could lose its advantage as the low-cost producer and face the possibility of competitive attack and financial ruin.

From an investment standpoint, of Warren's two business models, commodity-type businesses offer the least for future growth of shareholder value. First, these companies' profits are kept low because of price competition, so the money just isn't there to expand the business or to invest in new and more profitable business ventures. And second, even if they did manage to make some money, this capital is usually spent upgrading plant and equipment to keep abreast of the competition.

Commodity-type businesses sometimes try to create product distinction by bombarding the buyer with advertising in which manufacturers attempt to get the buyer to believe their product is better than the competition's. In some instances there are considerable product modifications to keep ahead of the competition. The problem, however, is that no matter what is done to a commodity-type product, if the choice the consumer makes is motivated by price alone, the company that is the low-cost producer will be the winner, and the rest end up struggling.

As an example of the poor investment qualities of the commodity-type business, Warren loves to use Burlington Industries, which manufactures textiles, a commodity-type product.

In 1964 Burlington Industries had sales of $1.2 billion and the stock sold for an adjusted-for-splits price of around $30 a share. Between 1964 and 1985 the company made capital expenditures of about $3 billion, or about $100 a share, on improvements to become more efficient and therefore more profitable. The majority of the capital expenditures were for cost improvements and expansion of operations. And even though in 1985 the company reported sales of $2.8 billion, it had lost sales volume in inflation-adjusted dollars. It was also getting far lower returns on sales and equity than it did in 1964. The stock in 1985 sold for $34 a share, or a little better than it did in 1964. Twenty-one years of business operations and $3 billion in shareholder money spent, and still the stock had given its shareholders only a modest appreciation.

The managers at Burlington are some of the most able in the textile industry, but the industry is the problem. Poor economics, which developed from excess competition, resulted in substantial overcapacity in the entire textile industry. Substantial overcapacity means price competition, which means lower profit margins, which means lower profits, which means a poorly performing stock and disappointed shareholders.

Warren is fond of saying that when management with an excellent reputation meets a business with a poor reputation, it is usually the business's reputation that remains intact.

IDENTIFYING A COMMODITY-TYPE BUSINESS

Identifying a commodity-type business is not that difficult; they usually are selling something that a lot of other businesses are selling. Characteristics include low profit margins, low returns on equity, difficulty with brand-name loyalty, the presence of multiple producers, the existence of substantial excess production capacity in the industry, erratic profits, and profitability almost entirely dependent upon management's abilities to efficiently utilize tangible assets.

The basic characteristics of a commodity business are

+ *Low profit margins.* Low profit margins are the result of competitive pricing—one company lowering the price of its products to compete with another company.

+ *Low returns on equity.* Low returns on equity are a good indication that the company that you are looking at is a commodity type. Since the average return on equity for an American corporation is approximately 12%, anything below that may indicate the presence of poor business economics created by commodity-type markets and pricing.

+ *Absence of any brand-name loyalty.* If the brand name of the product you just bought doesn't mean a lot, you can bet you are dealing with a commodity-type business.

+ *Presence of multiple producers.* Go into any auto supply store and you will find seven or eight different brands of oil, all of them selling for about the same price. Multiple producers breed competition, and competition breeds lower prices, and lower prices breed lower profit margins and lower profit margins breed lower earnings for the shareholders.

+ *Existence of substantial excess production capacity in the industry.* Anytime you have substantial excess production capacity in an industry, no one can really profit from an increase in demand until the excess production capacity is used up. Then and only then can prices start to rise. However, when prices rise, management will get the urge to grow. Grand visions of huge industrial empires may dance in management's heads. And with pockets full of shareholder's riches derived from the increase in demand and prices, management will set forth on the ultimate in grand illusions. They will expand production and in the process create even more production capacity.

The problem is that the guys down the street who are the competition also have the same idea. Soon everybody expands production and we are back in the position of overcapacity. Overcapacity means price wars, and price wars mean lower profit margins and profits. And then everything starts all over again.

+ *Erratic profits.* A real good sign that you are dealing with a commodity-type business is that the profits are wildly erratic. A survey of a company's per share earnings for the last seven to ten years will usually show any boom-or-bust patterns, which are endemic to the commodity-type business.

YEAR	EARNINGS
1987	$1.57
1988	.16
1989	.28
1990	.42
1991	(.23) (loss)
1992	.60
1993	1.90
1994	2.39
1995	.43
1996	(.69) (loss)

If yearly per share earnings of the business in question look like this——then you might suspect that it is a commodity-type business.

+ *Profitability almost entirely dependent upon management's abilities to efficiently utilize tangible assets.* Anytime profitability of a company is largely dependent upon the business's ability to efficiently utilize its tangible assets, such as plant and equipment, and *not* on such intangible assets as *patents, copyrights,* and *brand names,* you should suspect that the company in question is of the commodity type.

IN SUMMARY

Remember, if price is the single most important motivating factor in the purchase of a product, then you are most likely dealing with a commodity-type business. As such, the company probably will present you at best with only average results over the long term.

15

How to Identify the Excellent Business—The Key to Warren's Good Fortune

As we know, Warren is looking only for companies with great economics, companies for which he can reasonably predict future income. Throughout his investment career Warren has been able to find a number of these companies. He discovered that they all were selling a product or service that created what he calls a *consumer monopoly*.

The toll bridge is a classic form of the consumer monopoly. If you, the consumer, want to cross a river without swimming or using a boat, you very likely have to cross on a bridge, and to use the bridge you may have to pay the toll. The toll bridge has a kind of monopoly on crossing the river at that particular place. The same can be said when a large town has only *one* newspaper; if you want to advertise in the paper, you have to pay the advertising rate the paper is charging or you don't advertise. This consumer monopoly gives the toll bridge or the newspaper a greater freedom to price, which means greater profits for the shareholders.

In this chapter we shall address how to identify the exceptional business that has a consumer monopoly working in its favor. This is the "what Warren likes to buy" portion of the book. And what Warren wants to buy are companies that have products or services that create consumer monopolies.

WARREN IS SEARCHING FOR A COMPANY WITH A CONSUMER MONOPOLY

To get the mental juices flowing, lets take a quick jaunt back in time and take a look at some early thinkers who addressed the investment value of the consumer monopoly.

In 1938, an enterprising student by the name of Lawrence N. Bloomberg, who was attending Johns Hopkins University, wrote, as part of his doctoral dissertation, a paper on the investment value of the consumer monopoly. The paper, entitled "The Investment Value of Goodwill," compared the investment values of companies that had consumer monopolies to those of companies that were commodity-type businesses. Bloomberg thought it was consumer goodwill that created (as Warren calls it) the consumer monopoly. He wrote that though goodwill is a state of mind, it adheres to the company because of *some distinctive attributes that are particularly attractive to buyers, who then form an attachment to a company and the products it sells.*

Bloomberg thought consumer goodwill could be associated with a business's having a convenient location, courteous employees, prompt deliveries, and satisfactory products. He thought also that advertising may be so persistent and alluring that it causes the buyer to keep in mind a particular product or trade name when he makes his purchases. Or maybe, through the possession of a secret process or a patent, a company is able to supply an unusual or slightly different product—think of the secret process for making Coca-Cola.

Bloomberg said that because of the above factors a company could obtain superior results—which equated with higher returns on equity, superior earnings growth, and improved performance of the stock—and that stocks of such companies would outperform the rest of the market no matter whether the economy expanded or contracted.

Warren has developed a conceptual test to determine the presence of such a consumer monopoly. In testing for the presence of a consumer monopoly, he likes to ask this question: *If he had access to billions of dollars (which he does) and his pick of the top fifty managers in the country (which he does), could he start a business and successfully compete with the business in question?*

If the answer is a resounding no, then the company in question is protected by some kind of strong consumer monopoly.

In Warren's world the real test of the strength of a consumer monopoly is how much damage a competitor could do even if he didn't care about making money. Is it possible to compete with the *Wall Street Journal?* You could spend billions and still not put a dent in its readership. Could you start a chewing gum company and compete with Wrigley? Several have tried and several have failed. How about that Hershey chocolate bar? And what about Coca-Cola?

Driving in the high mountains of Indonesia last year, I pulled over to a roadside stand to get something to drink. At this small stand in the middle of nowhere, in a country with almost no signs of Americana, there was only one selection of soda, Coca-Cola.

Just think about Coca-Cola for a moment. Think about how many places sell it. Every gas station, movie theater, supermarket, restaurant, fast food joint, Kwik Shop, bar, hotel, and sporting arena sells Coca-Cola. In every office building in America you can bet that somewhere there is a Coca-Cola machine waiting to take your money. Coca-Cola is such a popular drink that stores and restaurants have to carry it. *They have to carry it!* They have to carry it because if they don't, they will lose sales. Can you name me one other brand-name product that every one of these vendors has to carry?

Try now to compete with Coca-Cola and you would need the capital base of two General Motors, and you probably would still fail. Talk about a consumer monopoly that is bombproof! I personally have consumed thousands of servings of the beverage. How about you? How about your children?

What about Marlboro cigarettes? Ever try to convince a Marlboro smoker to switch brands?

My personal test for a consumer monopoly is to ask this question: if someone gave me the rights to a particular brand name like Marlboro or Wrigley, or the rights to the name and secret formula of Coca-Cola, would the investment bankers at Salomon Brothers or Goldman Sachs consent to raise the billions I would need to start production? If the answer is yes, I know that I've got a winner.

If one were the owner of the only water company in town, one could make a ton of money. The only catch is that the populace long ago had the common sense to regulate the water industry. The same can be said for most utility companies. Great businesses, but regulations keep the owners from obtaining superior results. What you want is an unregulated water company.

The problem is that when companies like this are recognized by the investment community, the prices they sell at are usually astronomically high. Since the price you pay determines the rate of return you get, you will in effect be getting a smaller rate of return. So the trick is to find one that the rest of the world hasn't identified yet. You might say you are looking for a disguised water company.

Bloomberg thought that one of the reasons companies with strong consumer monopolies were so profitable was that they did not have to rely heavily on investments in land, plant, and equipment. Such fixed charges and property taxes loom large in the cost of production of their counterparts (the commodity-type businesses).

In contrast, the wealth of companies with consumer monopolies is principally in the form of intangible assets, such as the secret formula to Coca-Cola or the brand name Marlboro. Inasmuch as federal taxation is practically confined to earnings, the taxes paid by these companies tend to vary with profits, while the taxes paid by companies that have to make continuing heavy investments in physical assets, like General Motors, are not so flexible. Other than during the very early stages of a period of expansion, the physical asset/commodity-type business can meet the increasing demand for its products only by incurring heavy costs for plant expansion.

Companies that benefit from *consumer monopolies,* because of their large cash flows, are often nearly debt free. Companies like Wrigley (maker of chewing gum) and UST (maker of chewing tobacco) have little or no debt on their balance sheets; this gives them a great deal of freedom in pursuing other profitable ventures or purchasing their own shares. Additionally, they are often manufacturers of low-tech products, which don't require sophisticated manufacturing plants. Also, since there is little competition biting at their heels, they can get longer use out of their manufacturing facilities. Not having to compete means being free of the costs of constantly retooling and building new plants.

General Motors, a manufacturer of automobiles, a price-sensitive, commodity-type product, has to spend billions of dollars to retool and build new production facilities just to get a new model car to market. And it's a product that may stay competitive for only a few years before GM has to go back to the drawing board and build again.

It is worth noting that the history of commerce indicates that various forms of consumer monopoly have existed since the beginning of trade. From the Venetians, who profited greatly from their monopoly on trade with the Far East, to the British Empire's early consumer monopoly on high quality steel to the early American West, where the names Colt and Winchester meant quality firearms, to Germany's famed cannon maker Krupp, whose products were found on both sides in the two world wars—all of these businesses profited from the consumer's perception of a need for quality and services, for which they were willing to pay more.

Think of General Electric, the company that Thomas Edison helped start, and the profits it made electrifying the planet. You sell a country the know-how to make electricity and the products to wire it up and then you sell it electric appliances, light bulbs, power tools, and refrigerators. (It's like Gillette giving away the razor in order to get the customer to buy the razor blades.) GE to this day is one of America's most powerful commercial enterprises. Its power is derived in part from the huge amount of capital it acquired in the early part of this century, when it was the only game in town.

16

Nine Questions to Help You Determine If a Business Is Truly an Excellent One

There is a nature to the beast that we are stalking. Warren has discovered that the excellent business has certain other characteristics that help identify it.

I have found that it is easier to break this part of the analysis into a series of questions. Warren uses a similar line of questioning when he is trying to determine the presence of the consumer monopoly, exceptional business economics, and shareholder-oriented management.

Let's walk through the questions:

No. 1

Does the business have an identifiable consumer monopoly?

No. 2

Are the earnings of the company strong and showing an upward trend?

No. 3

Is the company conservatively financed?

No. 4

Does the business consistently earn a high rate of return on shareholders' equity?

No. 5

Does the business get to retain its earnings?

No. 6

How much does the business have to spend on maintaining current operations?

No. 7

Is the company free to reinvest retained earnings in new business opportunities, expansion of operations, or share repurchases? How good a job does the management do at this?

No. 8

Is the company free to adjust prices to inflation?

No. 9

Will the value added by retained earnings increase the market value of the company?

Nine thoughts to spark revelation. Kind of like trying to figure out if your blind date is a hopeful for the altar. Ever been married? Been to college? Has a good job? Does he or she snore?

We do the same thing when we allocate capital to investment. As Warren says, in the field of investing it is better that one act like a Catholic and marry for life. That way one makes sure going in that the partner chosen is one worth keeping—because there is no getting out.

So let's look at these questions in detail.

NO. 1

DOES THE BUSINESS HAVE AN IDENTIFIABLE CONSUMER MONOPOLY?

We have discussed the consumer monopoly and the concept of the toll bridge. It is the first question that you have to ask: Is there a consumer monopoly here? It will be either a brand-name product or a key service that people or businesses are dependent on. Products are much easier to identify than services, so let's start with those.

Go stand outside a convenience store, supermarket, pharmacy, bar, gas station, or bookstore and ask yourself, *What are the brand-name products that this business has to carry to be in business?* What products would a manager be insane not to carry? Make a list.

Now go into the establishment and examine the product, which usually has been shoved in your face by advertising. If it's got a brand name that you immediately recognize, then the chances are good there is some kind of consumer monopoly at work.

Name me a newspaper you can buy at any newsstand in America— *USA Today.* Name me a soda that you can buy anywhere in the world—Coca-Cola. Name me a brand of cigarette that every convenience shop carries—Marlboro. Who owns the rights to the *Little Mermaid* movie that your children can't seem to get enough of? Disney. What kind of breakfast cereal is your child eating? What kind of razor blades do you use every morning? Just take a walk around the local supermarket, and your imagination should go wild.

Companies that provide *services* that constitute consumer monopolies are much harder to identify. Key places to look are in the field of advertising—television networks and advertising agencies—and the financial services providers, such as credit card companies. (Don't worry, there is an entire chapter just ahead that tells you exactly where to look for companies that have consumer monopolies.)

But just because the business has a brand-name product working in its favor does not mean that it is an excellent business. There are dozens of ways for management to fail to maximize the magic of a consumer monopoly.

So after the product or service hits you in the face, you must begin a quantitative/qualitative process of analysis of the company and its management. A great product is where you start, but a great product doesn't necessarily mean a great company.

NO. 2

ARE THE EARNINGS OF THE COMPANY STRONG AND SHOWING AN UPWARD TREND?

A consumer monopoly is a great thing, but management may have done such a poor job running the rest of the company that annual per share earnings fluctuate wildly. Warren is looking for annual per share earnings that are strong and show an upward trend.

Does the per share earnings picture of the company in question look like Company I, or Company II?

Company I		Company II	
YEAR	PER SHARE EARNINGS	YEAR	PER SHARE EARNINGS
87	$1.07	87	$1.57
88	1.16	88	.06
89	1.28	89	.28
90	1.42	90	.42
91	1.64	91	(.23) loss
92	1.60	92	.60
93	1.90	93	1.90
94	2.39	94	2.39
95	2.43	95	.43
96	2.69	96	.69

Warren would be interested in Company I and not Company II. Company II's per share earnings have been way too erratic to predict with any certainty. Regardless of any competitive advantage Company II's products may have, something is going on to cause earnings to gyrate so much.

Company I shows a per share earnings picture that may indicate not only a company that possesses a consumer-monopoly product or products, but also a company whose management can turn that advantage into real shareholder value.

NO. 3

IS THE COMPANY CONSERVATIVELY FINANCED?

Warren likes companies that are conservatively financed. If a company has a great consumer monopoly, then more than likely it is spinning off tons of cash and is in no need of a long-term-debt burden. Warren favorites like Wrigley, UST, and International Flavor & Fragrances have little or no long-term debt. Warren's star performers like Coca-Cola and Gillette both carry long-term debt of less than one times current net earnings.

Sometimes an excellent business with a consumer monopoly will add a large amount of debt to finance the acquisition of another business, such as when Capital Cities more than doubled its long-term-debt burden to acquire the ABC television and radio networks. In a case like this you have to figure out if the acquisition is also a consumer monopoly, which it was in this case. But if it isn't, watch out!

When long-term debt is used to acquire another company, the rules are:

+ When two consumer monopolies go to the altar, it will more than likely be a fantastic marriage. With two consumer monopolies spinning off lots of excess profits, it doesn't take long for even mountains of debt to be reduced to molehills.
+ But when a consumer monopoly marries a commodity-type business, there is usually a mediocre result. This is because the commodity-type business will suck off the profits of the consumer monopoly business to support its poor economics, thus leaving little to pay down the newly acquired debt. The exception to this is when the management of a commodity-type company uses the company's cash flow to acquire a consumer-monopoly-type business and then after the mar-

riage, the management jettisons the cash-hungry commodity-type business.

✦ When a commodity-type business marries another commodity-type business, the result is usually a disaster. This is because neither can produce sufficient profits to climb out of debt.

When looking for an excellent business, look for companies that possess a consumer monopoly and are conservatively financed. If the company with a consumer monopoly is using large amounts of long-term debt, it should be only to acquire another company with a consumer monopoly.

NO. 4

DOES THE BUSINESS CONSISTENTLY EARN A HIGH RATE OF RETURN ON SHAREHOLDERS' EQUITY?

Warren has figured out that high returns on shareholders' equity can produce great wealth for shareholders. Thus, Warren is seeking to invest in companies that *consistently* earn high returns on shareholders' equity.

To fully understand why Warren is so interested in high returns on shareholders' equity, let us work through the following.

Shareholders' equity is defined as a company's total assets less the company's total liabilities. It's like the equity in your house. Let's say that you bought a house as a rental property and you paid $200,000 for it. To close the deal you invested $50,000 of your own money and borrowed $150,000 from a bank. The $50,000 you invested in the house is your equity in the property.

When you rent your house out, the amount of money that you earn from the rent, after paying your expenses, mortgage, and taxes, would be your *return on equity*. If you rented your house out for $15,000 a year and had $10,000 in total expenditures, then you would be earning $5,000 a year on your $50,000 in equity. Then the return on your $50,000 in equity would be the $5,000 you earned. This equates to a 10% return on equity ($5,000 ÷ $50,000 = 10%).

Likewise, if you owned a business and it had $10 million in

assets and $4 million liabilities, the business would have share-holders' equity of $6 million. If the company earned, after taxes, $1,980,000, we could calculate the business's return on share-holders' equity as being 33% ($1,980,000 ÷ $6,000,000 = 33%).

This means that the $6 million of shareholders' equity is earning a 33% rate of return.

Now, the average return on shareholders' equity for an American corporation over the last forty years has been approximately 12%. That means that as a whole, year after year, American business earns only 12% on its shareholders' equity base.

Anything above 12% is *above* average. Anything below 12% is *below* average. *And below average is not what we are looking for.*

What Warren is looking for in a business is consistently higher-than-average returns on equity. We are not talking about 12 or 13%, but, as we know, a rate of return of 15% and above—the higher the better.

Let's look at some of the companies that have caught Warren's interest in the past and see what kind of return on equity they were getting.

The General Foods Corporation was averaging an annual 16% return on equity during the time Warren was buying it. Coca-Cola's return on equity the year he started buying it was approximately 33%, and it had a 25% average annual return on equity for the preceding five years. Hershey Foods has long fascinated Warren. It has an average annual return on equity for the last ten years of 16.7%. A company like Philip Morris, the tobacco and food conglomerate, has had an average annual return on equity for the last ten years of 30.5%. Capital Cities had a return on equity of 18% when Warren took his present position (a position he swapped in 1995 for a billion in cash and big chunk of the ownership of Mickey Mouse—the Walt Disney Company). Service Master's return on equity was in excess of 40%, and UST's in excess of 30%. Gannett Corporation, one of his more recent acquisitions, had a return on equity of 25%.

Warren believes that a consistently high return on equity is a good indication that the company's management not only can make money from the existing business but also can profitably employ retained earnings to make more money for the shareholders.

Consistently *means* consistently. Warren is not after a company that occasionally has high returns, but one that consistently has high returns.

Analyzing the Company's Return on Equity

Does the *return-on-equity picture* of the company in question look like Company I, or Company II?

Company I		Company II	
YEAR	RETURN ON EQUITY	YEAR	RETURN ON EQUITY
87	28.4%	87	5.7%
88	31.2	88	1.6
89	34.2	89	2.8
90	35.9	90	4.2
91	36.6	91	2.3
92	48.8	92	7.0
93	47.7	93	9.4
94	48.8	94	9.3
95	55.4	95	4.3
96	56.0	96	6.9

Warren would be interested in Company I and not Company II. Company II's return on equity is way too low. Company I shows a very high rate of return on equity, which indicates that it benefits from possessing a very strong consumer monopoly.

There is a great deal more to understanding why Warren is interested only in companies that get high returns on equity, and we go into great detail on this subject in the second part of the book. High rates of return on equity are indicative of the excellent business.

NO. 5

DOES THE BUSINESS GET TO RETAIN ITS EARNINGS?

In the 1934 edition of *Security Analysis,* Graham introduces his readers to Edgar Lawrence Smith, who in 1924 wrote a book on investing entitled *Common Stocks As Long-Term Investments* (Macmillan, 1924). Smith put forth the idea that common stocks should in theory grow in value as long as they earn more than they pay out in dividends, with the retained earnings adding to the company's net worth. In a representative case, a business would earn a 12% return on equity, pay out 8% in dividends, and retain 4% to surplus. If it did this every year, the stock value should increase with its book value, at a rate of 4% compounded annually.

With this is mind, Smith explains the growth of common stock values as arising from the accumulation of asset values through the reinvestment of a corporation's surplus earnings in the expansion of its operations. Graham, however, warns us that not all companies *can* reinvest their surplus earnings in expansion of their business enterprises. Most, in fact, must spend their retained earnings on simply *maintaining* the status quo through the replenishment of expiring plants and equipment. (We will address this issue further on.) Predicting future earnings of any enterprise can be very difficult and given to great variance. This means that making a future prediction of earnings can be fraught with potential disaster.

Warren concluded that Graham's assessment of Smith's analysis was correct for a great majority of businesses. However, he found that under close analysis some companies were an exception to the rule. Warren found that these exceptions over a long period of time were able to profitably employ retained earnings at rates of return considerably above the average. In short, Warren found *a few businesses* that didn't need to spend their retained earnings upgrading plant and equipment or on new-product development, but could spend their earnings either on acquiring new businesses or expanding the operations of their already profitable core enterprises.

We want to invest in businesses that can retain their earnings and haven't committed themselves to paying out a high percentage of their profits as dividends. This way the shareholders can benefit from the full effects of compounding, which is the secret to getting really rich.

NO. 6

HOW MUCH DOES THE BUSINESS HAVE TO SPEND ON MAINTAINING CURRENT OPERATIONS?

As we said, *making money is one thing, retaining it is another, and not having to spend it on maintaining current operations is still another.* Warren found that in order for Smith's theory to work he had to invest in companies that (1) made money, (2) could retain it, and (3) didn't have to spend those retained earnings on maintaining current operations.

Warren discovered that the capital requirements of a business may be so demanding that the company ends up having little or no money left to increase the fortunes of its shareholders.

Let me give you an example. If a business makes $1 million a year, and retains every cent, but every other year it has to spend $2 million replacing plant and equipment that were expended in production, the company really isn't making any money at all; the business is only breaking even. The perfect business to Warren would be one that earns $2 million and spends zero on replacing plant and equipment.

Warren used to teach this lesson when he conducted a night class on investing at the University of Nebraska at Omaha Business School. He would lecture on the capital requirements of a company and the effect that it had on shareholder fortunes. He would do this by showing his students the past operating records of AT&T and of Thomson Publishing.

Warren would demonstrate that AT&T, before it was broken up, was a poor investment for the shareholders, because though it made lots of money, it had to plow even more money than it made into capital requirements—research and development and infrastructure. The way that AT&T financed the expansion was to issue more shares and to sell lots of debt.

But a company like Thomson Publishing, which owned a bunch of newspapers in one-newspaper towns, made lots of money for its shareholders. This was because once a newspaper had built its printing infrastructure it had little in the way of capital needs to suck away the shareholders' money. This meant that there was lots of cash to spend on buying more newspapers to make its shareholders richer.

The lesson is that one business grew in value without requiring more infusions of capital and the other business grew only *because of* the additional capital that was invested in it.

This same phenomenon can be seen in the financial records of the General Motors Company, which indicate that between the beginning of 1985 and the end of 1994 it earned in total approximately $17.92 a share and paid out in dividends approximately $20.60 a share. During this same time period the company spent approximately $102.34 a share on capital improvements. The question that should be running through your mind is, If General Motors' earnings during this time period totaled $17.92 and it paid out as dividends $20.60, where did the extra $2.68 that it paid out in dividends and the $102.34 that it spent on capital improvements come from?

From the beginning of 1985 to the end of 1994, General Motors added approximately $33 billion in debt, which equates to a per share increase in debt of approximately $43.70. The company also issued 132 million additional shares of its common stock. General Motors' per share book value also dropped $34.29 a share, from $45.99 in 1985 to $11.70 in 1994, as new-car-development costs sucked up retained earnings. What did all this do for increasing the shareholders' wealth? Nothing.

In the beginning of 1985 General Motors stock traded at $40 a share. Ten years later, at the end of 1994, the stock traded at, you guessed it, $40 a share. So after ten years of business activity, $33 billion in additional debt, and 132 million new shares issued, the market price of the stock did nothing. The sum annual return to investors was limited to the dividend payout of $20.60, which equates to an annual pretax compounding rate of return of approximately 5.8%. Factor in inflation and taxes, and your invested capital ends up losing real value.

General Motors has huge capital requirements because the products that it is making, cars and trucks, are constantly changing. This means GM's manufacturing plants constantly have to be retooled to accommodate the new design changes, which means an expenditure of great sums of money just for GM to stay in business.

One final story to drive home the point. About a year ago I was having lunch with the owner of a company that laid asphalt roads for the state. After talking for a while it became apparent that the owner was earning a yearly net profit of approximately $200,000. The owner confirmed this, but added that about every four years he had to replace all his equipment, which cost around $600,000. So in truth the owner was making only about $50,000 a year.

What Warren wants is a business that seldom requires replacement of plant and equipment and doesn't require ongoing expensive research and development. He wants a company that produces a product that never goes obsolete and is simple to produce and has little or no competition: the only newspaper in town, a candy bar manufacturer, a chewing gum company, a razor blade producer, a soda pop business, a brewery—basic businesses with products that people never want to see essentially change. Predictable product, predictable profits.

NO. 7

IS THE COMPANY FREE TO REINVEST RETAINED EARNINGS IN NEW BUSINESS OPPORTUNITIES, EXPANSION OF OPERATIONS, OR SHARE REPURCHASES? HOW GOOD A JOB DOES THE MANAGEMENT DO AT THIS?

Another of Warren's keys to defining a great business is that a company has the capacity to take retained earnings and reinvest them in business ventures that will give them an additional high return.

Remember young Warren and the pinball machine. If he just kept that one pinball machine and never expanded the business, all the money he earned from the single pinball machine would go into a bank account and earn whatever the rate of return the bank was paying.

However, if young Warren invested the earnings in new business operations that gave a better return than the bank account, he would achieve a higher return on equity *and in turn would become a richer owner/shareholder.*

Think of it this way. If I gave you $10,000 a year for ten years and you put that money in your dresser drawer, at the end of ten years you would have saved up $100,000.

If you put that $10,000 in a savings account paying 5% compounded annually, at the end of the ten years you would have $132,067.

Let's say you have the magic touch of Warren and you can reinvest earnings at a rate of return of 23% compounded annually. Then at the end of ten years the amount saved up would be $370,388—which is a couple of hundred thousand dollars more than either the $100,000 in the dresser drawer or the $132,067 in the bank account.

If you kept that 23% going for a period of twenty years, the wonders of compounding interest really would take hold, and the sum would rise to $3,306,059. That's a sum that is definitely greater than the $200,000 you would have had if you had kept your money in the dresser drawer for twenty years. It's also greater than the $347,193 you would have earned if you'd kept hauling those $10,000 payments for twenty years down to the local bank that was paying you 5%.

Warren believes that if a company can employ its retained earnings at above-average rates of return then it is better to keep those earnings in the business. He has stated many times that he is not at all unhappy when Berkshire's wholly owned businesses retain all of their earnings, as long as they can utilize internally those funds at above-average rates of return.

Warren has taken this philosophy and applied it to companies in which he has a small minority interest. He believes that if the company has a history of profitable use of retained earnings, or a reasonable promise of profitable use in the future, it would be to the shareholders' advantage to have the company retain all the earnings it can profitably employ.

Be aware that if a company has low capital requirements but no prospects for capital employment that would bring a high rate of return, or if the management has a history of investing retained earnings into projects of low profitability, then Warren believes that the most attractive option for capital employment would be to pay out the earnings via dividends or use them to repurchase shares.

When retained earnings are used to buy back shares, the company is in effect buying its own property and increasing future per share earnings of the owners who didn't sell. Think of it this way. If you have a partnership and there are three partners, you each in effect own one third of the partnership. If the partnership, using partnership funds, buys one of the partners out, then the two remaining partners would each own 50% of the company and split the partnership's future earnings fifty-fifty. Share repurchases cause per share earnings to increase, which results in an increase in the market price of the stock, which means richer shareholders. (Chapter 40 gives a detailed explanation of the economics that motivate share repurchase programs and why Warren is a big fan of them.)

Warren's preference is to invest in *cash cows;* these are very profitable businesses that require very little in further research and development or replacement of plant and equipment. The best cash cows have the ability to invest in or acquire other cash cows. Take RJR Nabisco and Philip Morris. Both own cigarette businesses that are cash cows and generate lots of retained earnings. If they decided to reinvest those earnings in, say, the automotive business, they could expect large expenditures for a long time before generating a profit from the operations. However, they have chosen instead to take their tobacco-generated earnings and acquire cash cow food companies like Nabisco Foods, General Foods, and Kraft Foods, as well as myriad other brand-name food purveyors. Another good example of this strategy is the Sara Lee Corporation, which not only makes brand-name cheesecake but has managed to build a portfolio of other consumer brand names such as L'eggs, Hanes, and Playtex.

Capital Cities, before it merged with Disney, used its cash cow cable TV business to buy the ABC television network, another cash cow. For a long time, acquiring other media properties was where it spent most of its money. It did this with its shareholders' money because for a long time TV and radio stations were fantastic cash cows. Build a TV station and it lasts for forty years. Up until recently, media properties' consumer monopoly was protected from competition by the federal government. However, recent expansion of cable, satellite, and interactive TV through the use of telephone lines calls into question whether or not the big three networks—ABC, CBS, and NBC—can protect their business from all the new competition.

There is a story about Tom Murphy, CEO of Capital Cities, sitting around Warren's home in Omaha, watching TV. Someone said to him, "Isn't it amazing that so many advances have been made in the field of broadcast technology?" He responded that he liked it better in the old days when there was only black-and-white TV and just three networks competing for the advertiser's dollar. Warren believes that the networks may not be the fantastic businesses that they once were but they are still great businesses.

Whether or not the management of the company can utilize its retained earnings is probably the single most important question you must ask yourself as a long-term investor in businesses. Commitment of capital to a company that has neither the opportunity nor the managerial talent to grow its retained earnings will cause your investment boat to become dead in the water.

NO. 8

IS THE COMPANY FREE TO ADJUST PRICES TO INFLATION?

Inflation causes prices to rise. The problem with the commodity-type business is that while prices for labor and raw material increase, it is possible that overproduction will create a situation in which the company has to drop the prices of its products in order to stimulate demand. In a case like this, the cost of production is sometimes in excess of the price the product will fetch in the marketplace. And so the company loses lots of money. This usually results in the company cutting back production until the excess supply dries up. But that takes time. The laws of supply and demand work, but not overnight. In the meantime the losses pile up and the viability of the business diminishes. (Ranchers are constantly faced with this dilemma. The price of live cattle is dropping, but the costs of feed, fuel, labor, insurance, veterinarians, and grazing land keep increasing. Miscalculate what the price of cattle will be next fall, and the family ranch may end up in foreclosure.)

This situation occurs periodically in the airline business. Airlines commit themselves to all kinds of heavy fixed costs. From airplanes to fuel to union contracts for pilots, ground crews, mechanics, and attendants—all cost lots of money, and they all increase in cost with inflation. But along comes a price war and the airlines have to start cutting ticket prices to stay competitive. Want to fly from New York to Los Angeles? There are a half dozen or more airlines competing for your business. If one drops prices significantly, they all end up losing. In the 1960s a round-trip airplane ticket from Omaha to Paris cost $1,000 or more. Recently, I bought one for $500. Even though the cost of airplanes, fuel, pilots, grounds crews, mechanics, and those terrible airline meals had more than quadrupled in the last thirty years, my ticket, thanks to a price war, got cheaper. But the airline that sold it to me didn't get any richer. Now you know why so many airlines go under.

With a commodity-type business it is possible to have the cost of production increase with inflation while the prices the business can charge for its products decreases because of competition.

To Warren the excellent business/consumer monopoly is one that is free to increase the prices of its products right along with inflation, without it experiencing a decline in demand. That way its profits remain fat, no matter how inflated the economy gets.

NO. 9

WILL THE VALUE ADDED BY RETAINED EARNINGS
INCREASE THE MARKET VALUE OF THE COMPANY?

Graham stated in his later life that he believed the market was made up of two components. One is long-term-investment oriented, so that over time the market price of a company's stock would reflect its intrinsic value. The other component is like a casino: people gamble on the short-term fluctuations of price. He believed that as a whole the casino side of the equation dominated, with people and institutions speculating on the impact that daily information would have on the value of the security.

Graham believed that it was this casino aspect that allowed the patient investor the opportunity to practice his craft. For while fear and greed dominated the floor of the casino, it offered the long-term investor the opportunity to buy companies at below their intrinsic value.

Warren subscribes to the same theory, with one addition. He believes that the long-term-investment nature of the market will continually ratchet up the price of a company's stock if it can properly allocate capital and keep adding to the company's net worth. A perfect example of this is his own Berkshire Hathaway, which in 1981 had a net worth of $527 a share and was trading at around $525. Sixteen years later, in 1997, it has a net worth of approximately $20,000 a share and is trading in the neighborhood of $45,000 a share. Warren expanded the company by allocating the company's retained earnings to the purchase of whole and partial interests in businesses that have exceptional economics. As the net worth of the company grew, so did the market's valuation of the company, thus the rise in the price of the stock.

Another great example of this long-term market phenomenon is the Philip Morris Company. This is a major manufacturer of cigarettes that over the last twenty years has had a dark cloud hanging over its head in the form of hundreds of lawsuits filed by people with cancer blaming their illness on Philip Morris and its very profitable product.

The market, being the skittish and fickle thing that it is, saw the lawsuits as the Grim Reaper and so valued Philip Morris at between eight and fourteen times earnings, even though it was consistently earning over a 21% return on equity. But the company kept making more money and acquiring more and more businesses. Its net worth and per share earnings continued to grow. So with the advance in the company's net worth and per share earnings, the company's stock increased in price as well, even though it continued to trade at between eight and fourteen times earnings.

Even though Philip Morris was stigmatized by the market, the long-term phenomenon of market price matching the intrinsic value of a business managed to increase the price of the stock, giving its shareholders over the last ten years an annual compounding rate of return of approximately 21.9%.

So remember, over the short term the market is manic-depressive, with irrational mood swings driving the prices of securities to foolish highs and insane lows. It is the market's manic-depressive behavior that offers opportunity to the investor. For the wise investor knows that over the long term the market will adjust the stock's price to reflect the real value of the business.

Warren is looking for a company that has a stock price that is responding to a real increase in the economic value of the company. He is not looking for a company that has a stock price that is increasing because of speculative pressure. One is a sure thing, the other is a bet at the race track.

SUMMARY

Warren is looking to invest in the business that has excellent economics working in its favor, which produces monopolylike profits. He has found that these excellent businesses usually have some kind of consumer monopoly, usually a brand-name product or service that consumers believe offers superior advantages over the competition.

Warren discovered that simply being able to retain earnings free of the burden of having to spend them on maintaining current operations was not enough. The management of the business must have the ability to allocate retained earnings to new moneymaking ventures that also give high rates of return on invested capital. If no new ventures are available, these excellent businesses engage in stock buybacks.

Warren also found that an excellent business, as a rule, will be conservatively financed and will have the freedom to adjust the prices of its product or services with inflation.

We now have an idea of what the beast looks like. In the next chapter we shall see what business fields it can be found hiding in.

17

Where to Look
for Excellent Businesses

Where do you find the excellent businesses that have created conceptual toll bridges? There are basically three types of toll bridge businesses that produce excellent results:

1

businesses that make products that wear out fast or are used up quickly, that have brand-name appeal, and that merchants have to carry or use to stay in business

2

communications businesses that provide a repetitive service manufacturers must use to persuade the public to buy their products

3

businesses that provide repetitive consumer services that people and business are consistently in need of

Let's examine each of these categories.

BUSINESSES THAT MAKE PRODUCTS THAT WEAR OUT FAST OR ARE USED UP QUICKLY, THAT HAVE BRAND-NAME APPEAL, AND THAT MERCHANTS HAVE TO CARRY OR USE TO STAY IN BUSINESS

Merchants (like the local supermarket), as opposed to manufacturers (like the Coca-Cola Company), make their profits by buying low and selling high. The merchant needs to pay as little for a product as possible and sell it for as much as possible. His profit is the difference between what he paid for the product and what he sells it for. If there are several manufacturers of a product, a merchant can shift from one to the other, shopping for the lowest price. However, if there is a product that only one manufacturer sells, then the merchant has to pay the price the manufacturer is asking; this gives the pricing advantage to the manufacturer and not the merchant. This means higher profit margins for the manufacturer.

Note also that when a great number of merchants need a particular product and there is only one manufacturer, the price competition is shifted to the merchants. Thus, different merchants cut the price of the product to stimulate sales. *But the manufacturer continues to charge all his stores the same price.* The price competition between the *different merchants* destroys the merchants' profit margins and *not* the manufacturer's.

Companies that manufacture brand-name products that wear out fast or are used up quickly and that merchants have to carry to be in business are, in effect, a kind of toll bridge. The consumer wants a particular brand-name product; if the merchant wants to earn a profit, he has to supply the consumer with that product. The catch is that there is only one manufacturer, only one bridge, and if you want that brand-name product, you have to pay the toll to *that manufacturer.*

Let's make a trip down to the local Kwik Shop or 7-Eleven. As you stand at the door, can you predict what brand-name products it has to carry to be in business? Well, it has to carry Coca-Cola, Marlboro cigarettes, Skoal chewing tobacco, Hershey's chocolate, Wrigley's chewing gum, and Doritos. Without these products the owner is losing sales and money. The manufacturers of all these products—the Coca-Cola Company, the Philip Morris Company (Marlboro cigarettes), US Tobacco (Skoal chewing tobacco), Hershey Foods (Hershey's chocolate), Wm. Wrigley Jr. Company (Wrigley's chewing gum), and the Pepsi-Cola Company (maker of Doritos)—all earn above-average rates of return on equity.

Name me eight brand-name products that every pharmacy has to carry. Crest toothpaste, Advil, Listerine, Coca-Cola, Marlboro cigarettes, Tampax tampons, Bic pens, and Gillette razor blades—without these products the drugstore merchant is going to lose sales. And the manufacturers of all these products earn high returns on equity.

When you eat out at a restaurant, you don't order your coffee by brand name. Nor do you order your hamburger and fries or BLT or shrimp fried rice by brand name. The company that sells the restaurant hamburger is not making above-average profit returns on equity, because nobody ever walks into a restaurant and asks for a hamburger ground up by Bob's Meats.

But you order your Coca-Cola by brand name. And if you own a restaurant and you don't carry Coca-Cola, well, you just lost some sales.

What brand-name products must most clothing stores sell? Fruit of the Loom or Hanes underwear and, of course, the ubiquitous Levi's. Both earn their manufacturers high rates of return on equity. How about stores that sell running shoes? Does Nike strike a bell? Nike earns excellent returns on equity. How about the corner hardware store? WD-40 and GE light bulbs. Both of these manufacturers earn, you guessed it, above-average returns on equity.

Think about the prescription drugs behind the druggist's counter. We live in an age where an overcrowded planet is connected by thousands of daily international flights; new diseases can jump from one country to another in a matter of hours. Throw in the fact that viruses can mutate into a new disease almost overnight, and it doesn't take a genius to see that these modern-day potion salesmen, the pharmaceutical companies, are going to have an ever-increasing demand for their lifesaving products. Products that people desperately need, protected by patents, mean that if you want to get well, you have to pay the toll.

The gatekeeper, the druggist, has to carry the products or he is going to lose business. All of the leading manufacturers of prescription drugs, such as Merck & Company, Marion Merrell Dow, Inc., Mylan Labs, and Eli Lilly and Company earn really high returns on equity. They are very profitable enterprises.

We should take special note of restaurant chains that have created brand-name products out of generic food. Restaurant chains, such as McDonald's, have taken the most ubiquitous of food, the hamburger, and turned it into a brand-name product. The key to their success is quality, convenience, consistency, and affordability. Take a bite out of a McDonald's hamburger in Hong Kong and it tastes just like the one you bit into the month before in the good old U.S.A. McDonald's consistently earns above-average rates of return on equity.

Advertising by manufacturers ensures that customers will demand the advertised products and that merchants can't substitute a cheaper product on which they can get a fatter profit margin. The merchant becomes the gatekeeper to the toll bridge, with the manufacturer being guaranteed his profit. Since these products are consumed either on the spot or within a short period of time, the gatekeeper and the manufacturer can expect many profitable trips across the bridge.

To Warren the brand-name consumer product is the kind of toll bridge business that he is interested in owning.

COMMUNICATIONS BUSINESSES THAT PROVIDE A REPETITIVE SERVICE MANUFACTURERS MUST USE TO PERSUADE THE PUBLIC TO BUY THEIR PRODUCTS

Long ago, the manufacturers of products reached their potential customers by having company salesmen call on customers directly. But with the advent of radio, television, newspapers, and a huge number of highly specialized magazines, manufacturers found that they could make their pitch directly to thousands of people with a single well-placed advertisement. Manufacturers found that these new mediums of reaching the customer worked, which meant increased sales and profits. Ultimately advertising became the battleground on which manufacturers competed with one another, with huge consumer corporations spending hundreds of millions of dollars a year on getting their "buy our product" message to the potential customer.

After a while these companies found there was no turning back; manufacturers had to advertise or they ran the risk that some competitor would sweep in and take over their coveted niche in the marketplace.

Warren found that advertising created a conceptual bridge between the potential consumer and the manufacturer. In order for a manufacturer to create a demand for its product, it must advertise. Call it an advertising toll bridge. And this advertising toll bridge profits the advertising agencies, magazine publishers, newspapers, and telecommunications networks of the world.

When there were only three TV major networks, each one made a great deal of money. Seeing this, Warren invested heavily in Capital Cities and then ABC. Now that there are sixty-seven channels to choose from, the networks don't do as well. They still make a ton of money, just not as much as when there were only three network toll bridges crossing the river.

The same can be said of the newspaper business. A lone newspaper in a good-size town can make excellent returns, but add a competitor and neither will do very well. This is what Warren experienced with the *Buffalo Evening News.* When there was a competitor in town, the paper was at best an average business. But since the competitor went out of business, the *Buffalo Evening News* has been getting spectacular results. Warren has found that if there is only one newspaper toll bridge in town, it can jack its advertising rates to the moon and still not lose customers. Where else are the manufacturers and merchants going to cross the river to reach the consumer by print media?

Advertising agencies that function on a world scale also enjoy high returns on equity by being in a unique position to profit from the huge consumer multinational companies that sell their products the world over. If one of these multinational companies wants to launch an advertising campaign, it has to use an advertising agency like Interpublic, the second-largest advertising agency in the world. Interpublic becomes the toll bridge to the consumer that the multinational manufacturer must cross. This is the line of reasoning that Warren followed when he bought 17% of Interpublic.

BUSINESSES THAT PROVIDE REPETITIVE CONSUMER SERVICES THAT PEOPLE AND BUSINESS ARE CONSISTENTLY IN NEED OF

Not products, but services. And the services provided can be performed by nonunion workers, often with limited skills, who are hired on an as-needed basis. This odd segment of the business world includes such companies as Service Master, which provides pest control, professional cleaning, maid service, and lawn care; Rollins, which runs Orkin, the world's largest pest and termite control service, and also provides security services to homes and businesses. We all know that at tax time H & R Block is there to save our necks by filling in all those blank lines with the right tax numbers. All of these companies earn high rates of return on equity.

This segment of Warren's toll bridge world also includes the credit card companies that he has invested in, such as American Express and Dean Witter Discover. Every time that you use one of these company's cards, it charges the merchant a fee, or toll. If you fail to pay your credit card bill within your grace period they get to charge you a fee as well. Millions of little tolls taxed to each transaction add up. Also, these strange credit card toll bridges don't need huge plants and equipment that suck up capital.

The key to these kinds of companies is that they provide necessary services but require little in the way of capital expenditures or a highly paid, educated workforce. Additionally, there is no such thing as product obsolescence. Once the management and infrastructure are in place, the company can hire and fire employees as the work demand dictates. You hire a person to work as a security guard for $8 an hour, give him a few hours of training, and then rent him out at $25 an hour. When there is no work, you don't have to pay him.

Also, no one has to spend money and energy on upgrading or developing new products. The money these companies make goes directly into their pockets and can be spent on expanding operations, paying out dividends, or buying back stock.

As long as the locusts keeping coming, the termites keep eating, the thieves keep thieving, shoppers keep using credit cards, and governments keep taxing us, these companies will make money. Lots of it, for a long time.

SUMMARY

The best way to start your search for the excellent business/toll bridge is to stand outside a supermarket, Kwik Shop, or 7-Eleven and try to name the brand-name products the store must carry to be in business. This mental process is much better than thumbing though endless financial magazines and guides searching for the elusive company of your dreams.

The products you will come up with will lead you to the companies that are sitting on consumer jackpots of gold and getting high returns on equity and superior results for their owners. So get a pen and paper out and start guessing.

Other companies of interest will be those that are uniquely situated to profit from providing advertising services to businesses, like the only newspaper in town.

Of special interest will be those companies that provide repetitive services that require neither products nor skilled labor, like Service Master, Rollins, H & R Block, and American Express.

18

More Ways to Find a Company You Want to Invest In

In the beginning of my education in Buffetology I went through the supermarket looking for goods that I bought or that other people were buying. I have to say that my stock selections were nothing less than spectacular. Try it and you'll see what I mean. Coca-Cola, Philip Morris, ConAgra, Kraft, General Foods, Hershey's chocolate, RJR Nabisco, Quaker Oats, Kellogg's, Campbell soups, Wrigley's chewing gum, and Sara Lee Corporation are just a few of the wonderful companies selling fantastic products right in your local supermarket. Every day of every week of every month of every year from now until the end of time, people will be spending their hard-earned dollars for a six-pack of Coca-Cola to cool off with on a hot summer's day, a pack of Marlboro cigarettes (to look cool), some oatmeal or Kool-Aid for the kids (growing children have hearty appetites), or maybe some gum.

My mother chewed Wrigley's chewing gum when she was a kid, I chewed it when I was young, and the other day my child offered me a piece. And what about that Oreo cookie? Do you think that those two thin wafers of chocolate with the icing in between are going to go obsolete in the next ten years, the way your computer or your car will? No way. As long as they keep making children, the good people at RJR Nabisco will be baking Oreos and selling them to our children. Personally, I still enjoy tearing them apart and eating the icing.

The point is that there are great ideas for stock investment, the partial ownership of a business, right at the end of your fingertips. Moreover, what chance do you have of understanding the workings of, say, a Genentech? And believe me, the stockbroker on the other end of the phone telling you about it doesn't either.

One of Warren's prerequisites for an investment is that he understand what the company makes and how the product is used. He likes products that don't become obsolete because of some technical advancement. This means a lot of high-tech companies are ruled out. It doesn't mean that you can't invest in them, using Warren's principles. It just means that if you don't understand what they do, you had better leave them alone. But who knows who will be reading this book?

Warren loves to tell the story of a friend who at one time was really hard up but who learned everything there was to know about water companies. This guy, as Warren tells the story, could tell how much money a certain water company would make every time someone flushed the toilet. After a while, the guy made a fortune investing in . . . what? You got it, water companies!

The trick is that you have to understand what you are investing in and never stray from this circle of competence. There are no ifs, ands, or buts about it. You have to know the nature of the game you are playing. Understanding the nature of the business is key to understanding the underlying economics of the business. And it is the economics of the company that will tell you whether it is a commodity- or a consumer-monopoly-type business. It will also tell you whether the management has the capacity to reinvest the retained earnings in a manner that will profit the investor. And it will give you an idea of what the company is worth and whether it is possible to predict the company's future stream of earnings, which is essential if you wish to calculate the company's value to you as an investor.

So, you want investment ideas? Start with the things that you use in your daily life. Divide them into two categories. One would be the commodity-type business, the other the consumer-monopoly type. Some of these companies will be publicly traded, which means that you can buy shares in them. Some, however, will be privately owned and will offer you no venue for investing.

Maybe you always have a Coca-Cola after work. Coca-Cola is a brand name and is known all over the world, so you would call this a consumer monopoly. Maybe you get the *Wall Street Journal.* Consumer monopoly. Maybe you buy gasoline for your car. Commodity. Or you use Chanel perfume. Consumer monopoly. Perhaps you have a fondness for Black & Decker tools or drive a Caterpillar at work. Everywhere you look in your daily life are businesses whose products you use and understand. Car mechanics know about the auto business, doctors about the medical business, and druggists about the drug business. A person working behind the counter at a Kwik Shop can tell you what the best-selling soft drink, beer, cigarette, or candy bar is without a moment's hesitation, and he has probably never read an analyst's report in his life.

A salesman in a computer store can tell you what companies sell the best computers and what the hottest-selling software is. If you work in a computer store and you realize that almost every computer other than Apple uses Windows 95 as an operating system, you may have a hunch that the guys who manufacture Windows 95 might be making some money. Do a little investigating and you end up with Microsoft, the manufacturer of Windows 95.

What I'm saying is that you have at hand hundreds of companies that you understand, which equate to hundreds of leads for potential investment opportunities.

But remember, these are just leads, and they require a great deal more investigation in order to determine their investment merit.

WHERE DO YOU GO FROM HERE?

Where do you go after you have found the name of a company that manufactures a product that you understand? You can start by looking at the package that the product came in to find out where it was manufactured. Then use the wonderful people at your long distance telephone company. Call information and get the phone number of the company in question. It just may be that the company you have chosen is the subsidiary of another corporation. For instance, Hanes hosiery is part of Sara Lee. Yes, the same people who are making your cheesecake are also draping women's legs in hosiery. It may also be that the address on the label was for a manufacturing plant and not the corporate offices.

All right, you call the company and ask them for the phone number of the home office. You then call the home office. Tell the receptionist that you would like a copy of the company's annual report. The receptionist will more than likely connect you with somebody in shareholder relations. If that happens, tell the person in that department that you would like a copy of the company's annual report. The person at the other end of the line will take your address and send you a copy free of charge.

That's right, free of charge.

The operator may tell you that the company is not publicly traded and doesn't issue an annual report to the public. This would be the case if you tried to get the annual report of, say, the Chanel Corporation, makers of that elegant fragrance Chanel No. 5. If that is the case, you would be out of luck and you should go on to your next company.

If, however, the annual report is in the mail and you know that the company is publicly traded and where its home office is, and you know one or several of the products it makes, you are in a position to start using some of the resources that the financial and information sectors offer.

Your first trip should be to the local library, where you will find a set of books called the *Guide to Business Periodicals.* This amazing set of books contains a listing by page, week, month, and year of every publication in which the company in question was mentioned. The guide dates back about thirty years, so you should start with the most recent and look for stories about your company that were published in major business periodicals like *Fortune, Business Week, Forbes,* and *Smart Money.* Though there may be countless other listings, these will more than likely give you a good overview of the company and the industry it is in.

It's really amazing, when you think about it. You get some hotshot reporter writing about the business you are interested in, a reporter who perhaps talked to the competitors, interviewed the head of the company, and gleaned the opinions of all the big-name analysts that cover the stock. And the really nice thing is, you don't have to pay a thing for this service, because after you get the listing for the story, you go to the periodical desk in the library and the librarian will tell you how to retrieve the story.

More than likely, the library will either have the magazine or will have a copy of it on microfilm. And all for free. (University libraries are often a better source of information than the local city library, especially if the university has a business school.)

As you are reading these stories, remember to take notes. List the names of the competitors and anybody quoted. You do this because at some future date you may want to contact them yourself and ask them a few questions. I know you're thinking, How can I call these people and ask them questions!? Just pick up the phone and dial! Tell them that you run a small fund—so what if your fund has only one investor, you? Tell them you are thinking about investing in the company. Nine times out of ten they will be happy to talk to you about the company.

Now that you have learned a little about the company, you can go back to the periodical desk at the library and inquire about a sourcebook of financial information called the *Value Line Investment Survey,* an investment advisory survey created by Arnold Bernhard, who in 1937 started compiling stock figures and publishing them. Bernhard was a contemporary of Graham's and sought a standard of value for stocks. He subscribed to the Grahamian concept of intrinsic value but had reservations about the methods Graham used to calculate the intrinsic value of a specific business.

Value Line covers seventeen hundred different companies and lists key financial figures dating back fifteen years. It is a key tool in the game and one that Warren regularly uses. It's full of important figures, such as the earnings per share and return on equity computations. I highly recommend it.

Another source of information is *Moody's Guide,* which can also be found at your library. *Standard and Poor's Stock Reports* also follows selected issues. Note that *Moody's, Standard and Poor's,* and *Value Line* offer subscriptions. If you are serious about investing, then they are worth, yes, the investment.

Look up the name of your company in *Value Line* and then turn to the page cited and read on. If you can't find the company listed in *Value Line,* try *Moody's.* There is one for New York Stock Exchange stocks and one for OTC stocks.

If you can't find your company listed by any of these services, call the company again and try to get annual reports dating as many years back as possible.

After you have read the stories you found through the *Guide to Business Periodicals* and have assembled the financial figures for the company for at least the last seven years, you are ready to answer some key questions about the nature of the business, namely, is it a commodity-type business, or a consumer-monopoly-type business, or is it something in between? You can also answer a few questions about the management: Does it have shareholders' interests at heart, or is it out to foolishly spend the shareholders' money on low-return projects?

If things look enticing, you will want to run figures for the return on equity and earnings growth over the last eight to ten years. You will also want to calculate the company's value to you as an investor, using the equations discussed in our section on mathematical tools. But remember, the earnings of a company have to have some strength and the company's products have to be of a nature that will allow you to project the company's future earnings with a fair degree of comfort.

Warren often refers to a *circle of competence*, using Bill Gates and his incredible company, Microsoft, as an example. He will say that Gates is probably the smartest and most creative manager in the business world today and that the company is super. However, Warren says he is unable to predict with any comfort what the future earnings of the company will be, and thus he can't calculate Microsoft's future value. If Warren is unable to calculate a company's future value, then the company will not fall in his circle of confidence and he will not consider it for investment. In Microsoft's case he says that he just doesn't understand the business well enough to evaluate it, and if he can't evaluate it, he's not going to invest in it.

Okay, let's say that, all things considered, the company looks like it might be what you are looking for. At this point you may want to go on to the next step.

The next step is really an adaptation of something the investment genius Philip Fisher wrote about in his enlightening sixties book *Common Stocks and Uncommon Profits*. In it he describes a process of investigation he calls the *scuttlebutt approach*. It is an investigative technique in which the prospective investor calls the competition and customers of a business and asks them about the company in question. It's not unlike having coffee with the ex-girlfriend or ex-boyfriend of someone you are thinking about dating.

Warren actually gets on the phone and calls the competition and asks what they think of a particular company. Or he may question someone he knows who has knowledge about a particular area of business. If you happen to be around Warren after he's got tanked up on four or five Coca-Colas he may regale you with some of his early scuttlebutt escapades from his days at the Columbia School of Business. My favorite is when Warren finds out that his favorite professor, none other than Benjamin Graham, is chairman of an insurance company called Government Employees Insurance Company (GEICO). Young Warren, upon learning this, ventured over to the Columbia library, looked up GEICO, and discovered that the company was located in Washington, D.C.

So, one Saturday, Warren hopped on a train and went down to Washington, D.C., arriving at GEICO's headquarters at about eleven o'clock in the morning. Upon finding the doors locked, he beat on the front door until a janitor answered. Warren asked the janitor in the building whom he could talk with about the company. The janitor, taking pity, told him a guy on the sixth floor might be able to help him. So Warren walked in, marched up to the sixth floor, and found none other than Lorimar Davidson, GEICO's chief investment officer, who later would become CEO. Davidson, flattered and impressed with Warren's desire to know about the company, spent four hours with him that day explaining the insurance business and how GEICO worked. And Warren became totally enamored of the company. As we noted, he later added GEICO to his circle of confidence and over the next forty years made over $1.7 billion on a $45 million investment in the company.

Do the scuttlebutt, yes!

A service that investment houses can provide you with is a list of all the institutions that own a particular stock. I have found it amazingly informative to call up those institutions and ask to talk to the analyst who follows the company I am interested in. I tell him

I run a small investment fund and that I am thinking about adding the company in question to my portfolio. I have yet to have an analyst turn me away. Analysts, as a lot, are a very talkative group, and invariably they will expound on the factors that made them interested in buying the stock. Sometimes you will find out why they wish they hadn't bought the stock. But remember, I have already done my homework on the company and I can talk intelligently about the business and ask pointed, timely questions.

Recently an investment fund manager told me that a business I had asked him about was not a very good one and had poor prospects for the future, but that the management was excellent and the CEO was the kind of guy you would want running your own business. This fund manager liked investing in companies whose management he could trust.

Another thing I like to do is go to a store that is selling the products of a business I am thinking of buying. I will ask the store manager how that particular product is selling.

When Philip Morris dropped the price of Marlboros to win back sales that were being lost to the bargain brands, I started asking Kwik Shop clerks if the drop in price of the Marlboros had stimulated sales. All said that it had. Weeks before the press reported to the public that the drop in sales price was stimulating sales and allowing Philip Morris to regain the market share, I already knew that their strategy was working.

Warren does the scuttlebutt, Philip Fisher does the scuttlebutt, David (my coauthor) and I do the scuttlebutt, and so can you. Be creative and have fun. The worst thing that will happen is someone won't answer your question. The best thing is that you may end up with a friend.

Anybody can do these things. You don't need an MBA and you don't need to work for a big Wall Street investment house. All you need to do is spend some time in the library reading and make a few phone calls. Don't be shy. After all, it is your money, and if you are not willing to do at least a little work on your investment decisions, then it probably won't be your money for very long.

19

What You Need to Know About the Management of the Company You May Invest In

Let's talk about those folks to whom you have entrusted your money—the management of the business you have invested in.

Poor businesses often are just that, and no amount of managerial talent is going to make a difference. Warren uses the analogy of ship captains to make his point. If you had two ship captains and one was much more experienced than the other, who do you think would win a race if you put the more experienced captain in a dinghy and the less experienced captain in a speedboat? It doesn't matter how good management is if the business suffers from inherently poor economics.

The same can be said of businesses with exceptional economics, in that it is hard for even inept managers to foul up the economics of the business. Warren once said that he is interested in investing only in businesses whose inherent economics are so strong that even fools can run them profitably.

It is the business's economics, not its management, that the investor should first look to in determining whether the business is one to be considered for investment. But as the old saying goes, not only do you want management that is hardworking and intelligent; it must be honest, too. For if it isn't honest, the first two qualities—hardworking and intelligent—are going to steal you blind.

Honesty probably is the single most important trait of management. Honest managers will behave as if they are owners. They are less likely to squander the shareholders' assets. One of the key ingredients to successful investing is that management function from the same premise that you and Warren are—*from a solid business perspective.*

The abilities that are easy to identify in a manager who has an owner's perspective include

+ profitably allocating capital
+ keeping the return on equity as high as possible
+ paying out retained earnings or spending them on the repurchase of a company's stock if no investment opportunities present themselves

Warren believes that one of the essential benchmarks that indicate management's good intentions is the use of excess retained earnings for the purchase of the company's stock *when it makes business sense to do so.*

When a company buys back its own stock at prices that give it a better return than other investments it could make, then it is a good thing for the investors who continue to own the stock. Their piece of the pie just got bigger, and they didn't have to do anything. Sounds good, doesn't it! Warren thinks so.

Let's look at Capital Cities' management to see how this works.

Capital Cities' management from 1989 through 1992 repurchased over 1 million shares of its own stock, spending in the neighborhood of $400 million. Its justification for spending the shareholders' money in this fashion was that since Capital Cities was a broadcasting business, it should be investing only in a business that it understands—in this case, broadcasting.

The problem is that broadcasting companies in the private market during this time were all selling at very high prices, in contrast with the public market (the stock market), in which companies were selling at a considerable discount from their non-publicly-traded, private-market cousins. Capital Cities' management saw that its stock was selling at a discount to the prices being paid in the private market. So the management of Capital Cities bought its own stock, which was a better deal than buying the stock of the privately held companies. This increased the wealth of the shareholders who kept their shares.

Again, you need honest management that views its function as increasing shareholder wealth and not fiefdom building. The great Wall Street sage of the 1920s and 1930s Bernard Baruch, when listing his investment criteria, said, "Most important is the character and brains of management. I'd rather have good management and less money than poor managers with a lot of money. Poor managers can ruin even a good position. The quality of the management is particularly important in appraising the prospects of future growth" (*My Own Story,* Holt, Rinehart & Winston, 1957).

In the end, management has complete control over your money. If you don't like what the managers are doing with it, you can either vote them out by electing a new board of directors or sell your stock and get out, which really is voting with your feet.

20

When a Downturn in a Company Can Be an Investment Opportunity

What throws most Warren watchers is that he will sometimes buy into a business when prospects seem the bleakest. He did this most recently with his early 1990s purchase of stock in Wells Fargo Bank. Previous investements of this kind include the purchase of stock in American Express in the late sixties, after the salad oil scandal (which will be explained later), and the purchase of his interest in GEICO in the seventies.

To understand this you have to remember that Graham believed that, since the majority of the players in the stock market were short-term oriented, they place 90% of their valuing effort into interpreting present results. That is to say, if a company had a bad year, the stock market would beat the price of the stock way down, even if all the preceding years had produced excellent results. To Graham this presented great opportunity to the investor who could take a long-term view. Warren discovered that short-term volatility is what creates opportunity for the long-term investor.

Let me give you a practical example. Let's say that you own a small ski resort. You have been in business for the last thirty years, and every year you made net profits of approximately $300,000. Occasionally you had a really great year and made around $600,000. You also occasionally had a really bad year when it didn't snow and you didn't make any money.

Would you value your ski resort business for less money in the year that it didn't snow and you didn't make any money? Probably not. You know that occasional weather cycles will once in a while bring you a really bad year, just as they will bring you an occasional really great year. Those are just the ups and downs of your business. And if you were valuing your business, you would take those ups and downs into account. Makes sense, doesn't it?

But if your ski resort was a publicly traded company, the stock market, being short-term motivated, would revalue your business every year as the earnings fluctuated. In really great years they would value the ski resort at a lot more and send the price of the stock sky-high. Likewise, in bad years, when it didn't snow, they would hammer the price of the stock into the ground.

This kind of event happens periodically to almost all businesses, regardless of whether they are the commodity type or have a consumer monopoly working in their favor. The television and newspaper industry are dependent on advertising to produce income. However, advertising rates and revenue fluctuate with the business activity of the entire economy. If the economy falls into a recession, then advertising revenues fall as well, and newspapers and television networks make less money. Seeing this loss of revenues, the stock market reacts, causing the stock price of the newspaper or television company to plummet.

Capital Cities/ABC Inc. fell victim to this weird manic-depressive stock market behavior in 1990. Because of a business recession, advertising revenues started to drop, and Capital Cities reported that its net profit for 1990 would be approximately the same as in 1989. The stock market, used to Capital Cities growing its per share earnings at approximately 27% a year, reacted violently to this news and in the space of six months drove the price of its stock down from $63.30 a share to $38 a share. Thus, Capital Cities lost 40% of its per share price, all because it projected that things were going to be the same as they were last year. (In 1995 Capital Cities and the Walt Disney Company agreed to merge. This caused the market-revalued Capital Cities to go upward, to $125 a share. If you bought it in 1990 for $38 a share and sold it in 1995 for $125 a share, your pretax annual compounding rate of return would be approximately 26%, with a per share profit of $87.)

The same kind of event can occur in the banking industry. Changes in interest rates can cause fluctuations in a bank's earnings for a particular year. Banks are also susceptible to the real estate cycle of boom and bust. The real estate market has periods of great expansion followed by periods of great contraction, which are followed by long periods of relative calm. But an industrywide recession is different from an individual bank becoming insolvent from poor business practice. To a large money-center bank, like Wells Fargo, such a problem is far more serious than it is to a middle-size regional bank. One brings the specter of an entire economy collapsing, the other a regional calamity.

Money-center banks are key players in the commercial world. These banks occupy a permanent and very vital niche in our economy. Not only do they do business with tens of thousands of individual customers and businesses; they also act as the banker to smaller banks. Most money-center banks are part of an elite group of financial institutions that are allowed to buy bonds from the U.S. Treasury and then resell them to other banks or institutions, kind of like a master toll bridge. In the eyes of the Federal Reserve Bank, they are the center of the financial universe. If one is poorly run and is likely to become insolvent, the Federal Reserve will do everything in its power to force it to merge with another money-center bank. But in a recession, when all banks are having problems, the Federal Reserve has only one solution, and that is to loosen the money supply and try to keep the money-center banks afloat.

What most people don't realize is that banks borrow money from other banks. The Federal Reserve Bank has what is called the discount window, which is where banks traditionally go when they are in trouble and need to borrow money. The discount window is a source of cheap money for banks. This allows them to borrow money from the Federal Reserve Bank and then loan it out at a profit. During periods of normal banking activity, if a bank shows up too many times at the discount window, a band of banking regulators will descend down upon it. But in times of a nationwide recession, the discount window is one way that the Federal Reserve Bank ensures that key money-center banks stay in business.

Remember, in an industrywide recession everyone gets hurt. But the strong survive and the weak are removed from the economic landscape. One of the most conservative, well-run, and financially strong of the key money-center banks on the West Coast, and the eighth largest bank in the nation, is Wells Fargo.

Wells Fargo, in 1990 and 1991, responding to a nationwide recession in the real estate market, set aside for potential loan losses a little over $1.3 billion, or approximately $25 a share of its $55 a share in net worth. When a bank sets aside funds for potential losses it is merely designating part of its net worth as a reserve for *potential* future losses. It doesn't means those losses *have* happened, nor does it mean they *will* happen. What it means is that there is a potential for the losses to occur and the bank is prepared to meet them.

This means that if Wells Fargo lost every penny it had set aside for potential losses, $25 a share, it would still have $28 dollars a share left in net worth. Losses did eventually occur, but they weren't as bad as Wells Fargo prepared for. In 1991 they wiped out most of Wells Fargo's earnings. But the bank was still very solvent and still reported in 1991 a small net profit of $21 million, or $.04 a share.

Wall Street reacted as if Wells Fargo were a regional savings and loan on the brink of insolvency, and in the space of four months hammered Wells Fargo's stock price from $86 a share to $41.30 a share. Wells Fargo lost 52% of its per share market price because it essentially was not going to make any money in 1991. Warren responded by buying 10% of the company—5 million shares—for an average price of $57.80 a share.

What Warren saw in Wells Fargo was one of the best-managed and most profitable money-center banks in the country selling in the stock market for a price that was considerably less than comparable banks were selling for in the private market. And though all banks compete with one another, money-center banks like Wells Fargo, as we said, have a kind of toll bridge monopoly on financial transactions. If you are going to function in society, be it as an individual, a mom-and-pop business, or a billion-dollar corporation, you need a bank account or a checking account, and maybe a car loan, or a mortgage. And with every bank account, checking account, car loan, or mortgage comes the banker, charging you fees for the myriad services he provides. California, by the way, has a lot of people, thousands of businesses, and lots of small and medium-size banks, and Wells Fargo is there to serve them all—for a fee.

Anyway, the loan losses that Wells Fargo anticipated never reached the magnitude expected, and seven years later, in 1997, if you wanted to buy a share of Wells Fargo, you would have to pay approximately $270 a share. Warren ended up with a pretax annual compounding rate of return of approximately 24.6% on his 1990 investment.

You have to know what you are interested in before you go shopping. But sometimes a twist in the business cycle creates a few down years for what is usually an excellent business. And the stock market flips out and slams the price of the stock into the ground.

For Capital Cities it was a general recession that caused a drop in advertising revenues. But this sort of thing has happened before. The same recession caused a collapsing real estate market and in the process caused the entire banking industry to suffer huge losses. But Wells Fargo wasn't going to vanish overnight; it was too well run and too key a player in the banking game. The weaker banks vanish long before the giants fall. The financial system's self-interest and the Federal Reserve see to that.

So, what's the point? The point is this: if you have identified the companies that have excellent management or a great consumer monopoly or both, it is possible to predict that they will most certainly survive a recession and more than likely come out of it in a better position than before. *Recessions are hard on the weak, but they clean the field for the strong to take an even larger share when things improve.*

THE INDIVIDUAL SCREWUP

Occasionally, a company with a great consumer monopoly going in its favor does something that is both stupid and correctable. From 1936 to the mid-1970s GEICO made a fortune insuring preferred drivers by operating at low cost and eliminating agents by operating via direct mail. But by the early 1970s new management decided that it would try and grow the company further by selling insurance to just about anyone who knocked on their door.

This new philosophy, of insuring any and all, brought GEICO a large number of drivers who were accident-prone. More accidents meant that GEICO would lose more money, which it did. In 1975 it reported a net loss of $126 million, which placed it on the brink of insolvency. In response to this crisis, GEICO's board of directors hired Jack Byrne as the new chairman and president. Once on board, he approached Warren about investing in the company. Warren had only one concern, and that was whether GEICO would drop the unprofitable practice of insuring any and all drivers and return to the time-tested format of insuring just preferred drivers at low cost by direct mail. Byrne said that was the plan, and Warren made his investment.

A different type of event occured at American Express in the mid-1960s. The company, through a warehousing subsidiary, verified the existence of about $60 million worth of tanks filled with salad oil, owned by commodities dealer Anthony De Angelis. De Angelis in turn put up the salad oil as collateral for $60 million in loans. When De Angelis failed to pay back the loans, his creditors moved to foreclose on the salad oil. But to the surprise of the creditors, the collateral they had loaned money against didn't exist. Since American Express had inadvertently verified the existence of the nonexistent oil, it was held ultimately responsible to the creditors for their losses. American Express ended up having to pay off the creditors to the tune of approximately $60 million.

This loss essentially sucked out the majority of American Express's equity base, and Wall Street responded by slamming its stock into the ground. Warren saw this and reasoned that even if the company lost the majority of its equity base, the inherent consumer monopolies of the credit card operations and travelers checks business still remained intact. This loss of capital would not cause any *long-term* damage to American Express. Seeing this, Warren invested 40% of Buffett Partnership's investment capital in its stock, thus acquiring for the Buffett partners approximately 5% of American Express's outstanding stock. Two years later the market reappraised the stock upward, and Warren sold it and pocketed a cool $20 million profit.

Think of it this way. Let's say you sued Coca-Cola and in 1993 won a judgment of $2.2 billion, or roughly what the company would have reported in net earnings that year. The stock market, hearing the news of your judgment, would kill Coca-Cola's stock price. But in truth this loss would have little or no effect on the amount of money Coca-Cola would make in 1994. The intrinsic consumer monopoly Coca-Cola possesses would still be intact. Effectively, your $2.2 billion judgment would be the same as if Coca-Cola had paid out a dividend of $2.2 billion in 1993. But instead of paying out the dividends to its shareholders, Coca-Cola would have paid it out to you. In the next year, 1994, Coca-Cola will show a net profit of $2.2 billion or better. By the time 1995 rolls around, no one will have remembered your 1993 judgment, and the price of Coca-Cola's stock will have returned to its pre-judgment price. How soon they forget!

The lesson here is that the volatility of a company's stock price caused by a recession, as in the case of Capital Cities or Wells Fargo, or the odd event, as in the case of GEICO or American Express, can create an opportunity for the business perspective investor who has an eye on the long term.

21

How Market Mechanics Whipsaw Stock Prices to Create Buying Opportunities

Warren believes that the technical mechanics of the stock market can create situations that will whipsaw security prices regardless of the underlying economics of the businesses. He believes this irrational economic behavior can create situations that present excellent buying opportunities for the practitioner of business perspective investing.

The stock-market-mechanics phenomenon is different from short-term-perspective profit seeking—which responds to individual business aberrations or general business cycles, just discussed. The stock-market-mechanics phenomenon is a quirk in the stock market infrastructure that occurs because of the ways and methods that securities are bought and sold. Also key in it are certain investment strategies, such as portfolio insurance and index arbitrage—two investment strategies that try to exploit the price movement of the whole stock market.

In these situations the stock of the individual businesses becomes a commodity, the demand for which is driven by forces that respond not to business values or economics or even the actual price of the security, but to the direction and the rate of speed at which the price level of the whole market changes.

This infrastructure problem can be the departure point for mass hysteria. When people experience a great loss of wealth for no apparent rational reason, they often panic, selling their securities and taking a position on the sidelines until the market stabilizes. The panic exacerbates the severity of the situation, a situation that offers us an opportunity to practice business perspective investing.

To explain the problem and the buying opportunity that it presents, we shall look at two different financial disasters that occurred as a result of these quirks in the stock market infrastructure.

THE MECHANICS

As we stated earlier, the many different stock market investment philosophies can be broken into two distinct and different strategies of exploitation. One is short-term oriented and the other long-term. Business perspective investing, from Warren's perspective, as we know, falls into the long-term category.

In a perfect world all the information about a particular company is interpreted and defined by these two different strategies. They, in turn, determine the market price for the stock of the company. We know that the short-term strategy is the dominant force in the marketplace and so will dominate the force that determines the stock's price. This is where the long-term business perspective buyer derives his or her buying opportunity.

There are, however, situations in which the information about the company has little to do with the forces that drive the stock's price. Such was the case in the Panic of 1901 and the most recent panic, of 1987. In both these situations a liquidity crisis arose among the market makers, which set off a market panic.

THE PANIC OF 1901

The Panic of 1901 is of interest to us because it lasted for only a week. It was caused by the battle between E. H. Harriman and James Hill (and their respective bankers, Kuhn, Loeb & Company and J. P. Morgan and Company) for control of the Northern Pacific Railroad.

In those days, when the titans of the railroad industry wanted to take over another railroad, they would go into the open market and quietly start buying the stock of the company desired until they acquired control. Today, under SEC regulations, anyone who acquires 5% or more of a company must make a public disclosure. In 1901 there was no such requirement, and it was often possible for a person or firm to slowly and quietly acquire controlling interest in a company before the general market became aware and accordingly bid up the price of the stock. This was the case with the Northern Pacific.

In the beginning of 1901, James Hill and J. P. Morgan and Company had large interests in the Northern Pacific Railroad, but they did not control a majority of the stock. In April of 1901, E. H. Harriman started secretly buying the stock, and during the month of April the price of the stock rose 25%. This didn't cause any alarm, because the overall level of the market had been rising. Since it wasn't apparent that a takeover was in the works, some traders thought that Northern Pacific's stock had risen too fast and started shorting it.

When one *shorts* a stock, he is in fact *borrowing* the security from someone and then *selling* it. If the price of the security then goes down, the person who shorted the stock can go into the market, buy the stock back, and tender the stock back to the person he borrowed it from, thus repaying the loan. One makes a profit if he shorts a stock and can later buy it back at a lower price. One loses money if he shorts a stock and has to buy it back later at a higher price.

On Monday, May 6, 1901, Northern Pacific's stock made a sudden and dramatic jump upward. No one seemed to know the cause of the stock's rise. The directors of the Northern Pacific didn't know, and their bankers were in the dark as well. Many thought it was a mere market manipulation, and accordingly the shorts increased their position—they shorted more of the stock.

On Tuesday, May 7, the stock continued to climb, from $117 a share to $143. By late afternoon it became apparent to all what was happening. Word got out that Harriman was making his final bid to take control of the company. Hill and Morgan heard this news and tried to stop him by putting in bids to buy as much of the stock as they could to keep it out of Harriman's hands.

By Wednesday, May 8, it became obvious to all concerned that the warring parties, Harriman versus Hill and Morgan, in their struggle for control, had cornered the market for the stock of Northern Pacific. This really wouldn't have had any effect on the overall stock market except for one thing: the people who had shorted the stock were *still* short—they hadn't covered their positions.

No one was selling, and big buyers were forcing the price through the ceiling. This meant the shorts were caught, and as the price of the stock rose, they started to panic. Understand that back in those days, people who sold short a stock had to deliver it the next day. If they didn't own it, they had to go borrow it. If they couldn't deliver it, the party they sold it to could go into the market and pay the market price for the stock and stick the bill to the person who shorted it but couldn't deliver.

On May 8 there were few if any sellers, and the shorts trying to cover their positions started to bid wildly for the stock. By the end of the day the stock was trading at $180 a share.

When the gong kicked off trading on Thursday morning, the ninth, the shorts had reached an intense state of fear, and panic swept like wildfire through their ranks. By noon the shorts had bid the stock to $1000 a share. When you have to have it, you have to have it.

At the same time a most interesting thing was occurring to the rest of the market. It started to nosedive. The shorts, caught in a very dangerous situation, began panic selling of their other holdings to raise money to cover their short positions. Dozens of large trading firms were caught with their pants down and now were scrambling to cover their butts.

Bernard Baruch was on the floor of the exchange that fateful day and later wrote, "On the Exchange floor fear had completely taken the place of reason. Stocks were being dumped wildly, dropping from ten to twenty points. There were rumors of corners in other stocks."

Before Harriman reached a truce the next day with Hill and Morgan, leading stocks fell as much as sixty points; and banks, who were charging 4% for money they loaned to traders, got scared and pushed their loan rates to as high as 60%. One stock goes through the ceiling and rest of the market gets tanked.

Here is the lesson. The drop in price of the other stocks was not caused by a recession or a lull in the business cycle, or by companies reporting lower earnings, or by a changing macroeconomic picture. It wasn't even because of a shift in the interpretation of the information available on these businesses.

What happened was that the investors who were short Northern Pacific stock were caught in a squeeze and were losing their shirts. This pushed them into a liquidity crisis, to which they responded by selling their *other* stock positions. They did this to generate cash to cover the losses they experienced because they were caught in a short position in Northern Pacific.

The rest of the traders, fearing similar situations in other companies, began freaking out and started a wave of panic selling.

Bernard Baruch realized what was going on. He knew that great companies were being sold at ridiculous prices and saw an opportunity to do some buying.

Thus the market mechanism that allowed someone to sell what he didn't own, combined with a sudden price rise in the stock of Northern Pacific, created an explosive situation, which led to a massive and irrational sell-off of the entire stock market. This strange bit of market dynamics in turn created a buying opportunity for Baruch. The market soon recovered and Baruch made his initial fortune.

Market mechanisms through unexpected interaction can cause wild price swings that have nothing to do with processing economic information.

THE PANIC OF 1987

You may be wondering what all this has to do with the market today. Didn't the SEC in the 1930s enact rules to prevent the kind of panic that occurred in 1901? The answer is yes. But things change and government bodies tend to legislate regulation after the fact. In the late 1980s, a new set of facts developed.

During the Panic of 1987, two new investment strategies, *index arbitrage* and *portfolio insurance,* came into play and started to dominate the stock market. Their interaction set into play dynamics that from October 13 to October 19, 1987, ripped the market apart.

The Presidential Task Force on Market Mechanisms, in what is popularly known as the "Brady Report," said:

> From the close of trading on Tuesday, October 13, 1987, to the close of trading on October 19, 1987, the Dow Jones Industrial Average "Dow" fell 769 points or 31 percent. In those four days of trading, the value of all outstanding US stocks decreased by almost $1 trillion [THAT'S $1 TRILLION!!!]. On October 19, 1987, alone, the Dow fell by 508 points or 22.6 percent. Since the early 1920's, only the drop of 12.8 percent in the Dow on October 28, 1929 and the fall of 11.7 percent the following day, which together constituted the Crash of 1929, have approached the October 19, (1987) decline in magnitude ("Brady Report," p. 1).

The precipitous market decline of mid-October 1987 was triggered by specific events: an unexpectedly high merchandise trade deficit, which pushed interest rates to new high levels, and proposed tax legislation, which led to the collapse of the stocks of a number of takeover candidates.

This initial decline ignited mechanical, value-insensitive selling by a number of mutual fund groups reacting to price reductions. Selling by these investors and the prospect of further selling by them encouraged a number of aggressive trading-oriented institutions to sell in anticipation of further market declines. These institutions included, in addition to hedge funds, a small number of pension and endowment funds, money management firms, and investment banking houses. This selling, in turn, stimulated further reactive selling by portfolio insurers and mutual funds.

To understand the madness of that October it is necessary to understand the buying and selling strategy of mutual and pension funds that use portfolio insurance. Portfolio insurance is a strategy that uses computer-based models to determine an optimal stock-cash ratio at various market price levels. This usually calls for selling as stock prices move downward and buying when stock prices move upward. In fact, two portfolio insurance users' programs involved in the crash of 1987 called for sales equaling 50% of their stock holdings in response to a 10% decline in the S&P 500 Index.

So if the price index of the S&P moves downward by 10%, then these two portfolio insurance users would sell 50% of their equity holdings. Hey, that makes sense, doesn't it? No, it doesn't.

And if the S&P rises by 10%, guess what they do then. That's right, they increase their equity holdings by 50%.

Does it sound stupid? Kind of like Dumb and Dumber running a pension fund? Well, get this! On a couple of the days during the crash, the same portfolio insurer was both the largest buyer and the largest seller of same securities. Look, Boss, the S&P Index is going down by 10%! Sell! Sell! Look, Boss, the S&P Index is going up by 10%! Buy! Buy! (Something akin to Chicken Little running an investment fund.)

Sound insane enough for you? Now get this. Instead of selling stocks directly, the portfolio insurers have figured out that it is cheaper for them just to sell an S&P 500 Index commodities contract. This allows them to sell millions of dollars' worth of stocks for just a few dollars down. Sounds cool, doesn't it? Let me explain the S&P commodities contract a little better.

Commodities like corn, sugar, cotton, and oil are traded on commodity future exchanges throughout the world. The biggest one is in Chicago. On these exchanges, contracts for the future delivery of a particular commodity are traded. If you are a maker of corn flakes and you want to buy 5,000 bushels of corn for delivery nine months from now, you can go to the commodities exchange, and for a little money down you can buy a contract that entitles you to purchase 5,000 bushels of corn nine months from now at a fixed price.

The person who sold you the contract is betting that the price of fulfilling the contract in nine months will be lower than the price on the contract he sold you. If it is lower, he makes money on the difference between the price terms agreed to on the contract and his cost to cover.

In the late 1980s a new type of futures contract developed, which allowed you to bet on the price direction of S&P 100 and S&P 500 market indexes. The contract was valued at a price that equaled the pool of stocks that made up a specific index. The contract's price would change minute by minute throughout the trading day, reflecting price changes in the underlying stocks that make up the index.

So if you believe that the general market was going up during, say, the next six months, you could buy a commodities-type contract representing a pool of securities making up the S&P 100 or the S&P 500 index.

With commodities contracts for such things as gold, cotton, wheat, and corn, you can actually take delivery of the underlying commodity. Contract to buy 10,000 bushels of wheat, and if you wanted, you could take delivery of 10,000 bushels of wheat. But with the S&P contracts, the delivery was the cash difference between the contract price and the price of the S&P contract on its execution date. Thus, a true casino developed, in which people and institutions could place large leveraged bets on the *direction* of the stock market.

In theory, since the S&P Index contract called for delivery in cash, there was no direct relationship between the S&P contract and the underlying stocks of the S&P Index, just wild betting by the investment world on the *direction* of the stock market.

The same type of stock index pool instrument developed in the options markets as well.

Now, the men and women on Wall Street, being the eager beavers they are, discovered that an arbitrage opportunity developed between the actual securities and the different index instruments.

Let me show you how this works. Let's say the S&P 500 Index contract was selling at a discount from what those five hundred different stocks would cost on the floor of the New York Stock Exchange. Wall Streeters would buy the S&P 500 contract and sell a like-kind pool of stocks on the New York Stock Exchange. The funny thing about this arbitrage game is that the players don't buy just one contract. They buy several thousand at a shot, which means that they have to sell tens of millions of dollars' worth of securities on the New York Stock Exchange at once. And if the game heats up, the selling can go into the hundreds of millions of dollars.

The catch is that portfolio insurers use the S&P 500 contract as a surrogate for the real thing. During Monday, October 19, 1987, portfolio insurers not only sold $2 billion in stocks on the New York Stock Exchange; they also sold 34,500 S&P 500 contracts representing some $4 billion in stocks on the Chicago commodities exchange. This massive selling by portfolio insurers drove the price of the S&P 500 commodities contract below the price that the basket of S&P 500 stocks was selling for on the New York Stock Exchange.

The index arbitrage program traders of the big investment banks then went to work buying the S&P 500 commodities contracts and selling the corresponding S&P 500 basket of securities on the New York Stock Exchange. This allowed them to take advantage of the price discrepancy between the two markets.

The index arbitrage program traders effectively transferred the portfolio insurers selling S&P 500 commodities contracts to the corresponding securities that made up the S&P 500 commodities contract. This put additional selling pressure on the individual stocks that made up the S&P 500 commodities contract, and before you knew it, the S&P 500 had dropped another 10% and portfolio insurers kicked in another round of selling. Getting dizzy yet?

This vicious cycle just kept playing itself out in a game of round-robin until the prices of the securities became so ridiculous that even an investor like Warren started perusing the market for possible buying opportunities. (One of his catches in 1987 turned out to be the Coca-Cola Company.)

Remember those market makers on the floor of the New York Stock Exchange, the ones who act as matchmakers? They have to buy those stocks that everybody is selling. Normally things go up a little and then down a little. This lets the market makers make their money and keep an orderly market. But when there is only selling going on, the stocks they bought in the morning are worth less in the afternoon. Additionally, if no one is buying, they have no way of selling the stocks they bought in the morning to generate cash to buy stocks people want to sell in the afternoon. And after five consecutive days of heavy selling, the market makers were running out of cash, which caused people to really panic. Normally the big Wall Street banks would have loaned them additional money, but in this case even the banks began to get scared.

About the time that the entire financial system was collapsing, the governing bodies of the New York Stock Exchange and the

Chicago Board of Trade shut down the computer system that supported the program trading. It took them only five days to figure it out! And the Federal Reserve Bank said that it was ready and willing to support the banks, which it did by infusing more money into the system through its open market operations.

To make a long story short, everything worked out, and you and I are still here, along with all the brilliant Gomer Pyles on Wall Street. "Hey, Gomer! S&P 500 is down 10%. Time to sell 50% of our investment portfolio."

Tim Metz of the *Wall Street Journal* wrote an excellent book about the subject entitled *Black Monday* (William Morrow & Co., 1988). I suggest you go check it out. Also, there is the "Brady Report," which is the official government explanation of what happened.

The lesson here is that there are *large forces* at work that buy and sell *huge* amounts of securities. And they couldn't care less about the economics of the businesses that they are buying and selling. And sometimes these forces go entirely out of whack and create wonderful opportunities for business perspective investing. It happened in 1901 for Bernard Baruch, and it happened in 1987 for Warren Buffett. And it will happen again and again and again. Fools and greed usually go hand in hand, which creates a field of opportunity for the rational man.

Inflation

To fully understand Warren's investment philosophy, you need to have an idea of what inflation is and how it is caused. To do this, you have to have an idea of what money is and how it works.

Long ago people traded goods with one another for different products and services: a pig for a plow, wheat for fish, a bit of wool to the local priest for a blessing. People found that it was hard to transport all this stuff around, so items of barter that retained their characteristics but were small and portable and would not spoil became a sort of currency. And still, to this day, in certain parts of the world, a man's wealth is measured in everything from salt to the number of camels he owns.

But gold and silver were the commodities chosen to function as currency more often than not. Gold and silver were semi-rare items of value that were easy to divide up, transport, and store. Thus gold and silver coins came into existence. And after a while the world started quoting prices not in olive oil and sheep but in pieces of gold and silver.

Then governments that were collecting taxes in gold and silver started minting their own coins when they paid money out of their treasury to their generals and armies and for the goods and services needed to run the country. The Romans were particularly good at developing a Roman currency of minted coins.

In the United States we developed the dollar, which was represented by gold coins of varying weights. A $20 gold piece was equal to an ounce of gold. In France it was the franc, and in England it was the pound, each representing a certain weight of gold or silver.

An odd thing happened in the early part of this century. Governments that were well established by this time in Europe started to butt heads, and in the process brought on World War I. Wars just don't happen for free. Somebody has to pay for them, and government, which controls the armies, is given the task.

Usually a government pays for a war out of its treasury, using taxation to generate the necessary money to pay the troops. However, as we approached the Industrial Age, the cost of going to war became more expensive. It's one thing to buy a thousand muskets and some cannons, it's another to have to finance the building of fleets of modern ships and airplanes. Today, a couple of cruise missiles cost more than both sides spent on the American Revolution.

The governments involved in the war had, of course, to strain every resource to get the funds for their necessary expenditures. An expedient means they all adopted was the issuance of paper money in exchange for gold coins. Let us consider the case of a country that had been doing business with a gold coin currency of, say, 100, using that figure to express the number of francs, marks, dollars, or other unit. If the government now printed 100 units of paper money and got the public to accept the 100 units of paper money in exchange for the 100 units of gold coin, then the government has effectively taken pieces of paper and traded them for pieces of gold.

This was done gradually. In America, the government ordered that the gold and silver coins were to be swapped for paper gold and silver certificates, which could be redeemed for their metal equals at your local Federal Reserve Bank. I'm comfortable with that, aren't you? Don't have to lug all those gold coins around, just nice, neat, clean dollar bills.

After a while people forgot about the redemption factor and the government quit offering it. One bright and sunny day in 1933, the American government ordered that all gold coin and bullion held by persons in the United States be turned over to the United States Treasury in exchange for—paper dollars. From 1933 to the time of the attack on Pearl Harbor, the United States Treasury's gold reserves increased from $8.2 billion to $22.7 billion. With a single sweep of the pen, the U.S. government effectively nationalized all the gold owned by the people of the United States.

With the gold neatly in the Treasury, the government could go out and spend it in other countries for the things needed to wage war. Governments knowledgeable about this neat trick of turning paper into gold, when dealing with a foreign government, insisted they be paid in gold—not in those funny paper things they had convinced their own citizens to use in place of the precious metal. As a result a gold standard between different countries developed. The British treasury could take the gold it acquired from its citizens and swap it with the Americans for paper dollars to buy war materials. After the United States entered World War II, the U.S. Treasury's gold reserves stopped increasing and started to decline, as the U.S. government spent its gold reserves overseas on the materials needed to build and keep the American military fighting a war on three continents.

Not only do governments engage in international trade, but businesses do as well, and a British businessman in need of American goods has to buy them with American dollars, and vice versa. In the old days, the British businessman could simply pay in gold or convert his gold into paper dollars. But since gold was no longer the medium of exchange, the Bank of England or the U.S. Federal Reserve Bank had to facilitate this exchange for him through his local bank.

So if you were a British businessman and you needed to buy American goods and you needed dollars to conduct the transaction, you would go to your local bank, which in turn would go to the Bank of England. The Bank of England would take your paper pounds and convert them to gold and then go buy paper dollars for you from the U.S. Federal Reserve Bank in New York City. The British businessman could now take his paper dollars and send them to America to buy the American goods.

All this buying and selling developed into a very efficient system. Any transaction could take place in a matter of minutes. In fact the Bank of England even kept a stock of American dollars on hand to facilitate transactions, just as the U.S. Federal Reserve Bank kept a stock of English pounds on hand. Big British businesses kept dollar-denominated bank accounts in America to facilitate the transactions, and American entities kept pound-denominated bank accounts in England.

However, after World War II, when the United States was the only country with a large industrial base left intact, the foreign business community had to buy almost all of its manufactured goods from America, which caused the central banks of these countries to exchange more of their gold for dollars than was normal—and after a while they ran out of gold. One by one the central banks of the world announced that they were off the gold standard and the value for their currency would be determined by supply and demand.

Many of these foreign central banks just let their printing presses run; if you need more money, you just print it. Eventually, the exchange value of these overprinted currencies began to fall in relationship to the dollar. Economists call this *devaluation of a currency*. The same thing happened in America in the early seventies, when Nixon took us off the international gold standard and let the international value of the dollar float against the other currencies of the world. If you remember, we had this little war going on in Vietnam, which was costing a fortune, and the U.S. government was paying for it by inflating the economy, pushing the rate of inflation into the double digits.

Now long ago, before there was paper money, if a government wanted to increase its wealth, it had to acquire more gold. It could do this by mining it, taxing the merchant class, or stealing it from another country. As we mentioned earlier, the famous Dutch East Indies Company was a publicly financed pirate operation, which built and operated pirate warships whose sole purpose was to rob Spanish galleons bringing back gold mined in the New World.

But with the invention of paper money a government merely had to crank up the printing presses to create new wealth. Fantastic, your own wealth-creating money machine! No need to go out and mine for gold. Instant wealth.

But an odd thing happens when a government just lets the printing presses run; it increases the supply of money. And when the supply of money increases, an even odder thing starts to happen—prices start to rise. That is inflation. Let's see how it works.

THE ROOTS OF INFLATION

To explain inflation I think it would be best if we start with a hypothetical. Suppose you live in an island country, and on this island there once was $100 million in gold coins circulating. Let's say that a $1 gold coin would buy you one dozen eggs. If the government replaced the $100 million in gold coins with $100 million in paper dollars, one paper dollar would still buy one dozen eggs. And everything is fine.

The rascals in the government, however, have figured out that they can print up extra dollars and spend them. The merchant believes he is being offered one of the original $100 million, and he gives the government one dozen eggs for $1. The government keeps doing this—getting something for nothing. After a while, instead of having $100 million in circulation, we have 200 million paper dollars in circulation.

When the government spends more money, business benefits—lots of big government contracts and lots of people making more money. The merchant who was pricing the eggs at $1 for a dozen one day notices that people suddenly have more money to spend and are much more willing to pay higher prices for his eggs. He finds that he can now charge $2 for a dozen eggs and people are still willing to buy as many eggs as when he was charging $1.

Imagine that you and I were at an auction and we both had $50 in our pockets and we were the only two people bidding on an item. The most money that would be paid for that item is $50. But if you have $100 dollars and I have $100, we can bid the price of the item up to $100.

The problem is that all prices rise to reflect the increase in the abundance of cash. The person selling eggs is not any richer in true purchasing power than he was when he was making $1 for a dozen eggs, because *he* has to pay the farmer more money for the eggs. And the farmer is not richer, because *he* has to pay more money for the chickens and the chicken feed. And the person with $200 in his pocket is not any richer than back when he had $100. *Both sums end up buying the same amount of goods.*

But the government's game is to get you to sell it your goods and services for inflated dollars at preinflated prices. Governments in effect have found a way to cheat you out of the real value of your money.

The governments of the world have been inflating their economies since World War I. This is why that candy bar you paid a nickel for in 1960 is now selling for 50 cents, or that McDonald's hamburger went from 15 cents to 75 cents, or a ski lift ticket went from $5 to $45. You can thank your Uncle Sam and those wonderful politicians who keep the printing presses running and continue to inflate the cost of everything.

In the United States the historic rate of inflation is running around 5% a year. In some other countries, like Germany during World War II and post–Cold War Russia, the inflation rate was in excess of 50% a year.

This hurts us as investors. If we hold on to dollars they will lose their value at the equivalent of the rate of inflation. So if inflation is running at 25%, your money will be losing its purchasing power at the rate of 25% a year. Thus, Warren believes that if you have an inflation rate of 25% you must get at least a 25% return on your investment in order for the real purchasing power of your wealth *to stay even with inflation.*

Warren believes that there will always be inflation. The reason for this is that the alternative, deflation, is political suicide for our politicians. Think about it. Inflation creates the illusion of wealth. The house you paid $100,000 for thirty years ago is now worth $500,000 and that makes you as the owner smile. You believe that you have become richer even though if you wanted to sell your home and buy a comparable one you would have to spend $500,000. Thirty years ago you made $20,000 a year and now you make $100,000. You think that you are making more money, yet $100,000 today doesn't have any more purchasing power than $20,000 did thirty years ago. You think that you are getting richer, but in truth all things remain the same. And if you are on a fixed income or you bought long-term bonds or you kept your money in cash, your actual wealth will more than likely decrease.

Financial institutions and corporations that have to borrow money have learned to use inflation to their advantage. They borrow your money today and promise to pay you back in the future with inflated dollars. Banks do it, insurance companies do it, real estate developers do it, and large manufacturing companies do it. Think about those hundred-year bonds that Wall Street occasionally sells. If I borrowed $100,000 from you and promised to pay it back in a hundred years, do you think it would have the same purchasing power as it does today? In a world with just 6% inflation, $100,000 in a hundred years will have the same purchasing power that $294 has today!

Of course, the alternative to inflation is *deflation*. This is when prices decrease. Sound great, doesn't it? Things just get cheaper. The problem is that your salary also goes down. Also, the value of your home decreases. But if you just borrowed $500,000 to buy a new home and suddenly your salary decreases to the point that you can't make your mortgage payment, then you are in trouble. The bank ends up foreclosing on your home. But because real estate prices are also deflating, the bank ends up losing money because it can't recoup what it loaned you. If this happens too many times, the bank becomes insolvent and collapses, and the people that invested in the bank lose all their money. If too many banks collapse and too many people lose all their money, the country ends up in a severe depression. A depression means mass unemployment, homelessness, bread lines, and a very angry voting population. And politicians start losing their jobs. That is something politicians just hate, losing their jobs. So if given a choice between inflation or deflation, the political animal will always choose inflation.

You may be wondering if a government can actually make this choice. You know that general inflation is caused by increasing the money supply. Back when the money supply was determined by the amount of gold a country possessed, to inflate the economy you had to increase the gold supply. (When Spain started extracting large amounts of gold from the New World it touched off a wave of inflation in Europe.) Increasing the money supply overnight by increasing the gold supply is practically an impossible thing to do. You just can't print more gold. But if your money supply is made up of paper dollars, you just start the presses running. Since deflation means political and financial ruin, given a choice, politicians will always choose the feel-good illusion of wealth that inflation creates over the disastrous effects of deflation.

For Warren inflation is a permanent part of the economic landscape. And so he takes its punitive effects into consideration whenever viewing a prospective investment.

A final note: It is now possible once again for Americans to own gold. Twenty years from now the federal government may tell us to trade in our gold again in exchange for . . . you got it, paper dollars. Fool me once, shame on you. Fool me twice, shame on me.

23

Inflation and
the Consumer Monopoly

Warren, for many years, felt that inflation was his worst enemy. And for the average investor it is. Promises today to pay sums of money tomorrow are invitations to folly in an economy racked with inflation. However, home owners who locked into thirty-year 5% mortgages in the 1960s benefited from inflation increasing their incomes while their mortgage payments remained fixed. Corporations also benefited in the sixties by convincing investors to loan them money for long periods of time at a fixed rate, which allowed them to pay back the loans in the future with inflated dollars. The people who got hurt were the investors, who experienced a real loss of purchasing power. That $4,000 they loaned GM (by purchasing a bond) back in the sixties would have bought them 100% of a new car. When GM paid it back to them in the nineties, the return of the $4,000 in principal would buy them only approximately 25% of a new car. Almost no investment escapes the taxation of inflation.

However, in 1983 Warren developed a theory that investments in companies that benefited from a strong consumer monopoly and required nominal incremental amounts of capital to continue operations actually benefited from the effects of inflation. Invest in these businesses and *inflation helps you as an investor. It makes you richer.*

Warren used See's Candy to explain this phenomenon. In 1972, See's was earning around $2 million on $8 million of net tangible assets (tangible assets are things like manufacturing plants and equipment, as opposed to intangible assets such as patents and copyrights). That means that See's plant and equipment and inventory produced, after all expenses and taxes, $2 million in net earnings. The company was earning 25% on its net tangible asset base ($2 million ÷ $8 million = 25%).

Berkshire Hathaway paid roughly $25 million in 1972 for See's, which equates to an after-tax rate of return of 8% ($2 million ÷ $5 million = 8%). Compare this to government bonds in 1972, which were paying a pretax rate of return of 5.8%, and See's after-corporate-income-tax annual rate of return of 8% doesn't look too bad.

Now let's say that a steel manufacturer with poorer economics than See's produced $2 million in net earnings, on $18 million in net tangible assets. (Blast furnaces for making steel cost considerably more than cooking pots for making candy.)

Two different businesses, both with net earnings of $2 million. The only difference is that See's produces its $2 million on a net tangible asset base of $8 million and the steel manufacturer produces its $2 million on a net tangible asset base of $18 million.

Now let's add in inflation. Over the next ten years, prices double, as do sales and earnings. Thus both our businesses experience a doubling of earnings, to $4 million. It's easy to figure out because all you have to do is sell the same number of units at the new inflated price, which everybody pays for with their new inflated salary.

But there is just one problem. Things wear out and eventually need to be replaced. When these two companies go to replace their net tangible asset bases, the one that had a base of $8 million, See's, is going to have to come up with $16 million. Prices doubled not only for candy but for plants and equipment. But the steel manufacturer with a net tangible asset base of $18 million is going to have to come up with $36 million.

Which company would you rather own—See's, which has to come up with $16 million, or the steel manufacturer, which has to come up with $36 million to stay in business? Get the point? The steel business manufacturer is going to require $20 million more of investment to produce the amount of earnings equivalent to See's.

Think of the advantages a business has if it almost never has to replace its plant and equipment and has the capacity to produce high rates of return on a small net tangible asset base—as See's does. The stock market sees this economic trick that inflation plays and responds by giving businesses like See's a *higher price-to-earnings valuation than it gives the steel business, which requires a higher net-tangible-asset base.*

Inflation, though harmful to a great many businesses, *can actually benefit the shareholders of companies that have a consumer monopoly working in their favor.*

24

A Few Words on Taxation

You know what taxes are. But then again, I really don't know the extent of your knowledge. So since this is a book for everyone interested in investing, I need to devote a page or two to discussing the effects of taxation on the investment process, something Warren thinks a great deal about. But don't worry, I'll keep it brief.

To the majority of investors taxes come as an afterthought. To Warren they play a very important role in the course of investment selection and the holding period.

When a corporation makes a profit for the year, it pays corporate income taxes. A company's net-income figure is an after-tax figure. The per share earnings figure is also an after-tax figure. So when we say that Company X has earnings of $10 a share, we are saying that it has made $10 a share *after paying its corporate income taxes.*

Once a company has paid its corporate taxes, it can do one of three things with its net earnings. It can pay them out as dividends, retain them and add them to its existing assets, or both.

Let's say the company we are looking at is earning $10 a share. So it can pay out all the earnings as a dividend, or retain all the earnings, or do a combination of both, paying out, say, $7 a share in dividends and retaining $3 a share.

(Companies need not always be profitable to pay out dividends. They can reach into their asset base and pay dividends from there. This, of course, lowers the net worth of the business.)

If the company pays out a dividend to the shareholders, the shareholders have to declare it as income and pay personal income taxes on it. If you own one share of Company X and it pays you a dividend of $10 a share, you will have to pay income taxes on that $10. If you are in a 31% tax bracket, you will have to pay $3.10 a share in taxes, thus reducing your take to $6.90 a share.

But if the company chooses to retain $10 a share in earnings, adding it to the company's asset base, then the shareholder is not taxed on the $10.

So if Company X retains its earnings, the effect of personal taxation is avoided.

When an investor, either a person or another corporation, sells the stock, the investor is subject to a capital gains tax on the profits. As of this writing, an individual must pay a maximum of 20%. A corporation is taxed at normal corporate income tax rates of up to 35%. Both the percentage of tax and the holding period change periodically, reflecting the whims of politicians and the government.

Interest payments made by a company to holders of its bonds are taxed to the recipient at personal or corporate income tax rates. Federal personal income taxes can run as high as 39.6%. The combined state and federal income taxes for individuals can run even higher. For corporations the federal income taxes run as high as 35%.

Dividend payments from one company to another are taxed at a combined federal and state tax rate of approximately 14%. For an individual they are taxed as regular income. This means that corporations have an advantage over individuals, who are stuck paying federal and state personal income taxes on dividend income they receive.

One could write volumes on the subject of taxation, but they would have to be rewritten every few years because the rates continually change. Be aware that taxes will always be there to take the government's cut of your investment profits. Accordingly, we address their impact on the investment process throughout this book.

The Effects of Inflation and Taxation on the Rate of Return, and the Necessity to Obtain a 15 % Return on Your Investment

Warren has often stated that real-world inflation and taxation greatly alter the investor's return. He argues that if we live in a world of 5% inflation, our assets decrease in real purchasing power by 5% every year.

For this *very* reason we invest our money. If we didn't, our wealth, held in cash, soon would lose its purchasing power.

If the value of our money depreciates at a rate of 5%, we have to have a return of at least 5% to offset inflation. But a return of 5% in a world of 5% inflation gives us a real growth in purchasing power of 0%. That is not good.

In a world of 5% inflation we need a return in excess of 5% to show a real growth in purchasing power. And in a world of 10% inflation we would need a return in excess of 10%.

THE EFFECTS OF TAXATION

Taxation adds another perspective to the situation. If we manage to obtain a 5% return on our money, income taxes can take 31% of that 5%, which means that we will be left with a real return of 3.45%. This means that in a world of 5% inflation, after paying income tax, we will be experiencing a real loss of purchasing power of 1.55% a year, also not good.

So in a world with 5% inflation and 31% income tax, we need an annual return on our investment of at least 7.2% just to stay even in the game and not have the purchasing power of our wealth diminish.

This means that if you want to increase your wealth, you must have an annual return in excess of 7.2%. If you invest in corporate bonds that pay an 8% return on your money, then, in effect, the return on your investment is—less personal income tax—approximately 31% (depending on which income tax bracket you fall in), which means you end up with an after-tax return of 5.5%. Subtract a 5% rate of inflation, and your real rate of return goes to 0.5%.

If you increased the rate of inflation to 9% and the tax rate to 40%, a situation we had in the early seventies, you must have a return of at least 15% for the real purchasing power of your wealth to stay intact (15% – 40% tax rate = 9%; 9% – 9% rate of inflation = 0%).

During the last twenty years in American history, we have seen double-digit inflation and tax rates of 50% and higher on personal income. Warren has come to believe that politicians will constantly try to inflate the economy and at the same time raise taxes. So he set up the minimum possible pretax annual compounding rate of return he wanted to achieve on his investments—approximately 15%.

It is interesting to note that Graham felt that the "long-term trend is toward inflation, punctuated by equally troublesome periods of deflation," and, "common stocks are by no means an ideal protection or 'hedge' against inflation, but they do more for the investor on this point than either bonds or cash" (*Security Analysis,* 1951, p. 8).

So, in summary, if you desire to have a real increase in your purchasing power, then *it is necessary that the return on your wealth be at least equal to the effects of inflation and taxation.*

26

The Myth of Diversifications Versus the Concentrated Portfolio

Warren believes that diversification is something people do to protect themselves from their own stupidity. They lack the intelligence and expertise to make large investments in just a few businesses, so they must hedge against the folly of ignorance by having their capital spread out among many different investments.

As we know, Graham's investment strategy required that he have literally one hundred or more stocks in his portfolio. He did this to hedge against the possibility that some of his investments would never perform, as businesses and as stocks. The nature of the business, he felt, was locked into *the numbers,* and he was not all that concerned with really getting to know the businesses he owned.

Warren followed Graham's strategy for a while but in the end found that it was more like owning a zoo than a stock portfolio. And as he shifted his method of analysis to the Munger/Fisher format, he found that he had to have a better understanding of the businesses he was investing in than Graham did.

Fisher, though agreeing that some diversification was necessary, thought that diversification as an investment principal was way oversold. (He pointed out that some cynics thought this was because it was a simple enough theory for even stockbrokers to understand.) Fisher agreed that investors, responding to the horrors of putting all their eggs into one basket, ended up spreading out their eggs into dozens of different baskets, with many of the baskets ending up containing broken eggs. Also, it was impossible to keep an eye on all the eggs in all the baskets. Fisher thought that most investors had been so oversold on diversification that they ended up owning so many stocks that they had little or no idea of what kind of businesses they had invested in.

Warren was greatly influenced by the writings of the late, great British economist John Maynard Keynes. Keynes, a person of noted expertise in the field of investments, said he had made the majority of his money in just a few different investments—the underlying businesses whose investment value he understood.

Warren has adopted the concentrated-portfolio approach, which means that he holds a small number of investments he really understands and intends holding for a long period of time. This allows the question of whether to allocate capital to an investment to be approached with the utmost seriousness. *Warren believes that it is the seriousness with which he addresses the questions of what to invest in and at what price that decreases the risk.* It is his commitment to the strategy of investing only in exceptional businesses at prices that make business sense that reduces his chances for loss.

Warren has often said that a person would make fewer bad investment decisions if he were limited to making just ten in his lifetime. Just ten. You would put a little work into making those ten decisions, don't you think?

It's amazing that intelligent, hardworking individuals think nothing of taking a large portion of their net worth and investing it in a company they know little or nothing about. If you ask them to invest in a local business, they would pepper you with questions. But let some stockbroker call them on the phone, and the next thing you know, they are partial owners of some exotic business.

Baruch said: "Time and energy are required to keep abreast of the forces that may change the value of a security. While one can know all there is to know about a few issues, one cannot possibly know all one needs to know about a great many issues" (*My Own Story*, Holt, Rinehart & Winston, 1957).

Baruch, by the way, lived to be a very old and a very, very wealthy man.

27

When Should You Sell
Your Investments?

The investment business is said to be 50% science and 50% art and 100% folklore. The Wall Street folklore that surrounds selling has something to do with the old adage that no one ever went broke by selling at a profit. Warren might respond that no ever got really wealthy that way either. (That last sentence should have caused a *big* question mark to appear in your head. Curious? Let us see why Warren thinks that this old adage won't make you superrich.) *Please note:* Parts of this chapter appear in other sections of the book. We thought it would be beneficial to bring all thoughts on selling under one roof. So if it looks familiar, it probably is.

THE GRAHAM APPROACH TO SELLING

Warren originally followed Graham's approach to selling. Graham, as we know, advocated selling a security when it reached its intrinsic value. Graham reasoned that a security had little or no profit potential past that point, and that one would be better off finding another undervalued situation.

If Graham had purchased a stock for $15 a share and assigned it an intrinsic value with a range of $30 to $40 a share, when the stock reached the price of $30 a share, he would sell it. He would take the proceeds and reinvest them in another undervalued situation.

As we noted earlier, Graham discovered that when you bought a stock that was selling below its intrinsic value, the longer you had to hold the stock, the lower the projected annual compounding rate of return on your investment would be. If you bought a stock for $20 a share and it had an intrinsic value of $30 a share, and if it rose to $30 a share the first year, your rate of return would be 50%. However, if it took two years for the share price to rise to the stock's intrinsic value, then your *annual* compounding rate of return would drop to 22.4%. If it took *three* years, your *annual* compounding rate of return would drop to 14.4%, in four years it would drop to 10.6%; in five to 8.4%, in six to 6.9%, in seven to 5.9%, and in eight to 5.1%. The longer it took, the lower your annual compounding rate of return. Graham's solution to this problem was to buy a company's stock only when its market price was sufficiently below the stock's intrinsic value to afford you a *margin of safety*. The margin of safety was there to protect you if the stock took a long time to realize its full intrinsic value. How long you thought the investment would take to rise to its intrinsic value determined the size of the margin of safety needed. If a long time is anticipated, then a large margin of safety is needed; but if a short time is expected, then a smaller margin of safety is probably adequate.

Graham, however, had one additional problem. What happens if the stock price never rises to its intrinsic value? What happens if the market refuses to realize the stock's full intrinsic value? How long should one wait? Two years? Five years?

His answer was two to three years. He reasoned that if the stock hadn't reached its intrinsic value by then, it probably never would. In that case, it was better to sell the stock and find a new situation.

WARREN'S APPROACH

Warren found that these remedies didn't really solve the *realization-of-value* problem. He found that more often than not, he was left holding dogs that never rose to their projected intrinsic value. And even if they did, once he sold them, the IRS would slap him with a capital gains tax. So, he found Graham's solutions to be wanting.

Charlie Munger and Philip Fisher advocated another solution to this problem. They argued that if one bought an excellent business that was growing, and the management functioned with the shareholders' financial gain as their primary concern, then the time to sell the business was never—unless these circumstances changed or a better situation availed itself. They believed that superior results could be had by following this strategy, which allowed for the investor to fully benefit from the compounding effect of the business profitably employing its retained earnings.

In order for Warren to implement this strategy he was required to leave the Graham fold and stop buying any situation solely on the basis of price. He began to base his investment decisions on the economic nature of the business. The excellent business with high rates of return on equity, identifiable consumer monopoly, and shareholder-oriented management became his primary target.

Price still dictated whether the stock would be bought and what Warren's annual compounding rate of return would be. But once the purchase was made, it could be held for many years as long as the economics of the business didn't change dramatically for the worse.

Using this strategy, Warren has held on to some of his greatest investments, including the *Washington Post* and GEICO, both of which have given him an annual compounding rate of return of 17% or better, for the last twenty years. These are companies that he sees as having an expanding value that will benefit him greatly over the long term. Even though they periodically sell at prices in excess of their Grahamian intrinsic value, Warren has continued to own them. One removes weeds from the garden, not the shoots of green that are flowering and bearing fruit.

BEAR AND BULL MARKETS—WHEN TO SELL

Many investors continually fall victim to the threat that the next bear market is right around the corner. Maybe it starts in the *Wall Street Journal* or on *Wall Street Week*. Your stockbroker is calling to tell you to take a defensive position, which means you have to move some of your assets into cash. (Brokers love this because it lets them earn a commission on the sale of the stocks that produce the cash. They also make another commission later on when they reinvest the cash for you.)

Fisher thought this was a stupid way to conduct your affairs. First of all, it is unlikely that the bear market will ever occur on schedule; and that the Wall Street fortune-tellers are wrong as much as they are right. And if you sell your great investment, that bear market just around the corner may end up being a bull market instead, and you just missed it.

But wait, you say, I'll just get back into the stock if the bear market doesn't materialize, and if it does, I can buy it back at a lower price. First of all, when you sold the stock, you got whacked for a capital gains tax and a broker's commission, which means that you don't have as much money as you started out with. If the bear market doesn't materialize, you have to come up with more money. Additionally, if the bear market does come, and you want to rebuy the stock, your stock has to drop considerably in price to make up for the capital gains tax and the broker's commission you paid.

Fisher also argues that people he knows seldom get back into their investments even if the bear market shows up. People who react to fear usually are left in a state of paralysis when soothsayers' predictions come true.

Bernard Baruch summed up his feelings on this subject with this advice: "Don't try to buy at the bottom and sell at the top. This can't be done—except by liars."

Warren's solution to all this bear/bull market twaddle is to totally ignore it. He can do this because he buys into a business on the basis of price. If the price is too high, the investment won't offer a sufficient rate of return and he won't buy in. Where the market is on any given day doesn't really matter to him. He doesn't think about it. Instead, he thinks about the business he is considering investing in and whether he can get it at the right price.

Warren is aware that great buys can show up even in a raging bull market, but he has also found that a bear market, where lots of companies are being sold cheap, offers him his greatest opportunity to find a really spectacular deal.

In the great crash of 1987, when all the market went crazy, running off a cliff, Warren was standing at the bottom of that deep abyss waiting for a business he was in love with to drop by. And sure enough, as we told you, the price of Coca-Cola stock got hammered and Warren jumped on it with a billion dollars. No, he didn't sell out and move into cash, and no, he didn't stand there with his hands in his pockets. His eyes saw opportunity where others saw only fear. And he could do this because his investment decisions are made from a business perspective.

SUMMARY

As we said, Warren is interested only in long-term ownership of businesses that possess some sort of consumer monopoly and allow for continuous per share earnings growth, through either expansion of operations or stock buybacks. Because continuous per share earnings growth eventually equates to higher per share prices for the company stock, Warren discovered that it makes more sense to hold an investment for as long as possible, even when the market places a very high value on the stock.

Warren wants the compounding to go on as long as possible. Sure, over the short term he could sell and make a handsome profit, but he is after an outrageous profit, the kind that makes you one of the richest people in the world. To get that rich you have to get your capital to compound at a high annual rate of return for a long time!

Warren's Different Kinds of Investments

Warren Buffett has made his fortune investing in the securities of many different types of businesses. We know that his preference is to purchase 100% of a business that has excellent business economics and management. When that is not possible, his second choice is to make a long-term investment in the common stock of a company that also benefits from excellent business economics and management.

Warren also invests in:

+ long-term fixed-income securities
+ medium-term fixed-income securities
+ short-term cash equivalents
+ short-term arbitrage commitments

These investments are not his favorites, nor do they bring him the largest profits. But they do offer a profitable use of assets while he waits for a chance either to buy an entire business or to make a long-term common stock commitment. It is these kinds of investments that confuse the press and public at large. They fail to see that the kind of company in which Warren is willing to take an *arbitrage position* may not be the kind of company in which he is willing to make a *long-term investment*.

The major portion of this book concerns Warren's business perspective investment strategy for long-term investments in common stocks. In this chapter we would like to examine some of Warren's other investments and explore how business perspective investing plays a role in their selection.

LONG-TERM FIXED-INCOME SECURITIES

As a rule Warren will almost never invest in long-term fixed-income securities (long-term bonds). The reason is that they require the long-term commitment of capital to an investment that usually offers a low rate of return. Warren also believes that the specter of inflation is a permanent part of our political economy and that high rates of inflation could easily strip away the value of any investment in long-term fixed-income securities.

The exception to this is when the market offers a unique circumstance that carries an acceptable amount of risk and an adequate rate of return. Warren's investment in Washington Public Power Supply System (WPPSS) bonds was one of those rare circumstances.

From October 1983 to June 1984, Warren purchased $139 million in WPPSS bonds for Projects 1, 2, and 3. WPPSS had just defaulted on $2.2 billion in bonds issued to build Projects 4 and 5.

Warren extended the criteria that he uses in buying an entire business to the purchase of the WPPSS bonds. His $139 million in WPPSS bonds would give him a tax-free annual interest payment of $22.7 million. Warren figured that this equated to an annual after-tax rate of return of approximately 16%.

Warren, using the rationale of business perspective investing, calculated that it would take about $45 million in pretax earnings for a normal business to produce $22.7 million in after-tax earnings in 1984. Warren estimated that the purchase of a whole business that produced $22.7 million in after-tax earnings would cost approximately $250–$300 million, or *nearly twice what he was paying for the WPPSS bonds.*

Thus, the theory of business perspective investing produced for Warren the subtheory of the *bond as a business.* Warren noted that this bond/business had a maximum value of $205 million—the face value of the bonds—which was only 48% higher than the $139 million he paid for the bonds. Warren also noted at the time that most businesses have a limited upside potential unless you invest additional capital in them. So the limited growth potential didn't bother him. Besides, the WPPSS bonds paid their interest in cash, so Warren could effectively remove the earnings from the business and reallocate them elsewhere.

Warren will invest only in bond situations that offer him an absolutely better opportunity to profit than other business ventures might.

MEDIUM-TERM FIXED-INCOME SECURITIES

Warren has always considered medium-term fixed-income tax-exempt securities to be a viable alternative to cash equivalents, such as T-bills, issued by the U.S. Treasury. In 1986 he purchased about $700 million in tax-exempt bonds, most with a maturity of between eight and twelve years. Warren considers these bonds to be mediocre investments, but they were the best alternative to keeping his assets in cash equivalents, such as treasuries.

He bought them with the intention of selling them as he needs the capital for other investments. With this strategy it is possible for Warren to show a loss if he sells them after interest rates have risen. Warren believes that any loss that would occur would be offset by the potential gain that a long-term investment in an excellent business, like Coca-Cola, would bring.

Warren considered his investments in the convertible preferred stocks of Champion International, Salomon Brothers, and USAir to fall into this category of medium-term fixed-income securities. Warren watchers for the longest time have been baffled by these convertible preferred investments. They scramble to find some kind of consumer monopoly or great underlying business economics, when there aren't any. What enticed Warren into these investments is the tax advantage that is given the dividend of a preferred stock and the marginal upside potential of the stock that the preferred will convert into. Note that I said "marginal"! Champion International, Salomon Brothers, and USAir are at best just average businesses that produce average returns for their investors. *They are not exceptional businesses,* compared to some of his other choices.

So why did Warren invest in them? Well, in the case of Salomon Brothers, he bought $700 million worth of 9% preferred stock at a per share price of $1,000. The terms of the preferred were that it could be converted, at Warren's option, after three years into Salomon common stock. Also, under the terms of the deal, if Warren elected not to convert the preferred, Salomon had to start redeeming it in 1995 at a rate of 140,000 preferred shares annually for the next five years. What this means is that if Warren wanted to, he could exchange the $700 million in Salomon preferred stock for $700 million in Salomon common stock—which equates to approximately 18.5 million shares of Salomon common stock. Or if he chose to keep the preferred, he had the option of either cashing out or converting to Salomon common stock under the annual redemption terms of the deal, which started in 1995. (In case you are wondering, Warren chose the cash in 1995; he said he had a better use for it. In 1996 he chose the Salomon common stock, which he used to secure the issuance of $500 million worth of Berkshire notes that convert into Salomon stock. The convertible Berkshire notes are really just a very clever way for Warren to sell 8,825,000 shares of Salomon common stock without dumping it directly on the market.)

From an economic standpoint, the Salomon preferred pays to Berkshire a 9% annual dividend yield. Dividends to an individual shareholder, like yourself, are taxed as income, which means that you end up paying approximately 31% of your yield to the IRS. This means that your 9% yield is really an after-tax yield of 6.21%, if it is paid to the individual shareholder.

But in Warren's case, his holding company, Berkshire Hathaway, bought the Salomon 9% convertible preferred. The advantage here is that corporations are given a tax break on income received from another corporation. In fact, Berkshire must pay only an effective tax of 14% on dividends it receives from another corporation.

This means that Berkshire's after-tax return on the 9% Salomon convertible preferred is approximately 7.7%. For Berkshire to earn an after-tax return of 7.7% on operational income it would have to have a pre-tax return of approximately 11.8%. So from a business perspective, Warren just bought a "convertible preferred business" that earned an annual pretax return of 11.8% and an after-tax return of 7.7%.

Warren was well aware when he made the investment in the

Salomon 9% convertible preferred stock that it would not produce the returns that Berkshire was achieving by investing in excellent businesses that were selling at attractive prices. He was aware also that the Salomon investment would not produce the kinds of returns that Berkshire's wholly owned subsidiary companies were producing.

What Warren did know was that the Salomon 9% convertible preferred investment would produce a return that was in excess of Berkshire's usual fixed-income portfolio, which was valued at $1.2 billion in 1986, the year before Berkshire bought the Salomon 9% convertible preferred. The convertible preferred investments offer Warren a profitable place to *park* large amounts of capital until something else comes along.

SHORT-TERM CASH EQUIVALENTS

Warren will periodically hold large amounts of cash in short-term notes of the United States government, other select businesses, and certain municipalities. None of these obligations would have a maturity of over a year. Think of it as short-term parking. Not very profitable, but better than stuffing the money under the mattress at home.

SHORT-TERM ARBITRAGE COMMITMENTS

This is one of the most important tools in Warren's investment arsenal. So we have decided to give short-term arbitrage commitments a chapter of its own, in which we go into great detail about Warren's use of arbitrage. Because the chapter is filled with equations, we have placed it in the Advanced Buffettology section, the second part of the book. If you are curious now, just turn to Chapter 43 and arbitrage away.

Now that you know what kind of company to invest in, it is time to learn how to figure out what price to pay. It is time to go on to Advanced Buffettology. Turn the page.

PART II

Advanced
Buffettology

You have just finished the qualitative portion of the book. What lies ahead is the quantitative portion. It is the math segment. It contains the equations that you will need to master to determine if a stock's market price makes business sense. This part of the book is essential to your reaching a full understanding of Buffettology. You have to have these skills to profitably implement a business perspective investment program. We have worked hard to make the equations very accessible. If you have the financial calculator we recommended earlier, the math becomes a breeze.

Now the key to this part of the book is the mathematical tools section, which includes, first, a number of small chapters instructing you in the use of mathematical tests that help determine at what price a potential investment makes business sense. This is introduced by a chapter on the analyst's role in ascertaining earning power. Following this is a chapter of case studies, which show you how to apply what you have learned, and then a chapter entitled "How Warren Got Started: The Investment Vehicle," which is about how to start your own investment partnership, just like Warren. And last, but not least, we close with a chapter that contains fifty-four companies to look at, which is a list of companies in which Warren has invested in the past and that your authors believe are still part of his investment universe, and a chapter entitled "Waiting for the Perfect Pitch."

Are you ready? Let's begin.

29

The Analyst's Role
in Ascertaining Earning Power

Warren uses a series of mathematical valuation techniques to ascertain the earning power of a business in which he is interested. By ascertaining the earning potenial of the business, he can then estimate the annual compounding rate of return that he expects the investment to earn. Warren, just as Graham did, has found that it is possible to predict the earnings and dividends a number of years ahead for some businesses.

Wall Street, though the home of many a financial analyst, has never been fond of making long-term projections for business. They argue that it is hard enough to estimate the current or coming year's earnings with any accuracy. As a rule, Wall Street analysts prefer to calculate future earnings of a company for only a relatively short period of time, usually twelve months or less. This is the end of the quantitative inquiry.

Graham stated in *Security Analysis* that the rest of the Wall Street analyst's study is qualitative in nature and "leads to an overall opinion, stated primarily in descriptive terms, about the standing and prospects of the enterprise." Graham further stated,

> The typical study of this kind will culminate in a buying recommendation, which is only rarely developed in a careful and thoroughgoing manner. . . . In some cases the stock is called "cheap" and "attractive" because it is selling at what seems a low price in relation to current earnings or those about to be realized. While such a measurement is important, it is hardly adequate for an investment decision, since value cannot soundly be established on the basis of earnings over a short period of time.

Graham went on to say: "The analyst could do a more dependable or professional job of passing judgment on a common stock if he were able to determine some objective value, independent of the market quotation, with which he could compare the current price."

In Graham's world next year's profits were of importance only if they could be viewed as indicative of the longer-term earning power of the business. The greatest chance for the investor to profit was to formulate a long-term opinion on the earning prospects of the business in question.

This is where Warren has made the greatest inroads and advancements in the theory of security analysis. Warren has developed the selective criteria for the identification of the businesses whose long-term earning power can be identified and projected. With this advancement, he has been able to see the long-term investment value of these businesses better than the run-of-the-mill, shortsighted analyst.

Your role, then, as an analyst/investor, is to identify those businesses that have long-term earning power. Then, depending on the return they offer, you make your investment decision.

To gain a perspective on the prospective return a business may offer and whether or not its long-term prospects are decipherable, it is necessary that we learn to use several different mathematical equations. These equations will help us get a better understanding of the economic realities of the business in question.

30

The Mathematical Tools

The mathematical tools that you will need in order to evaluate whether a potential investment makes business sense at a given price are for the most part fairly simple.

Before you start tapping away on your calculator, you must have established the nature of the company and answered the key questions necessary to determine the predictability of the company's future earnings. Then you must decide whether the company is an excellent business that benefits from a consumer monopoly or a commodity-type business that is doomed to average results. You must also determine if the company is managed by people who are honest and competent and who function with their shareholders' best interests in mind.

Although, as we know, Warren believes that it is hard to damage a great consumer monopoly by poor management, poor management can make it difficult for the investor to profit from the economics of a great consumer monopoly. As we observed, Coca-Cola in the seventies is a prime example of this phenomenon. Coca-Cola has a fantastic consumer monopoly but was run in the seventies by management that seemed uncertain about how to increase the per share value of the business. As a result, the company sat dormant, awaiting more enlightened management. It arrived with the appointment of Roberto Goizueta as Coca-Cola's president in 1980. Goizueta immediately picked up the ball and ran for touchdown after touchdown, which produced an increase in Coca-Cola's per share earnings, which caused the price of the stock to shoot up like rockets.

You, the investor, must also figure out if the company's management has the ability to effectively allocate capital in a profitable fashion. This can be determined with the help of a number of calculations. After the economic nature of the business is determined, you can use several other calculations, explained in detail on the pages that follow, to determine whether the stock is selling at an attractive price.

31

Test #1, to Determine at a Glance the Predictability of Earnings

This is the simplest test you can perform and it is probably the most basic. Although every security analyst performs it the first time his or her eyes scan a *Moody's* or *Value Line,* few will acknowledge it as a calculation. But it is, because it is the first place you must start the process of statistical analysis. To put it simply, you merely look at and compare the reported per share earnings for a number of years. Are they consistent or inconsistent? Do earnings trend upward, or do they jet up and down like a roller coaster?

The investment survey services, such as *Moody's* and *Value Line,* make this comparison of yearly figures very easy by providing you with a list of earnings dating back a number of years.

Does the earnings picture of your company look like Company I, or Company II?

Company I		Company II	
YEAR	PER SHARE EARNINGS	YEAR	PER SHARE EARNINGS
1983	$1.07	1983	$1.57
1984	1.16	1984	.16
1985	1.28	1985	.28
1986	1.42	1986	.42
1987	1.64	1987	(.23) loss
1988	1.60	1988	.60
1989	1.90	1989	1.90
1990	2.39	1990	2.39
1991	2.43	1991	(.43) loss
1992	2.69	1992	.69

Company I has more predictable earnings than Company II.

You don't need to be a genius to see that. From the looks of the earnings of Company I, you can tell that per share earnings have increased every year but 1988, in which there was a drop from $1.64 to $1.60 a share. A look at the earnings of Company II indicates that they are all over the place, with no trend being apparent.

Fast question: for which company at this very moment would you be willing to predict future earnings?

You should have picked Company I. Even though all you know about the company is its ten years of earnings, you know that they (1) are strong and (2) have an upward trend. Your next question should be, What were the economic dynamics that created this situation?

Company II, from a Grahamian point of view, may have some investment merit. From a Buffett point of view, the lack of strong earnings indicates that Company II's future earnings would be impossible to predict with any degree of comfort. Thus, Graham may have considered for investment both Company I and Company II. But Warren at first glance would have considered only Company I.

We've mentioned that Graham used to say that you didn't need to know someone's weight to know he was fat. The same holds true in reviewing the earnings history of a company. The first thing you should do when investigating the earnings history of a company is gather together the per share earnings figures for the last seven to ten years and see if they present a stable or unstable picture. There will be lots of black-and-white examples, but also quite a few that fall into a gray area. If something seems fishy, don't be afraid to move on. But knowing what you know now, if something smells interesting, don't be afraid to go on and dig a little deeper.

APPLICATION OF
EARNINGS PREDICTABILITY AT A GLANCE

Let's apply this test to Warren's most recent purchase of Coca-Cola common stock. (All Coca-Cola examples have been adjusted to reflect all stock splits through 1996.)

On August 8, 1994, Warren purchased 257,040 shares of Coca-Cola's common stock for $21.95 a share.

When Warren first took a look at Coca-Cola's yearly per share earnings, this was what he saw:

It's easy to see that Coca-Cola's per share earnings for the period of 1983 to 1994 are consistent, strong, and growing at a steady rate.

Coca-Cola in 1994 passes Warren's first test.

Year	Earnings
1983	$.17
1984	.20
1985	.22
1986	.26
1987	.30
1988	.46
1989	.42
1990	.51
1991	.61
1992	.72
1993	.84
1994	.98 (est.)

32

Test #2, to Determine Your Initial Rate of Return

This calculation tells you the *initial* rate of return that you can expect at a particular price.

Say that in 1979 Capital Cities was trading at $3.80 a share (which it was) against estimated earnings for the year of $.46 a share. This means that in 1979, if you paid $3.80 for a share of Capital Cities stock you could calculate that your initial rate of return would be 12.1% ($.46 ÷ $3.80 = 12.1%).

With Warren's 1988 purchase of Coca-Cola stock for $5.22 a share, against 1988 earnings of $.36 a share, he could calculate that his initial rate of return would be 6.89% ($.36 ÷ $5.22 = 6.89%). With his 1994 purchase of Coca-Cola stock for $21.95 a share, against 1994 earnings of $.98 a share, his initial rate of return equated to 4.5% ($.98 ÷ $21.95 = 4.5%).

Warren couples this initial rate of return with the estimated earnings growth figure to come up with the perspective that he is buying in 1994 a Coca-Cola equity/bond that pays a 4.5% rate of return, and that rate of return will expand as Coca-Cola's per share earnings grow at an estimated rate of 17% to 19% a year.

This is where Warren and Graham initially derive the theory that the price you pay will determine your rate of return. The higher the price, the lower the rate of return. The lower the price, the higher the rate of return.

33

Test #3, to Determine the Per Share Growth Rate

Management's ability to grow the *per share earnings* of a company is key to growth of the shareholders' value in the company. In order to get per share earnings to grow, the company must employ its retained earnings in a manner that will generate more earnings per share. The increase in per share earnings will, over a period of time, increase the market valuation for the company's stock.

A really fast and easy mathematical method of checking the company's ability to increase per share earnings is to figure the annual compounded rate of growth of the company's per share earnings for the last ten years and the last five years. This will tell you the annual compounding rate of growth of the earnings over the long and short run. We use the two numbers to allow us to see the true long-term nature of the company and to determine whether management's near-term performance has been in line with the long term.

Let's get on with some examples and then we can do some in-depth analysis. We'll go back and look at the yearly per share earnings of General Foods:

To calculate the company's per share earnings annual compounding growth rate, treat the first year as your pre-

Earnings for General Foods, 1970–80	
YEAR	PER SHARE EARNINGS
1970	$2.38
1971	2.36
1972	2.21
1973	2.40
1974	2.00
1975	3.02
1976	3.56
1977	3.40
1978	4.65
1979	5.12
1980	5.14

sent value, in this case the 1970 earnings of $2.38. Then use the 1980 earnings of $5.14 as the future value. The number of years is ten. Now you punch these values into your calculator while it is in its financial mode and hit the CPT key followed by the %i key and get the annual compounding rate of growth for the ten years, which is 8%.

Now do the same for the five-year period between 1975 and 1980, using as the present value the 1975 earnings of $3.02. The future value will be the earnings for 1980, $5.14. Five is the number of years. Punch the CPT key followed by the %i key and the calculator will tell you that your annual compounding rate of growth will be 11.2% for the five-year period between 1975 and 1980.

These two numbers tell you several different things. The first is that the company has had a higher rate of earnings growth in the last five years, 1975 to 1980, than it did in the ten-year period from 1970 to 1980. The question you need to ask is, Why the change? And what effect will past economics have on our ability to predict the company's future earnings? What were the business economics that caused this change? Was General Foods buying up its own stock, or was it finding new business ventures to be profitably involved in?

APPLICATION OF THE
PER SHARE EARNINGS GROWTH TEST

Here is an application of the per share earnings growth test to Warren's purchase of 257,640 shares of Coca-Cola stock in 1994.

A check of Coca-Cola's per share earnings indicates the following:
Coca-Cola's per share earnings grew at an annual rate of 17.2% a year for the period 1984 to 1994 and at an annual rate of 18.4% a year for the period 1989 to 1994.

To perform this calculation, treat the 1984 per share earnings as the pre-

YEAR	EARNINGS
1983	$.17
1984	.20
1985	.22
1986	.26
1987	.30
1988	.46
1989	.42
1990	.51
1991	.61
1992	.72
1993	.84
1994	.98 (est.)

sent value and the 1994 per share earnings as the future value; ten is the number of years; then all you have to do is punch the CPT key followed by the %i key, which would give you the annual rate of growth. So, if you have a Texas Instruments BA-35 Solar calculator, you would go to the financial mode. Punch in $.20 into the PV (present value) key; $.98 into the FV (future value) key; 10 into the N (number of years) key. Then punch the CPT (compute) key and the %i (interest) key, and you will get 17.2% as the annual rate of growth for Coca-Cola's earnings from 1984 to 1994.

To get the value for the five-year period from 1989 to 1994, punch in $.42 for the PV; $.98 for the FV; 5 for the N. Hit the CPT key followed by the %i key, and you get 18.4%.

Warren could reason that in 1994, if he paid $21.95 for a share of Coca-Cola stock that had per share earnings of $.98 a share, he would in effect be getting an initial after-corporate-tax return on his investment of 4.5% ($.98 ÷ $21.95 = 4.5%). And this rate of return would expand because Coca-Cola's per share earnings were growing at an annual compounding rate of 17.2% to 18.4% a year.

34

Determining the Value of a Company Relative to Government Bonds

A way of establishing the value of a company relative to government bonds is to divide the current per share earnings by the current rate of return for government bonds. This allows you to quickly compare them.

In the case of Warren's investment in Capital Cities in 1979, the per share earnings were $.47 a share. Divide $.47 a share by the rate of return on government bonds, which was approximately 10% in 1979, and you get a relative value of $4.70 a share ($0.47 ÷ .10 = $4.70). This means that if you paid $4.70 for a share of Capital Cities, you would be getting a return equal to that of the government bonds, which was 10%. This means that Capital Cities has a value relative to government bonds of $4.70 a share.

In 1979 you could have bought Capital Cities stock for less than $4.70 a share. (In fact, the stock traded for a price of between $3.60 and $4.70 a share. This means that you could have bought the stock at a price that was below its relative value to the return being paid of government bonds in 1979. This means also that your rate of return would have been greater than 10%.) This is where you use the annual per share earnings growth rate. The annual per share earnings growth rate for Capital Cities stock from 1970 to 1979 is equal to approximately 21%.

Thus you can ask yourself this question: what would I rather own— $4.70 worth of a government bond with a static rate of return of 10% or a Capital Cities equity/bond with a return of 10% or better, whose per share earnings are growing at an annual rate of approximately 21%? You may not want to own either, but given a choice between the two, the Capital Cities equity/bond has much more enticing qualities.

Many analysts believe that if you divide the per share earnings by the current rate of return on government bonds you end up with the intrinsic value of the company. But all you end up with is the value of the company relative to what the return is on government bonds.

The same thing applies to the theory that the intrinsic value of a business is its future earnings discounted to present value. If you use the rate of return on government bonds to determine the discount rate, what you end up with is a discounted present value relative to the rate of return on government bonds.

Also, remember that the return on government bonds is a pre-income-tax return and the net earnings figure of a corporation is an after-corporate-tax return. So, comparing the two without taking this into account is fraught with folly. Still, it is a method that has a place in our box of tools.

35

Understanding Warren's Preference for Companies with High Rates of Return on Equity

To understand Warren's preference for businesses that have a high return on equity, you must remember that Warren views some common stocks as a sort of bond. He calls the stock an *equity/bond* if it has an interest rate equal to the yearly return on equity the business is earning. The earnings per share figure is the equity/bond's yield. If the company has a shareholders' equity value of $10 a share and net earnings of $2.50 a share, Warren would say that the company is getting a return on equity of 25% ($2.50 ÷ $10 = 25%).

But since a business's earnings are given to fluctuation, the return on equity is not a fixed figure as it is with bonds. Warren believes that with an equity/bond, one is buying a variable rate of return, which can be positive for the investor if earnings increase, and negative for the investor if earnings decrease. The return on equity will fluctuate as the relationship of equity to net earnings changes.

As we know, shareholders' equity is defined as a company's total assets *less the company's total liabilities*. Let's say you own a business; we will call it Company A. If it has $10 million in assets and $4 million liabilities, the business would have a shareholders' equity of $6 million. If the company earned, after taxes, $1,980,000, we could calculate the business's return on shareholders' equity as being 33% ($1,980,000 ÷ $6,000,000 = 33%).

This means that the $6 million of shareholders' equity is earning a 33% rate of return.

Now imagine that you own another business; call it Company

B. Also imagine that it too has $10 million in assets and $4 million liabilities, which, as with Company A, gives it $6 million in shareholders' equity. But imagine that instead of making $1,980,000 on an equity base of $6 million, it makes only $480,000. This means that Company B would be producing a return on equity of 8% ($480,000 ÷ $6,000,000 = 8%).

	Company A	Company B
ASSETS	$10 million	$10 million
LIABILITIES	$4 million	$4 million
SHAREHOLDERS' EQUITY	$6 million	$6 million
AFTER-TAX EARNINGS	$1,980,000	$480,000
RETURN ON SHAREHOLDERS' EQUITY	33%	8%

Both companies have exactly the same capital structure, yet Company A is four times as profitable as Company B. That's the easy part of this trick. Of course the better company is Company A.

Now let's say that the management at both Company A and Company B are really good at what they do. Company A's management is really good at getting a 33% return on equity, and Company B's management is really good at getting an 8% retrun for equity.

What company would you rather invest more money in—Company A, whose management will earn you a 33% return on your newly invested money, or Company B, whose management will earn you only an 8% return? You, of course, choose Company A, whose management is going to earn you a 33% return on your new investment.

Now, as the owner of Company A, you have the choice of either getting a $1,980,000 dividend from Company A at the end of the year or letting Company A retain your earnings and letting its management earn you a 33% return. What do you do? Do you take the dividend, or do you let Company A's management continue earning you a 33% return? Is a 33% rate of return sufficient enough for you? Of course it is. Company A is making you very rich. So you let it keep the money.

Also, as the owner of Company B, you have the choice of either getting a $480,000 dividend at the end of the year or letting Company B retain your earnings and letting the management earn you an 8% return. Do you take the 8% return? Is an 8% rate of return sufficient enough for you? The picture in not nearly as clear as it is with Company A. Let me ask you this: If I told you that you could take Company B's dividend and reinvest it in Company A, would that help you make up your mind? Of course it would. You would take your money out of Company B, where it was earning only an 8% rate of return, and reinvest it in Company A, where it would earn a rate of return of 33%.

By now you can start to see why companies that earn high returns on shareholders' equity are big on Warren's list. But there are a few more twists to the wealth-creating power that high returns on equity will produce. Let's look deeper.

Let's pretend that you don't own either Company A or Company B. Easy enough. But you are in the market to buy a business. So you approach the owners of Company A and Company B and tell them that you interested in buying their business and ask them if they are interested in selling.

Now, Warren believes that all rates of return ultimately compete with the rate of return that is paid on government bonds. He believes that the government's power to tax ensures the bonds safety, and investors are very aware of that. He believes that this competition of rates is one of the main reasons that the *stock market goes down when interest rates go up* and *why the stock market goes up when interest rates go down*. A stock investment that offers a 10% rate of return is far more enticing than a government bond offering a 5% rate of return. But jack up interest rates to the point that the government bond is offering you a 12% rate of return, and the stock's rate of return of 10% suddenly loses its appeal.

Keeping this in mind, the owners of Companies A and B compare what they could earn by selling their businesses and putting their capital into government bonds. This means that they could forget about the hassles of owning a business and still earn the same amount of money. Let's say that at the time you made your offer to buy, you could buy government bonds and earn an 8% rate of return.

In the case of Company A, which is earning $1.98 million a year, it would take $24.75 million worth of government bonds to generate $1.98 million in interest. So the owner of Company A says that he will sell you his company for $24.75 million. This means that if you pay $24.75 million for Company A, you would be paying roughly four times shareholders' equity of $6 million, or 12.5 times Company A's current earnings of $1.98 million.

In the case of Company B, which is earning $480,000 a year, it would take $6 million worth of government bonds to generate $480,000 in interest. So the owner of Company B says that he will sell you his company for $6 million. This means that if you pay $6 million for Company B, you will be paying one times shareholders' equity of $6 million, or 12.5 times Company B's current earnings of $480,000.

Two companies, A and B, both with the same capital structure—but A is worth, relative to the return on government bonds, $24.75 million, and B is worth $6 million. But if you paid $24.75 million for Company A, you could expect a return of 8% in your first year of ownership. And if you paid $6 million for Company B, you could also expect an 8% return in your first year of ownership.

One of the keys to understanding Warren is that he is not very interested in what a company will be earning next year. *What he is interested in is what the company will be earning in ten years.* While Wall Street is focusing on next year, Warren realizes that to let compounding work its wonders he has to focus on predicting the future. That is why companies that have consumer monopolies and are earning high rates of return on shareholder equity are so very important to him.

Warren would find Company A far more enticing than Company B. The economics of Company A are such that it can earn a 33% return on shareholders' equity. This means that if management can keep this up, the retained earnings will earn 33% as well. And so, every year the shareholders' equity pot is going to grow. *It is the growing equity pot and the earnings that go with it that Warren is interested in.* Let me show you.

(Now take a moment and look at the equity and earnings projections for Company A found on the chart that follows.)

		Company A	
YEAR	EQUITY BASE*	R.O.E†	EARNINGS *(Added to Next Year's Equity Base)*
1	$ 6,000,000	33%	$ 1,980,000
2	7,980,000	33	2,633,400
3	10,613,400	33	3,502,422
4	14,115,822	33	4,658,221
5	18,774,043	33	6,195,434
6	24,960,478	33	8,239,927
7	33,209,405	33	10,959,104
8	44,168,509	33	14,575,608
9	58,744,117	33	19,385,559
10	78,129,675	33	25,782,793
11	103,912,470	33	34,291,115

*Beginning year equity base   †Return on equity

What you are seeing is the shareholders' equity base compounding at a 33% rate of return. (Remember that Warren is after the highest compounding rate of return possible.)

By the beginning of Year 11, Company A will have an equity base of $103,912,470 and expected Year 11 earnings of $34,291,115. If government bonds are still at 8%, it would take approximately $428 million in government bonds to annually produce $34,291,115.

If you paid $24.75 million for Company A at the beginning of Year 1 and sold it for its equity value of $103,912,470 at the beginning of Year 11, effectively holding the investment for a full ten years, your annual compounding rate of return would be 15.4%. If you sold it for $428 million, the amount of government bonds that it would take to earn the $34,291,115 Company A is projected to earn in Year 11, your annual compounding rate of return would be approximately 33%.

Now let's compare this to Company B. The economics of Company B are such that it can earn only an 8% return on shareholders' equity. This means that if management keeps this up, the retained earnings will earn only 8% as well. This means that every year the shareholders' equity pot is going to grow by 8%. (Take a moment

			EARNINGS
YEAR	EQUITY BASE*	R.O.E†	(Added to Next Year's Equity Base)

Company B

YEAR	EQUITY BASE*	R.O.E†	EARNINGS (Added to Next Year's Equity Base)
1	$ 6,000,000	8%	$ 480,000
2	6,480,000	8	520,000
3	7,000,000	8	560,000
4	7,560,000	8	600,000
5	8,160,000	8	650,000
6	8,820,000	8	710,000
7	9,520,000	8	760,000
8	10,280,000	8	820,000
9	11,110,000	8	890,000
10	11,990,000	8	960,000
11	12,950,000	8	1,036,000

*Beginning year equity base   †Return on equity

and study the equity and earnings projections for Company B found on the next page.)

By the beginning of Year 11, Company B will have an equity base of $12,950,000 and expected Year 11 earnings of $1,036,000. If government bonds are still paying 8%, it would take $12.95 million in government bonds to produce $1,036,000.

If you paid $6 million for Company B at the beginning of year 1 and sold it for its equity value of $12.95 million at the beginning of Year 11, effectively holding your investment for a full ten years, your annual compounding rate of return would be approximately 8%. If you sold it for $12.95 million, the amount of government bonds that it would take to earn the $1,036,00 Company B is projected to earn in Year 11, your annual compounding rate of return would still be approximately 8%.

Suppose you say to yourself that you have only $6,187,500, and wouldn't it be better to spend it buying all of Company B instead of spending it to buy 25% of Company A? Warren has figured out that even 25% of Company A is a better investment than owning 100% of Company B. If you paid $6,187,500 to buy 25% of Company A and you sold it for 25% of its equity value—$25,978,000—in the beginning of the eleventh year, then your annual compounding rate of return would still be 15.4%. If you sold it for 25% of the government bond value—$107 million—your annual compounding rate of return would remain approximately 33%.

Now, you may have figured out by now that paying $24.75 million, or 12.5 times earnings, for Company A is a fantastic deal if you expected to be earning a 33% compounding annual rate of return for ten years. In fact, Company A may be worth a whole lot more. The question Warren must address is, How much more? Let's figure it out.

Let's say that instead of paying $24.7 million or 12.5 times earnings, for Company A, you paid $59.4 million, or thirty times Company A's Year 1 earnings of $1.98 million. And let's say you sold it at the beginning of Year 11, which means you effectively held the investment for ten years, for 12.5 times Year 11's projected earnings of $34,291,115 ($34,291,115 × 12.5 = $428,638,937). If you paid $59.4 million, or thirty times earnings, for Company A in Year 1 and sold it in ten years for $428,638,937, your compounding annual rate of return would be 21.8%.

If you paid forty times Company A's Year 1 earnings—$79.2 million—and then sold Company A in ten years for $428,638,937, your compounding annual rate of return would be 18.3%. A compounding annual rate of return of 18.3% for ten years is something investment managers dream about.

The secret that Warren has figured out is that excellent businesses that benefit from a consumer monopoly, that can consistently earn high rates of return on shareholders' equity, are often bargain buys even at what seem to be very high price-to-earnings ratios.

I know that some of you are thinking that the above example is just a hypothetical and that this kind of thing never happens in real life, and that the market is efficient and never offers this kind of return.

Consider this.

In 1988 Coca-Cola had shown a consistent capacity for earning high rates of return on shareholders' equity—in the neighborhood of 33% annually. If you invested $100,000 in Coca-Cola stock in 1988 and held it for eight years, to 1996, your $100,000 investment would have grown to approximately $912,280 in stock market value. This equates to a before-tax annual compounding rate of return of 31%. Invest $100,000 in Coca-Cola stock, and eight years later you are worth $912,280. Add in the dividends that you would have received—approximately $40,524—and your before-tax compounding annual rate of return goes to 32.5%.

In 1988 Warren saw Coca-Cola's consumer monopoly and the high rates of return that it was earning on shareholders' equity and bought $592.9 million worth of the stock, and the rest is the stuff investment legends are made of.

APPLICATION OF RETURN-ON-EQUITY TEST

Here is an application of the return-on-equity test to Warren's purchase of 257,640 shares of Coca-Cola stock in 1994. A check of Coca-Cola's annual return on equity indicates that for each of the six years prior to 1994, it was in excess of 30%. This means that it was way above the 12% average for most businesses. In 1994 Coca-Cola passed Warren's requirement that a company show consistently above-average annual rates of return on equity.

36

Determining the Projected Annual Compounding Rate of Return, Part I

Now, before we jump into projecting the annual compounding rate of return we expect a potential investment to produce, you should understand that all these mathematical equations serve merely to give you a better picture of the economic nature of the beast. Each of the calculations will tell you a little something different. Yet each describes the same business and each gives you another perspective of the business's earning power. Earning power is the key to predictability, and predicting future results is the job of the security analyst.

Warren has defined the intrinsic value of a business as the sum of all the business's future earnings discounted to present value, using government bonds as the appropriate discount rate. Warren cites *The Theory of Investment Value* by John Burr Williams (Harvard University Press, 1938) as his source for this definition. John Burr Williams, on the other hand, cites Robert F. Wiese, "Investing for Future Values" (*Barron's*, September 8, 1930, p. 5), as his source for this definition. Wiese stated that "the proper price of any security, whether stock or bond, is the sum of all future income payments discounted at the current rate of interest in order to arrive at the present value." (It is interesting to note that both Williams and Wiese were referring to future dividends paid out and not the future earnings of the company. Warren treats it as future earnings, regardless of whether or not they are paid out.)

We all know that projecting a business's earnings for the next one hundred years is impossible. Sure, you could try, but the realities of the world dictate that some change will occur and destroy or change the economics of the business in question. Just look at the television industry. It was hardly a bump on the economic landscape in the 1940s. In the 1960s and 1970s it was a fantastic business for anyone involved. After all, there were only three channels. So great was the networks' monopoly position that Warren said in the early eighties that if he had to invest in just one company and then go away to a deserted island for ten years, it would be Capital Cities. Quite a strong vote of confidence.

But by 1992 Warren was of the opinion that the television business was no longer what it used to be. Dozens of channels had been started up, all competing for ad revenue. Absolutely unsinkable businesses are hard to find. (Coca-Cola may be one of the few.)

History tells us that even if your name is Medici, Krupp, Rothschild, Winchester, or Rockefeller, the wheels of commerce may not always turn in your favor. The monopoly that once was enjoyed, like that held by the early television networks, can vanish almost overnight due to a change in technology or the hands of government regulators. The Medici family of Italy spent the last five hundred years trying to get over the fact that the Dutch sailed around the horn of Africa and destroyed Venice's monopoly on trade with the Orient. Things change, and though commerce has elements of repetition, fortune favors the brave, and the brave constantly test the fertile waters of commerce, looking for new ways of making a buck.

Keeping this in mind, you would invite sheer folly by thinking you had a chance in a million of projecting a company's earnings fifty to one hundred years and then discounting them back to present value. There are just too many variables. It may be true in theory—but in reality, summing up all a company's future earnings and discounting them to present value creates impossible number combinations, especially if you are factoring a constant rate of growth.

It is of interest that Graham also noted the insane valuations that discounting a company's future earnings to present value often creates, especially when the earnings are constantly growing.

Some analysts try to solve this problem by dividing the future earnings into two different periods. The first period is assigned the high growth rate and the second period is assigned a lower growth rate. The problem here, as Williams discussed, is that anytime you have a rate of earnings growth that is less than the rate of interest used in the discounting equation, the stock will end up having a value of zero, even though growth continues on without limit. (See *The Theory of Investment Value,* p. 89.)

An additional problem is the discount rate chosen. If you choose the rate of return being paid on government bonds, you are in effect discounting the business's future earnings at a rate of return that is relative to the government bond rate of return. Also, if the rate of interest changes, your evaluation changes as well. The higher the interest rate, the lower the valuation. The lower the interest rate, the higher the valuation.

One other problem with using government bonds as a discount rate is that their yield is quoted in pretax terms. So a government bond that is paying a return of 8% will earn the individual investor only an after-tax return of 5.52%. The future earnings of the company that are being discounted are quoted in after-corporate-income-tax terms, which means that an 8% return will remain an 8% return unless it is paid out as a dividend.

What Warren does is to project the per share equity value of the company in question for a period of, say, five to ten years. This is done by using historical trends for the return on equity less the dividend payout rate.

Warren figures out approximately what the equity value of the company will be at the future date, say, in ten years, and then he multiplies the per share equity value by the projected future rate of return on equity ten years out, which gives him the projected future per share earnings of the company. Using the projected per share earnings of the company, he is then able to project a future trading value for the company's stock. Using the price he paid for the stock as the present value, he can then calculate his estimated annual compounding rate of return. Warren then compares this projected annual compounding rate of return to other rates of return being offered in the market and to what his needs are to keep ahead of inflation.

Let me show you, using Berkshire Hathaway as an example. In 1986, Berkshire Hathaway had stockholders' equity of $2,073 a share. For the period from 1964 to 1983, Berkshire's rate of return for stockholders' equity was 23.3% compounded annually. If you want to project the company's equity per share figure for

1996, all you have to do is get out the old and trusted Texas Instruments BA-35 Solar financial calculator and switch to the financial mode and perform a future value calculation. Let's do it.

First, you punch in the 1986 per share equity value of $2,073 as the present value (PV key), then the rate of growth for the interest rate, 23.3% (%i key), then the number of years, 10 (the N key). Then you hit the calculation key (CPT) and the future value key (FV), and the calculator tells you that in the year 1996 Berkshire should have a per share equity value of $16,835.

The question that you should be asking yourself is how much money you are willing to pay in 1986 for the right to own $16,835 in shareholders' equity in 1996. First of all, you need to ask yourself how much return you are looking to get. If you are like Warren, then 15% is the minimum return you are willing to take. So, all you have to do is discount $16,835 to present value, using 15% as the appropriate discount rate.

First, clear your calculator of the last calculation. Now punch in $16,835 as the future value (FV), then the discount rate, 15% (%i), and the number of years, 10 (N). Hit the compute button (CPT) and the present value button (PV). The calculator will tell you that in 1986 the most money you can spend on a share and expect to get a 15% annual rate of return over the next ten years is $4,161 a share.

A check of the local newspaper in 1986 would tell you that the market was selling a share of Berkshire's stock for around $2,700 a share that year. You think, Wow, I might be able to get an even better return than the 15% I'm looking for. To check it out, you punch in $2,700 for the present value (PV), $16,835 for the future value (FV), and 10 for the number of years (N). Then you hit the compute button (CPT) and the interest button (%i), and the calculator will tell you that you can expect a compounding annual rate of return of 20%.

By 1996 Berkshire ended up growing its per share equity value at a compounding annual rate of approximately 24.8%. With a compounding annual rate of return of approximately 24.8%, Berkshire grew its per share equity base to $19,011 in 1996.

But get this. While you were patiently waiting for the value of Berkshire to grow, the market decided it really liked Berkshire and bid the stock to $38,000 a share by 1996. If you paid $2,700 a share for a share of Berkshire in 1986 and sold it in 1996 for $38,000 a share, this would equate to an annual compounding rate of return of 30.2% on your money for the ten-year period.

To get the rate of return, you would assign $2,700 as the present value (PV), $38,000 as the future value (FV), and 10 as the number of years (N). Then you would punch the compute key (CPT) and the interest key (%i), which will compute the compounding annual rate of return—which is 30.2%.

Let's say that you paid $38,000 for a share of Berkshire Hathaway in 1996. What would your annual rate of return be if you held the stock for ten years?

We know that Berkshire has a per share equity value in 1996 of $19,011 and that it has grown at an average annual compounding rate of approximately 23% a year for the last thirty-two years. Assuming this, we can project that in ten years—in the year 2006—the per share equity value for a share of Berkshire Hathaway will be $150,680.

If you paid $38,000 in 1996 for a share of Berkshire that will have a per share equity value of $150,680 in the year 2006, what is your compounding annual rate of return? Punch in $150,680 for the future value (FV), $38,000 for the present value (PV), 10 for the number of years (N). Then hit the CPT key, followed by the interest key (%i), and presto—your annual compounding rate of return is 14.76%.

You can make a market price adjustment to this calculation by figuring that over the last thirty-two years Berkshire has traded in the market for anywhere from approximately one times its per share equity value to double its per share equity value. If this trend continues you could project that in the year 2006 Berkshire will trade between $150,680 a share, its projected per share equity value, and $301,360 a share, double its projected per share equity value.

If you paid $38,000 in 1996 for a share of Berkshire and sell it for $150,680, its per share equity value in the year 2006, your annual compounding rate of return would be 14.72%. If you sell it for $301,360, or double its projected per share equity value of $150,680 in 2006, your annual compounding rate of return would be 23%.

So, depending on the market value for Berkshire, you can project a before-tax annual compounding rate of return of somewhere between 14.72 and 23%.

Any hope of doing better than that is wishful thinking.

Determining the Projected Annual Compounding Rate of Return, Part II

In the preceding chapter we learned how to calculate the future value of Berkshire Hathaway by projecting its future per share equity value. We also saw that once a future value is determined, it is possible to project the annual compounding rate of return the investment will produce.

In this chapter we will project the future per share earnings of a company and then determine its future market price. We will then use the results of these calculations to project the annual compounding rate of return that the investment in question will produce.

I think it would be very instructive at this point if we explored a real-life example of Warren's decision making. In the following we shall explore in depth the financial reasoning that led Warren to take his initial position in the Coca-Cola Company. (*Please note:* This is a very important chapter because it brings to light several key concepts that have escaped many students of Warren's methods. All the historical figures given for Coca-Cola have been adjusted to reflect stock splits through 1996.)

THE COCA-COLA COMPANY—1988

In 1988, Warren, using his equity-as-a-bond rationale, had his holding company, Berkshire Hathaway, buy 113,380,000 Coca-Cola equity/bonds (stock) at $5.22 a share, for a total investment of $592,540,000. Coca-Cola, in 1988, had shareholders' equity of $1.07 a share and net earnings of $.36 a share. From Warren's point of view each Coca-Cola equity/bond that he just bought had a coupon attached to it that paid $.36. This means that each of Warren's equity/bond shares was yielding 33.6% return on equity ($.36 ÷ $1.07 = 33.6%), of which approximately 58% was retained by the company and 42% was to be paid out as a dividend to the shareholders.

Thus, in theory, when Warren bought his Coca-Cola equity/bond share with a per share equity value of $1.07, he calculated that his $1.07 equity/bond would be effectively earning a 33.6% return. He also figured that this 33.6% return was divided into two different types of yields.

One yield would represent 58% of the 33.6% return on equity and would be retained by the company. This amount is equal to $.21 of the $.36 in per share earnings. This portion of the yield is the after-corporate-tax portion and is subject to no more state or federal taxes.

The other yield is the remaining 42% of the 33.6% return on equity, which is paid out as a dividend. This amount is equal to $.15 of the $.36 per share earnings. This portion of the return is subject to personal or corporate taxes for dividends.

So, our 33.6% return on equity is two different yields. One is a 19.4% return on equity equal to $.21, which is retained by the Coca-Cola Company and added to Coca-Cola's equity base.

The other is a 14.2% return on equity equal to $.15, which is paid out to the shareholders of Coca-Cola as a dividend.

1988

Coca-Cola's $1.07 per share equity value × .336 return on equity = $.36 a share earnings.

The $.36 is divided into two portions. One portion is retained by the company and is equal to 58% of the per share earnings, or $.21. The other portion is paid out as a dividend to the shareholders and is equal to 42% of the per share earnings, or $.15.

$.21 retained to equity
and
$.15 paid out as a dividend

Now, if we assume that Coca-Cola can maintain this 33.6% return on equity for the next twelve years, and will continue to retain 58% of this return and pay out as a dividend the other 48%, then it is possible to project the company's future per share equity value and its per share earnings.

This is done by taking 58% of the 33.6% return on equity, or 19.4%, and adding it to the per share equity base each year.

So, if in 1988 Coca-Cola had a per share equity value of $1.07, we would increase the $1.07 by 19.4%, which would give us a projected per share equity value for 1989 of $1.28 ($1.07 × 1.194 = $1.28).

This same calculation can be done with your calculator by punching in $1.07 as the present value (PV), and 19.4 as the compounding rate of interest (i%), and 1 for the number of years (N). Then hit the CPT key and future value key (FV). This will give you a per share future value of $1.28 for 1989.

If you want to know *what the per share equity value will be in 1998,* all you have to do is punch in $1.07 for the present value (PV), 19.4 as the compounding rate of growth (i%), and 10 for the number of years (N). Then hit the CPT and future value (FV) keys, and this will give you a projected per share equity value of $6.30 for 1998.

If you want to project the per share earnings, all you have to do is multiply the per share equity value by 33.6%. In the case of 1989 we would multiply the per share equity value of $1.28 by 33.6% and get a projected per share earnings of $.43. To do this for the year 1998, we would multiply the projected per share equity of $6.30 by 33.6% and get projected per share earnings of $2.12.

Let's do the calculations and project out the per share equity value and per share earnings of Coca-Cola for twelve years, beginning in 1988 and ending in 2000.

Projections usually aren't worth the paper they are written on. Most financial analysts are willing to project earnings only for a year or two in advance, and then they give you an overview of the company and pronounce it a buy. But Graham felt that the real role of the analyst was to ascertain the earning power of the business and make a long-term projection of what the company was capable of earning (*Security Analysis*, 1951, p. 412).

In the following table we have projected per share earnings for

		Projections for 1988 to 2000		
YEAR	EQUITY VALUE	PER SHARE EARNINGS	DIVIDENDS PAID OUT	RETAINED EARNINGS
1988	$1.07	$ .36	$ .15	$ .21
1989	1.28	.43	.18	.25
1990	1.53	.51	.21	.30
1991	1.83	.61	.26	.35
1992	2.18	.72	.30	.42
1993	2.60	.87	.37	.50
1994	3.10	1.04	.44	.60
1995	3.70	1.24	.52	.72
1996	4.42	1.48	.62	.86
1997	5.28	1.77	.75	1.02
1998	6.30	2.12	.90	1.22
1999	7.52	2.53	1.07	1.46
2000	8.98	3.02	1.27	1.75
			Total: $7.04	$9.66

twelve years. In most situations this would be an act of insanity. However, as Warren has found, if the company is one of sufficient earning power and earns high rates of return on shareholders' equity, created by some kind of consumer monopoly, chances are good that accurate long-term projections of earnings can be made.

Since we have projected Coca-Cola's per share earnings from the year 1988, we can find out if our analysis has any validity to it. To do this we can compare our projected per share earnings for 1988 to 1996 against the actual results reported by Coca-Cola for 1988 to 1996.

We can see that our margin of error is running between 0% and 5.4% on projections running forward for eight years. Not bad. If Coca-Cola can maintain a 33.6% return on shareholders' equity in twelve years from 1988, we can project that the company will be earning approximately $3.02 a share in the year 2000. (*Please note:* The further forward you go, the greater chance for variation in *actual* results versus *projected* results. This is not a game of absolutes.)

By the year 2000, Warren will have also developed an after-tax pool of dividend payouts equal to $686 million (dividend pool of $7.04

Comparisons of Coca-Cola
Per Share Earnings Projections to Actual Results

Year	Projected Earnings	Actual Earnings	Margin of Error
1989	$ .43	$ .42	2.3%
1990	.51	.51	0%
1991	.61	.61	0%
1992	.72	.72	0%
1993	.87	.84	3.5%
1994	1.04	.99	5%
1995	1.24	1.19	4%
1996	1.48	1.40	5.4%

× 113.38 million shares – income tax on dividends of approximately 14% = $686 million).

So Warren can also project that by year 2000 his investment in Coca-Cola will have paid back his original investment of $592,401,000, and he will still get to keep the 113.38 million shares of Coca-Cola stock as profit. If the company is trading at a historically conservative rate of fifteen times our projected earnings of $3.02 a share, the 113.38 million shares of the Coca-Cola stock should be worth $45.30 a share (15 × $3.02 = $45.30), or $5.136 billion ($45.30 × 113.38 million shares = $5.136 billion). Not bad for a day's work.

Please note: When you are choosing a price-to-earnings ratio—P/E—to multiply your projected future per share earnings by, you get the best perspective by running your calculations with the average annual P/E ratio for the last ten years. You should also run your equations with the high and the low P/E ratio for the last ten years, just to give you a better perspective of how well you might or might not do. But be warned, *stocks* don't always *trade at their historically high P/E. To be overly optimistic in using a historically high P/E ratio can create projections that lead to disaster. Stick with the average annual P/E ratio for the last ten years, especially if there has been a huge spread between the high and the low P/E ratio within the last ten years. When in doubt, choose the middle road.*

Now, if we are projecting per share earnings for Coca-Cola in the year 2000 to be $3.02, we can estimate that the market price for the stock will range between fifteen and twenty-five times per share earnings. (This equates to a P/E ratio of between 15 and 25.) This means that in the year 2000 the stock is projected to be trading in a price range of between $45.30 (15 × $3.02 = $45.30) and $75.50 (25 × $3.02 = $75.50) a share. We also know that Warren's initial investment was $5.22 a share.

To determine the annual compounding rate return for the period of 1988 to 2000, all we have to do is take out the calculator and punch in 12 for the number of years (N), $5.22 for the present value (PV), and either $45.30 or $75.50 for the future value (FV). Then hit the CPT key and the interest key (i%). This will give you the annual compounding rate of return, which in this case will be either 19.7% for a per share market price of $45.30 or 24.9% for a per share market price of $75.50. Thus, Warren could project an annual compounding rate of return of between 19.7 and 24.9% for the twelve-year period between 1988 and the year 2000.

We can adjust these numbers to reflect the dividends Coca-Cola paid out and any taxes Warren would have to pay if he sold the stock in the year 2000. To do this you take the $45.30 and subtract the amount Warren has invested in the stock, $5.22 (the $5.22 is not taxed). This will give you $40.08, the amount of Warren's profit. You then subtract 35% for corporate taxes on the gain, which leaves you with $26.05. Then add in the after-tax pool of Coca-Cola dividends that Warren has been collecting for the twelve years, $6.05 ($7.04 − 14% = $6.05). This gives you an after-tax profit of $32.10 ($6.05 + $26.05 = $32.10). You then add back in the $5.22, which gives you an after-tax total proceeds from the sale of $37.32 ($32.10 + $5.22 = $37.32).

With a cost basis of $5.22 a share and total after-tax sale proceeds of $37.32, total after-tax profit from the sale will be $32.10. This equates to an after-tax annual compounding rate of return of 17.8%. Thus, in the year 2000, if Coca-Cola is trading at fifteen times earnings and Warren elects to sell his stock, his annual compounding rate of return after taxes will be 17.8% for the twelve years from 1988 to 2000.

You can run the same sequence of calculations for a P/E of 25, which equates to a market price of $75.50 a share in the year

2000. After you take out taxes and add in the after-tax dividend pool, you end up with a total return of $51.79, which equates to an annual compounding rate of return of 22% for the twelve-year period. (*Note:* Even if Coca-Cola's stock is trading at only nine times earnings in the year 2000, Warren can still project an after-tax annual compounding rate of return of 14.4%.)

Now, imagine if I came to you and said that I wanted to sell to you, at par value, a noncallable twelve-year Coca-Cola bond that paid a tax-free, fixed annual rate of return of 14.4% or, even better yet, 17.8%. Or how about 22%? Mouth starting to water yet? What would you do? I'd mortgage the farm, house, and kids, and buy all I could. But I can tell you that the likelihood of that ever happening is nil.

However, back in 1988, you could have bought the stock in the Coca-Cola company and essentially got a tax-free equivalent annual compounding rate of return of between 14.4 and 22%, provided you were willing to hold the investment for a period of twelve years. (*Note:* As luck would have it, the stock market started valuing Coca-Cola stock in 1996 and 1997 at historically high price-to-earnings ratios of 40 and better. This has enabled Warren to show a higher annual compounding rate of return than is projected here for the period of between 1988 and 1997. Be warned that using Coca-Cola's historically high P/E ratio of 40 and better as a current multiplier may be a bit too optimistic. *Use the average annual P/E ratio for the last ten years instead.*)

What creates all this wealth is Coca-Cola's ability to take its retained earnings and earn a 33.6% rate of return on shareholders' equity. Then it can retain 58% of the 33.6%, which is added, free of personal income taxes, to the shareholders' equity base in the company. This effectively compounds the retained earnings by adding them to the base sum from which they were created.

And that, folks, is how it works.

APPLICATION TO
WARREN'S 1994 PURCHASE OF COCA-COLA STOCK

On August 8, 1994, Warren bought 257,640 more shares of Coca-Cola stock for $21.95 a share. What Warren saw were per share earnings of $.99 that had been growing at an annual rate of between 17 and 18% for the last ten years and a return on equity that had been for the last four years in excess of 40%. Warren also saw a market price for the stock that for the last seven years had been trading at an average P/E of 21.

Let's say that even with Coca-Cola's increase in its return on equity to over 40%, Warren still wants to stay with his original schedule of projected earnings, created for 1988 to 2000, found in the table on page 224. Let's say also that he wants to hold his 1994 purchase only until the year 1999. What would his expected rate of return be if he sold his 1994 purchase of Coca-Cola stock in 1999?

The table indicates that per share earnings in the year 1999 are projected to be $2.53. If we multiply $2.53 by the average P/E of 21, we get a projected market price for 1999 of $53.13. Punch in $21.95 for the PV, $53.13 for the FV, 5 for the number of years, and hit the CPT and i% keys, and you get Warren's projected annual compounding rate of return, which is 19.33%.

To adjust for taxes and dividends, you would add in an after-tax pool of dividends of $3.86 to an after-tax adjusted total proceeds from the stock sell of $42.21, which equals total proceeds of $46.07. A total return of $46.07 equates to an annual compounding after-tax rate of return of 15.98%. Punch in $21.95 for the PV, $46.07 for the FV, 5 for the number of years, and hit the CPT and %i keys, and you get Warren's projected annual compounding after-tax rate of return, which is 15.98%. Thus Warren could project in 1994 that if he held his investment to 1999, it would produce for him an after-tax annual compounding rate of return of 15.98%.

An after-tax compounding annual rate of return of 15.98% doesn't interest you? Remember that if it was a government bond it would have to have a *before-tax annual rate of return of 24.58% to give Warren an after-tax compounding annual rate of return of 15.98%*. See any government bonds paying a 24.58% rate of return? How about corporate bonds? I don't. Now do you see why Warren keeps going to the soda fountain and ordering more Coca-Cola? Things do go better with Coke, including your money.

38

The Equity/Bond
with an Expanding Coupon

Warren has more than one way of looking at an investment situation. One of these ways is to view a stock as an equity/bond with an expanding coupon. Let's see how this works with the Coca-Cola situation. (You might be wondering where the *coupon* concept comes from. Bonds used to come with dozens of coupons attached to them. You'd clip a coupon and send it to the company that issued the bond, and they would send you the fixed rate of interest the bond had earned for a particular period of time. That way the company didn't have to keep track of who owned the bond. Today, bonds are *registered* with the company that issued them and a bondholder gets the interest checks in the mail without doing anything. In Warren's world, the equity/bond of certain companies has a coupon that is increasing. Each year the equity/bond pays you a little more. Thus, the equity/bond with an expanding coupon.)

Now, remember what we said earlier: what you pay for a stock determines your rate of return. When Warren purchased his initial interest in Coca-Cola in 1988, the company had an equity/book value of $1.07 a share and earnings of $.36 a share. This equates to Coca-Cola in 1988 earning a 33.6% return on equity. If you paid $1.07 for a share of Coca-Cola stock, you would be buying it at its per share equity value of $1.07, which would give you an initial rate of return of 33.6% ($.36 ÷ $1.07 = 33.6%). However, Warren didn't pay $1.07 a share; he paid approximately $5.22 a share, which means that his rate of return on his Coca-Cola equity/bond would be approximately 6.89% ($.36 ÷ $5.22 = 6.89%), or well below the 33.6% Coca-Cola was earning on its equity base in 1988.

Now, an initial rate of return of 6.89% is not all that great. But Warren was projecting that Coca-Cola's per share earnings would continue to grow and in the process cause an annual increase in his rate of return. Sound enticing? Let's look more closely.

We can explain Coca-Cola's economics from several vantage points, but the key is the return on equity and retained earnings. In 1988 Warren will earn $.36 a share on his original investment of $5.22, which equates to a 6.89% rate of return. If Coca-Cola *retains* approximately 58% of that $.36, or $.21 ($.36 ×.58 = $.21), Coca-Cola will have effectively reinvested $.21 of Warren's money back into the company. (*Note:* the other 42% of the $.36, or $.15, is paid out as a dividend.)

So, at the beginning of 1989, Warren will have invested in his Coca-Cola stock his original 1988 investment of $5.22 a share, plus 1988's retained earnings of $.21 a share, for a total investment of $5.43 a share ($5.22 + $.21 = $5.43).

At the beginning of 1989, Warren's total investment in Coca-Cola is projected to be:

Original 1988 investment	$5.22
Retained earnings for 1988	+ .21
1989 total per share investment	$5.43

We can project that in 1989 the original $5.22 portion of the $5.43 that Warren now has invested in Coca-Cola stock will still earn $.36, or 6.89%. Now, if Coca-Cola can maintain a 33.6% return on equity, we can project that in 1989 the $.21 of retained earnings from 1988 will earn a rate of return of 33.6%. So $.21 a share in retained earnings will produce $.07 a share in new earnings in 1989 ($.21 × .336 = $.07). This means projected 1989 earnings will be *$.43* a share ($.36 + $.07 = $.43).

Warren will be earning 6.89%, or $.36, on his original 1988 investment of $5.22 a share, and a return of 33.6%, or $.07 a share, on retained earnings of $.21 a share. This means in 1989 his Coca-Cola stock will earn $.43 a share, which will give him a 7.9% rate of return on his initial investment plus retained earnings of $5.43 a share ($.43 ÷ $5.43 = 7.9%).

Projected Per Share Return on Invested and Retained Capital for 1989

Original 1988 investment	$5.22 × 6.89%	=	$.36
Retained earnings for 1988	+ .21 × 33.6%	=	.07
1989 total per share investment	$5.43 Earnings Per Share		$.43

Rate of return on total capital invested for 1989: earnings per share of $.43 ÷ invested and retained capital of $5.43 = 7.9% rate of return.

The same analysis can be run for 1990 as well. Coca-Cola will retain 58% of the $.43 per share earnings from 1989, or approximately $.25. This will add $.25 to the $5.43 Warren already has invested in Coca-Cola. So his investment in Coca-Cola stock at the beginning of 1990 will be the original 1988 investment of $5.22, plus the retained earnings from 1988, $.21, plus the retained earnings from 1989, $.25, for a total of $5.68 ($5.22 + $.21 + $.25 = $5.68).

Total Per Share Investment in Coca-Cola at the Beginning of 1990

Original 1988 investment	$5.22
Retained earnings for 1988 and 1989	+ .46
1990 total per share investment	$5.68

We can project that in 1990, Warren's original investment of $5.22 a share will earn 6.89% or $.36 a share. But the retained earnings from 1988, $.21 a share, and from 1989, $.25 a share, *will each earn the current rate of return on equity, which is projected to be 33.6%*. This $.46 a share ($.21 + $.25 = $.46) in retained earnings from 1988 and 1989 will produce earnings of $.15 a share in 1990 ($.46 × .336 = $.15). Thus, total earnings for 1990 are projected to be $.51 a share ($.36 + $.15 = $.51). This means that in 1990 Warren's projected rate of return on invested and retained capital of $5.68 a share will be $.51 a share. This equates to a 8.9% rate of return on his initial investment plus retained earnings from 1988 and 1989 ($.51 ÷ $5.68 = 8.9%).

Projected Per Share Return on Invested and Retained Capital for 1990

Original 1988 investment	$5.22 × 6.89%	= $.36
Retained earnings for 1988 and 1989 +	.46 × 33.6%	= .15
1989 total per share investment	$5.68 Earnings Per Share	$.51

Rate of return on total capital invested for 1989: earnings per share $.51 ÷ invested and retained capital of $5.68 = 8.9% rate of return.

I'm sure you noticed the increasing rate of return, but what I really want you to see here is that Warren's original investment in Coca-Cola is fixed at a rate of return of 6.89%, but the retained earnings are free to earn the full 33.6%. Think of it as if you bought a Coca-Cola equity/bond that paid a return of 6.89% and every time you got an interest check in the mail you could reinvest that interest check in a new Coca-Cola equity/bond that paid a 33.6% annual compounding rate of return. The only catch to getting the 33.6% annual compounding rate of return is that you have to first buy the Coca-Cola equity/bond that is paying 6.89%.

You pay a steep price to get in the door, but once you get in it's bliss. And the longer you stay, the better it gets.

39

Using the Per Share Earnings
Annual Growth Rate to Project
a Stock's Future Value

It is possible to project that future price of a company's stock by using the company's per share earnings annual growth rate. By using the per share annual growth rate we can project a future year's per share earnings and then project the stock's price. If we know the stock's future price, the price we paid for it, and the number of years the investment is held, then we can project the annual compounding rate of return the investment will give us.

For this explanation I want to use Capital Cities as an example. Capital Cities had very consistent per share earnings growth for the ten-year period of 1970 to 1980. We will project per share earnings from 1980 ten years forward, to 1990. Then we will project a price range that Capital Cities stock will be trading at in 1990. We will then project the compounding annual rate of return you would have earned if you had bought a share of Capital Cities in 1980 and sold it in 1990. (Please note: All stock prices and per share earnings for Capital Cities reflect a 10 for 1 stock split in 1994.)

TO PROJECT CAPITAL CITIES'
FUTURE PER SHARE EARNINGS FOR 1990

From 1970 to 1980, Capital Cities' per share net income grew from $.08 to $.53, or at an annual compounding rate of approximately 20%. If we projected the per share earnings of Capital

Cities forward ten years from 1980, to the year 1990, using the rate of growth of 20%, we would get projected per share earnings of $3.28 for 1990. PV = $0.53, N = 10, %i = 20. Punch the CPT and the future value (FV) buttons and you get a calculated $3.28. This means that we can project that in 1990 Capital Cities will have per share earnings of $3.28.

TO PROJECT THE MARKET PRICE OF CAPITAL CITIES STOCK IN 1990

A review of the price-to-earnings ratio for Capital Cities for the period of 1970 to 1980 indicates that the stock traded at anywhere from nine times earnings to twenty-five times earnings. Let's say for argument's sake that we are as conservative as old Ronald Reagan and that the low end of the P/E range, nine times earnings, is what we are going to value Capital Cities' 1990 projected per share earnings at. Thus, our projected 1990 earnings of $3.28 a share equates to a projected 1990 market price for the stock of $29.52 ($3.28 × 9 = $29.52).

TO PROJECT THE ANNUAL COMPOUNDING RATE OF RETURN YOU WOULD HAVE EARNED IF YOU BOUGHT A SHARE OF CAPITAL CITIES IN 1980 AND SOLD IT IN 1990

By looking in the *Wall Street Journal,* one could see that he or she could buy Capital Cities stock in 1980 for around $5 a share. Get out your calculator and punch in PV = $5, FV = $29.52, N = 10. Hit the CPT key and the interest key (%i) and you get an annual compounding rate of return of 19.4%. This means that if you spent $5 a share for Capital Cities stock in 1980, you could project an expected annual compounding rate of return of 19.4% for the next ten years.

Since we are using past data for this Capital Cities example, let's look and see what really happened to the $5 a share investment we made in 1980. In 1990 the company had earnings of

$2.77 a share, compared to the estimate of $3.28 a share. (Okay, it's not an exact science.) The stock in 1990 traded in a price range of between $38 and $63 a share, compared to our estimate of $29.52 a share. Let's say you sold your stock at $38 a share in 1990. To calculate your annual compounding rate of return on the $5 investment you made in 1980, PV = $5, FV = $38, N = 10. Hit the CPT key and %i key and you get 22.4%. So your pre-capital-gains-tax annual compounding rate of return would have been 22.4% for the ten-year period between 1980 and 1990. If you had sold it in 1990 for the high price of $63 a share, your pre-capital-gains-tax annual compounding rate of return would have been 28.8% for the ten-year period between 1980 and 1990.

Thus, in the case of Capital Cities, the stock market revalued the stock to a higher price multiple than projected and in the process increased our fortunes above our expectations.

In case you are wondering, if you had invested *$100,000* in Capital Cities at $5 a share back in 1980, it would have compounded annually at 22.4% and grown to be worth approximately *$754,769.21* by 1990.

You should understand that Warren is not calculating a specific value for the stock, as is believed by many Warren watchers and writers. Warren is not saying that Capital Cities is worth X per share and I can buy it for half of X, as Graham used to do. Warren is instead, saying, If I pay X per share for Capital Cities stock, given the economic realities for the company, what is my expected annual compounding rate of return going to be at the end of ten years? After determining the expected annual compounding rate of return, Warren then compares it to other investments and the annual compounding rate of return that he needs to stay ahead of inflation.

By functioning in this manner, Warren can buy a stock and not care if he ever sees what Wall Street is valuing it at. Warren knows approximately what his long term annual compounding rate of return is going to be. He also knows that over the long term the market will value the company to reflect this increase in the company's net worth.

If Warren bought from the Grahamian point of view, then if a share of a company was worth $10 and he was able to buy it for $5 a share, he would have to sell that share when the market valued the company at $10 a share. If this were the case, Warren would have to have his nose glued to the *Wall Street Journal* every day to see what the market was valuing the stock at.

40

How a Company Can Increase Its Shareholders' Fortunes by Buying Back the Company's Stock

Now, if you compare our projected per share equity value for the Coca-Cola Company from 1988 to 1993, found in the table on page 224, with the actual per share equity values reported by Coca-Cola, you will find the following:

Year	Projected Per Share Equity Value	Actual Per Share Equity Value
1989	$1.28	$1.18
1990	1.53	1.41
1991	1.83	1.67
1992	2.18	1.49
1993	2.60	1.77

You can clearly see a considerable discrepancy between our projected per share equity values and the actual reported values. Were our projections inaccurate? A review of our projections for per share earnings indicate that they were extremely accurate.

Year	Projected Earnings	Actual Earnings	Margin of Error
1989	$ .43	$ .42	2.3%
1990	.51	.51	0%
1991	.61	.61	0%
1992	.72	.72	0%
1993	.87	.84	3.5%

What is going on here is that the Coca-Cola Company has been expending its equity base on retiring its common stock. In fact, from 1984 to the end of 1993, Coca-Cola expended approximately $5.8 billion of its equity buying back its common stock. From 1984 to the end of 1993, Coca-Cola managed to shrink the number of its outstanding common shares from approximately 3.174 billion in 1984, to approximately 2.604 billion by the end of 1993. This represents a reduction of approximately 570 million common shares, or 21% of all the common stock the company had outstanding in 1984.

If one considers that Coca-Cola had 3.174 billion outstanding shares in 1984 and that Coca-Cola spent $5.8 billion of its shareholders' money over the next nine years on share repurchases, you can argue that Coca-Cola spent approximately $1.82 a share of its shareholders' money buying back its own shares ($5.8 billion ÷ 3.174 billion shares outstanding in 1984 = $1.82 a share).

In 1993 Coca-Cola posted a total net income of approximately $2.176 billion. If you divide the total net income for 1993 by the total number of common shares outstanding at the end of 1993, which was 2.604 billion shares, you get an earnings per share figure of $.84. This means that in 1993, with 2.604 billion common shares outstanding and net income of $2.176 billion, the company posted per share earnings of $.84 a share (total 1993 net income of $2.176 billion ÷ 2.604 billion outstanding shares = $.84 a share).

Now consider this: if at the end of 1993 there had been as many shares outstanding as there were in 1984, which was approximately 3.174 billion shares, with Coca-Cola's 1993 total net income being $2.176 billion, Coca-Cola would have reported in 1993 per share income of $.68 (total 1993 net income of $2.176 billion ÷ 3.174 billion outstanding shares = $.68 a share).

This means that the $1.82 a share in shareholders' equity that Coca-Cola spent buying back its shares from 1984 to 1993 caused in 1993 a per share earnings increase of $.16 (EPS in 1993 without share repurchases $.84 − EPS in 1993 with share repurchases $.68 = $.16 increase in per share net income).

Coca-Cola, based on 3.174 billion shares outstanding in 1983, spent approximately $1.82 a share to cause a per share earnings increase of $.16. This equates to an approximate rate of return of 8.7% ($.16 ÷ $1.82 = 8.7%). Doesn't sound all that rewarding, does it? In fact, what seems to be a marginal allocation of capital on Coca-Cola's part is actually economic brilliance when you consider how the stock market interprets this $.16 per share increase in earnings.

In 1993, the stock market valued Coca-Cola's stock at twenty-five times per share earnings. This means that a $.16 increase in the per share earnings caused a $4.00 increase in market value of the stock. Let me show you how this works.

In 1993 without share repurchases: 1993 total net earnings of $2.176 billion ÷ 3.174 billion shares = per share earnings of $.68 in 1993. If you multiply $.68 by a P/E of 25 you get a per share market price of $17.00 ($.68 × 25 = $17.00).

In 1993 with share repurchases: 1993 total net earnings of $2.176 billion ÷ 2.604 billion shares = per share earnings of $.84 in 1993. If you multiply $.84 by a P/E of 25 you get a per share market price of $21.00 ($.84 × 25 = $21.00).

The difference between the two is $4.00 ($21.00 − $17.00 = $4.00).

Remember that Coca-Cola spent only $1.87 a share of shareholders' money in the repurchase of its stock. Thus, the $1.87 a share of shareholders' money spent produced a $4.00 increase in Coca-Cola's per share market price. By spending its equity base to retire its common stock, Coca-Cola effectively shrunk both its equity base and the number of outstanding shares. Though this doesn't effect total net earnings, it does increase per share earnings, because the number of shares have decreased. The pie remains the same size. The pieces have just gotten bigger because there are fewer slices.

Also, since the equity base has decreased, the return on equity will increase as well. (Remember, the return on equity is found by dividing the net earnings by the equity value. You can increase the rate of return on equity by increasing the net earnings or by decreasing the amount of equity in the company.)

The bottom line here is that Coca-Cola spent $1.87 a share of its shareholders' money to repurchase its stock, which caused per share earnings to increase by $.16, which in turn caused a $4.00 increase in the stock's market price. You double your money and you get to own a bigger piece of the pie.

Understand that as total net earnings increase over time, the reduction in the number of outstanding shares will cause an even larger increase in the market value of the stock. As an example, let us say that in ten years, the year 2003, Coca-Cola's total net earnings have increased at an annual rate of 15%, from $2.176 billion 1993 to $8.403 billion in 2003. Now let's run the per share figures for Coca-Cola in 2003 as if it still had the same number of shares it had outstanding in 1984, which was 3.174 billion shares. We will also run the per share figures for Coca-Cola in 2003, with only 2.604 billion shares outstanding, reflecting the share repurchases that took place between 1984 and 1993.

In 2003 without share repurchases: total net earnings of $8.403 billion ÷ 3.174 billion shares = per share earnings of $2.65 in 2003. If you multiply $2.65 by a P/E of 25 you get a per share market price of $66.25 ($2.65 × 25 = $66.25).

In 2003 with share repurchases: total net earnings of $8.403 billion ÷ 2.604 billion shares = per share earnings of $3.23 in 2003. If you multiply $3.23 by a P/E of 25 you get a per share market price of $80.75 ($3.23 × 25 = $80.75).

The difference between the two is $14.50 ($80.75 − $66.25 = $14.50).

In 2003, without the share repurchases, per share earnings will be approximately $2.65, which equates to a market price of $66.25 a share. But with share repurchases the per share earnings in 2003 will be approximately $3.23, which equates to a market price of $80.75 a share. This means that the $1.87 a share in shareholders' equity that was spent retiring Coca-Cola stock between 1984 and 1993, in this hypothetical, is projected to produce, in 2003, an increase of $14.50 in the market price for the stock. This would give the shareholders an approximate annual compounding rate of return of approximately 15% on the $1.87 of their money that Coca-Cola spent buying back its shares.

If Coca-Cola paid out as a dividend the $5.8 billion that it spent on buying back its own stock, the stockholders would have had to pay personal income tax on the $5.8 billion they received. Income taxes would have reduced the shareholders' take to approximately $4 billion, or $1.26 a share.

So the choice that you, the investor, have to make is, Do you want the $1.26 a share in your pocket, or do you want Coca-Cola to spend it on increasing the size of your portion of the Coca-Cola pie? If you let Coca-Cola keep the after-tax $1.26, it can spend it buying back its own stock, which will increase per share earnings, which increases the value of your stock.

Since Warren bought into Coca-Cola and obtained a seat on the board of directors, the company has been an aggressive buyer of its own stock. During this same period the stock market has increased its valuation of the company from a price-to-earnings ratio of 18 in 1988 to a price-to-earnings ratio of 40 in 1997. The stock market just loves fat increases in per share earnings and high rates of return on equity. For Warren, Coca-Cola's stock repurchase program made a good thing an even better thing.

41

How to Determine If Per Share Earnings Are Increasing Because of Share Repurchases

We have discussed how to determine the annual compounding growth rate of per share earnings over a number of years. We have discussed also how a company can increase the annual compounding growth rate on per share earnings by decreasing the number of shares outstanding. But when you analyze a security you need to know what is causing any increase in per share earnings. Is it the economic engines of the business that are creating the increase? Or is it the manipulation of the financial mechanics? Or is it some combination of both?

The way that this is done is to compare the company's actual net earnings annual compounding growth rate against the annual compounding growth rate for per share earnings. Understand that the per share figure is derived from taking the company's net earnings and dividing it by the number of shares the company has outstanding.

Thus, in 1986, the Washington Post Company had total net earnings of $100.2 million. Divide this by the number of shares outstanding, 12.83 million, and you get a per share figure of $7.80. If you decreased the number of shares outstanding to 10 million, you would get a per share earnings figure of $10.02. Decrease the number of shares, and the per share earnings figure goes up. Increase the number of shares, and the per share figure goes down.

It's a neat trick and is one of the ways that management can effectively use capital to increase the shareholders' wealth. But it also can downplay mediocre results.

Let's say in 1980 Company X had net earnings of $100 million and 10 million shares outstanding, which equates to per share earnings of $10 ($100 million ÷ 10 million = $10). Now, let's say that in 1990 the company reports net earnings of $75 million and has 5 million shares outstanding, which equates to per share earnings of $15.

So, even though Company X actually had a decline in actual net earnings over the ten-year period between 1980 and 1990, from $100 million a year to $75 million a year, the company still reported an increase in per share earnings, from $10 a share in 1980 to $15 a share in 1990.

This means that Company X had an annual growth rate for per share earnings of 4.13%. But actual net earnings had an annual *loss* of 2.83%. Managements, being the creative devils that they are, use this technique to keep their shareholders in line. Hey, per share earnings increased 4.13% last year. Not bad! Now go back to watching TV and leave us alone.

You think I'm kidding don't you? No one would be silly enough not to check actual net earnings versus per share earnings. I know you have probably been to Disneyland, but have you ever been to Wall Street?

Raytheon, the makers of the Patriot missile, clever rocket scientists that they are, managed to get their per share earnings to grow from 1985 to 1995 at an annual compounding rate of 11.2%, which is great. Management can point to a chart with pride and tell its shareholders that per share earnings increased from $2.30 a share in 1985 to $6.65 a share in 1995. Give those guys a raise! But in truth Raytheon's *actual net earnings* grew only at an annual rate of 7.8%. In case you are wondering, 7.8% is nothing to rave about; it just stays a little ahead of inflation. The reason that per share earnings rose so dramatically is that Raytheon shrunk the number of its outstanding shares by 24%, from 155 million in 1985 to 117 million in 1995.

Not only can share repurchases downplay a mediocre increase in total earnings; they can also accent a spectacular performance. From 1985 to 1995, the Coca-Cola Company reported that per share earnings grew at an annual compounding rate of 19.5%, which is fantastic. Actual net earnings during the same period grew at an annual compounding growth rate of 15.2%, which is also outstanding. Coca-Cola has grown its actual net earnings at an impressive rate, but its per share growth rate was given an added boost by a decrease in the number of shares outstanding from 3.087 billion in 1985 to 2.475 billion in 1995.

Philip Morris Company reported that its actual net earnings grew at an annual compounding rate of 16% for the period between 1985 and 1995. Its *per share earnings,* however, grew at an annual compounding rate of 18.35%, which is smoking hot. This was due in large part to Philip Morris decreasing the number of shares that it had outstanding by 13%, from 954 million in 1985 to 823 million in 1995.

Sometimes the capital needs of a company are so extreme that instead of buying back its shares it issues more. This creates more outstanding shares and helps drive down the annual per share growth rate. Just as a decrease in the number of shares outstanding doesn't affect the growth rate for actual net earnings, an increase in the number of shares has no effect either. General Motors is a perfect example of this.

From 1985 to 1995 GM reported a 4.82% annual rate of growth of its net earnings. But its per share earnings grew only at an annual rate of 2.68%. This is because GM increased the number of shares outstanding from 682 million in 1985 to 755 million in 1995. This is a good indication that GM's increase in earnings can be attributed to an increase in its capital base and not the economics of its business.

Bank holding companies are especially good at this. They grow not because they have some fantastic business spinning off tons of cash, but by having investors invest more money in the business. Norwest, the thirteenth-largest bank holding company in the United States, for the period between 1985 and 1995 reported a per share earnings annual compounding growth rate of 21% and an actual net earnings annual compounding growth rate of 28%. Its outstanding shares for this period increased from 178 million in 1985 to 325 million in 1995. What Norwest does is print up new stock certificates and exchange them for other banks. If Norwest gets good value for its shares, the new banks will add value to Norwest, which increases its per share earnings.

42

How to Measure Management's
Ability to Utilize Retained Earnings

When a company earns a profit, it has to decide what to do with it. As a rule, a portion of the profit must be used to replenish capital equipment of the core business that produced the profit. Warren considers these earnings to be restricted earnings.

An example of restricted earnings would be that Company A earns $1 million in 1992 but in year 1993 anticipates that it will have to replace a generator at its main plant at a cost of $400,000. This means that in 1993 the company has to come up with $400,000 to replace the generator or it is out of business. If the company hasn't saved $400,000 in its bank account, it will have to go out and raise the money. But Company A earned $1 million in 1992, so at the end of 1992, when it is trying to figure out what to do with this $1 million, the management of the company will allocate $400,000 of the $1 million in earnings to the purchase of the new generator in 1993.

This means that $400,000 of Company A's $1 million in earnings is now restricted. Thus, Company A earned $1 million in year 1992, $400,000 of which is restricted for the purchase of a new generator in 1993, and $600,000 of which can either be paid out as a dividend to Company A's shareholders or be spent on new business ventures.

It is the $600,000 in unrestricted earnings that Warren finds so interesting. What Company A's management does with it will determine whether Company A grows in value for the shareholders or not.

Warren believes that management should use the unrestricted earnings to give the shareholders the best value.

Company A's management has the choice of either paying out the unrestricted earnings as a dividend to its shareholders or retaining the unrestricted earnings and spending them either on share repurchases or on new business ventures.

Warren believes that management should retain unrestricted earnings only if it can earn a higher rate of return on the unrestricted earnings than the shareholders could earn on the outside.

Let's assume that Company A's management is able to employ the $600,000 in unrestricted earnings in a manner that would earn the company an annual return of 15%. But, the shareholders, if they received the $600,000 as a dividend, may not be able to do as well. Then it would make more sense for Company A to keep the unrestricted earnings than to pay them out as a dividend. (This example ignores the effects of taxation to keep things simple.) Warren believes that a company should retain unrestricted earnings only if it is reasonable to project that the management would be able to do a better job investing those unrestricted earnings than would the shareholders.

If the reverse is true and the shareholders could earn a return of 15% and Company A's management could reinvest the earnings only at a rate of 5%, then it would make more sense to pay out the unrestricted earnings as a dividend to the shareholders.

Our problem as investors is that it is hard to determine if the management of a company is doing a superior job of allocating its unrestricted earnings. This is because a company with exceptional economics in its core business can produce tons of excess cash and in the process cover up any mistakes that management makes in allocating capital. As noted, a tremendous business can be so strong that it can hide even inept management.

Inflation also helps hide management's performance by increasing the level of earnings on the core business, even though unit sales remain the same. A 10% increase in the price level could equate to a 10% increase in the price of the company's products and a 10% increase in earnings. If the core business is one that requires very little in new capital investment, then this increase in earnings created by inflation could be incorrectly attributed to management's ability to allocate unrestricted earnings.

So that is the problem. How do we as investors measure a company and its management's ability to profitably allocate unrestricted earnings?

There is a simple mathematical way of measuring management's performance. It's simple in that the core business and inflation can still cause the end figure to be anything but a close approximation of what is going on. Still, necessity is the mother of all invention and our need for some measure of performance is great. So until accounting and reporting standards change to allow a more detailed analysis, we are stuck making rough estimates of management's performance.

What we do is take the *per share earnings retained by a business for a certain period of time, then compare it to any increase in per share earnings that occurred during this same period.*

Let's look at several examples to give you a better idea of how this works.

In 1983 Coca-Cola made $.17 a share. This means that all the capital invested in Coca-Cola up until the end of 1983 produced for its owners $.17 a share in 1983. Now, between the end of 1983 and the end of 1993, Coca-Cola had total earnings for this ten-year period of $4.44 per share. Of that $4.44, Coca-Cola paid out in dividends between 1983 and 1993 a total of $1.89 a share. This means that for the ten-year period between 1983 and 1994, Coca-Cola had retained earnings of $2.55 a share ($4.44 − $1.89 = $2.55).

So, between the end of 1983 and the end of 1993, Coca-Cola earned a total of $4.44 a share, paid out in dividends a total of $1.89 a share, and retained to its capital base a total of $2.55 a share.

Between 1983 and 1993 Coca-Cola's per share earnings rose from $.17 a share to $.84 a share. We can attribute the 1983 earnings of $.17 a share to all the capital invested in Coca-Cola up to the end of 1983. We can also argue that the increase in earnings from $.17 a share in 1983 to $.84 a share in 1993 was caused by Coca-Cola's management doing an excellent job of utilizing the $2.55 a share in earnings that Coca-Cola retained between 1983 and 1993.

If we subtract the 1983 per share earnings of $.17 from the 1993 per share earnings of $.84, we find that the difference is $.67 a share. Thus we can argue that the $2.55 a share that was retained between 1983 and 1993 produced $.67 in additional income for 1993. This means that the $2.55 in retained earnings earned $.67 in 1993 for a total return of 26.2% ($.67 ÷ $2.55 = 26.2%).

Thus, we can argue that Coca-Cola's management earned a 26.2% return in 1993 on the $2.55 a share in shareholders' capital that Coca-Cola retained from 1983 to 1993.

Let's compare this to a company like General Motors, which had total per share earnings of $37.67 between 1983 and 1993, of which $22.18 was paid out in dividends and $15.49 was retained by the company. Per share earnings for General Motors, however, decreased from $5.92 in 1983 to $2.13 in 1993. General Motors' management kept $15.49 per share of shareholders' earnings and allocated it in such a manner that per share earnings actually dropped. This makes you wonder about the underlying economics of the auto business.

If we ran General Motors' numbers forward to 1995, when it earned $7.28 a share, we would see that from 1983 through 1995 General Motors retained approximately $26.27 in shareholders' earnings and increased its per share earnings from $5.92 in 1983 to $7.28 in 1995. This means that General Motors kept $26.27 in shareholders' earnings and in the process managed to increase per share earnings by $1.36 ($7.28 − $5.92 = $1.36). Thus we can argue that the $26.27 a share that was retained between 1983 through 1995 produced $1.36 in additional income for 1995. We can argue that the $26.27 in retained earnings earned $1.36 in 1995, for a rate of return of 5.1% ($1.36 ÷ $26.27 = 5.1%).

Cray Research, which builds supercomputers, had from 1983 to 1993 total per share earnings of $31.67 a share and it retained every penny. From 1983 to 1993 earnings increased $1.44 a share, from $.89 in 1983 to $2.33 in 1994. Thus, Cray Research retained $31.67 a share in shareholders' earnings, which in 1993 produced $1.44 a share, for a return of 4% on the total retained earnings for the period of 1983 to 1993 ($1.44 ÷ $31.67 = 4.5%).

Compare Cray Research with the Gannett Corporation, which as we know publishes roughly 190 newspapers. Gannett from the end of 1983 to the end of 1993 produced total per share earnings of $20.88 a share, of which $10.37 was paid out as dividends. This means that between 1983 and 1993 the Gannett Corporation retained $10.51 a share in shareholders' earnings. From 1983 to 1993 per share earnings increased by $1.59 a share, from $1.13 in 1983 to $2.72 in 1993.

We can argue that Gannett Corporation kept $10.51 a share in shareholders' earnings, which in 1993 produced $1.59 a share, for a rate return of 15.1%. But Cray Research kept $31.67 a share in shareholders' earnings, three times what Gannett did, and produced only $1.44 increase in per share earnings, for a rate of return of 4%.

Even if we have no idea what business these four companies are in, we can still tell that the Coca-Cola Company and Gannett Corporation appear to do a much better job of profitably allocating their retained earnings than do General Motors and Cray Research.

A check of the per share market prices on these four companies indicates that both General Motors and Cray Research traded in 1993 at about the same price that they traded at in 1983. This means that even though General Motors kept $15.49 in shareholders' earnings and Cray Research kept $10.49, neither could produce any significant increase in long-term value for their shareholders.

But both Coca-Cola and Gannett saw significant increases in the market price of their stocks from 1983 to 1993 and thus added real value to their shareholders' interests.

This test is not perfect. One must be careful that the per share earnings figures used are not aberrations. One has to make sure that the per share figures used are indicative of any real increase or decrease in earning power. The advantage to this test is that it gives you, the investor, a really fast method of determining whether or not a company and its management have the ability to allocate retained earnings in a fashion that increases the wealth of the company's shareholders.

43

Short-Term Arbitrage Commitments

One of Warren's hidden talents is his success in the field of arbitrage—or, as he calls it, *workouts*. These arbitrage, or workout, opportunities arise from corporate sellouts, reorganizations, mergers, spin-offs, and hostile takeovers. Warren prefers to commit capital to investment for the long term, but when no opportunity for long-term investment presents itself, he has found that arbitrage, or workout, opportunities offer him a vastly more profitable venue for utilizing cash assets than other short-term investments. In fact, over the thirty-odd years that Warren has been actively investing in these types of arbitrage situations, he estimates that his average annual pretax rate of return has been in the neighborhood of 25%. That's real money in anybody's book.

In the early days of the Buffett Partnership, up to 40% of the total partnership funds in any given year may have been invested in arbitrage, or workout, situations. And in dark years like 1962, when the whole market was headed south, it was the profits from workouts that saved the day. They allowed the partnership to be up 13.9% compared to the Dow's miserable performance of being down 7.6%. (However, the Buffett Partnership's investments in normal operations actually lost money in 1962. It was the arbitrage/workout profits that turned a disaster into the stuff financial legends are made of.)

Though there are many types of arbitrage/workouts, or "special situations," as Graham called them, Warren has come to be very comfortable with what Graham called *cash payments on sale or liquidation*. In this type of arbitrage, a company sells out its business operations to another entity or decides to liquidate its operations and distribute the proceeds to its security holders.

Warren's purchase in 1988 of 3,342,000 shares of RJR Nabisco stock for $281.8 million after the announcement of the RJR management's bid for the company is a good example of a company selling out to another entity.

Warren's purchase of General Dynamics stock was motivated by the company's announcement that it was going to liquidate certain business properties and disburse the proceeds to its shareholders.

An investment opportunity arises for the arbitrageur in the price spread that develops between the announced sale or liquidation price and the market price for the company's stock before the sale or the liquidation.

As an example, Company X announces it will sell all its stock to Company Y for $120 a share at some date in the future. But the arbitrageur is able to buy the stock for $100 a share before the close of the transaction, so the arbitrageur will make a profit of $20 a share—the difference between the market price paid, $100, and the sale price of $120 ($120 − $100 = $20). The question becomes, When will the transaction close so the arbitrageur can cash out at $120 a share and make the $20 a share profit?

Thus, the big question is one of time. The longer the time from the purchase date to the date the transaction closes, the smaller your annual rate of return. Let me show you.

If you paid $100 a share and the company is going to sell out in twelve months at $120 a share, your profit would be $20 and your pretax annual rate of return would be 20%. But what would happen if because of some complication the transaction didn't close for, say, two years? Your pretax *annual* rate of return would drop to 10%.

Likewise, if you got lucky and the transaction closed in six months instead of twelve, then your pretax annual compounding rate of return would jump to 40%.

The arbitrage/workout situation is essentially an investment with a timetable. The amount you are going to earn is fixed—in our example, $20. The length of time that the security is held will determine the pretax annual rate of return. The shorter the length of time, the larger the pretax annual rate of return. The longer the length of time, the smaller the pretax annual rate of return.

There are certain risks to investing in these types of situations. One, as we already discussed, is that the transaction may take longer than expected. The other is that the transaction may fail to occur at all, which is, as we used to say, a major bummer.

There are hundreds of reasons why these transactions can take longer than expected or not take place at all. Sometimes the shareholders reject the offer; other times the government antitrust people kill the party; and there are times when the IRS takes an eternity issuing a tax ruling. Anything and everything can go wrong.

One way that Warren has come to protect himself from some of the risk is to invest only in situations that have been announced. This sounds like the normal, intelligent thing to do. What kind of fool would invest in a transaction that hadn't been announced? Care to take a guess? You got it. Wall Street! Yes, they have worked their brains overtime and have figured out that they can really make a lot of money by investing in companies that are *rumored* to be takeover candidates. Trading on rumors can mean big profits, but it also means greater risk.

Warren has found, after being involved in literally hundreds of arbitrage/workout situations, that an almost certain annual rate of return of 25% is usually more profitable than a 100% annual rate of return that is a big maybe. The gnomes of Wall Street can trade on rumors, but Warren will invest only after the sale or merger has been announced.

During the Buffett Partnership years, from 1957 to 1969, Warren was of the opinion that the arbitrage/workout category of investment would produce year to year the most steady and absolute profits for the partnership, and in years of market decline give the partnership a big competitive edge.

You should understand that when the stock market is going down, shareholders and management start to worry about the sinking price of the company's stock and therefore are more willing to entertain selling out, liquidation, or some form of reorganization. Thus, when the market starts to sink, the opportunities in the field of arbitrage should start to rise.

THE GRAHAMIAN EQUATION

Warren learned the arbitrage/workout game from Graham. Graham, who was influenced by Meyer H. Weinstein's classic 1931 treatise on the subject, *Arbitrage in Securities* (Harper Brothers), expounded brilliantly on the subject in his 1951 edition of *Security Analysis*.

Graham noted that in the case of a sale for cash of a going concern, large profits were to be found if the security was bought *before* the announcement. Graham also noted that after the announcement—but before the consummation of the sale—an interesting spread often developed between the market price of the security and the announced sale price. This is the kind of arbitrage Warren found most profitable.

Because of the complexity of the investment and the different variables that come into play, Graham developed a general formula to determine the profit potential of a particular transaction. It is this formula that he taught to Warren. The formula is as follows:

G = the expected gain in the event of success

L = the expected loss in the event of failure

C = the expected chances of success, expressed as a percentage

Y = the expected time of holding, in years

P = the current price of the security

$$\text{Annual return} = \frac{CG - L(100\% - C)}{YP}$$

The formula takes into account the possibility for loss, which should be weighed into any transaction of this type. Let's take a look at how it works.

EXAMPLE OF THE USE
OF THE GRAHAM ARBITRAGE FORMULA

On February 13, 1982, Bayuk Cigars Inc. announced that it had approval from the Justice Department to sell its cigar operations to American Maize Products Co. for $14.5 million, or approximately $7.87 a share. It announced also that it was adopting a plan of liquidation and would distribute the proceeds from the sale to its shareholders.

Shortly after the announcement, Warren bought 5.71% of Bayuk Cigar's outstanding stock for $572,907, or $5.44 a share. Warren was arbitraging the difference between the current market price of $5.44 a share and the future distribution to the shareholders of the proceeds from the sale of Bayuk's assets, which was estimated to be $7.87 a share.

In applying the above Graham equation for arbitrage situations, the first thing Warren must do is to calculate his prospective per share profit. This can be done by subtracting from the sale price, $7.87 a share, the market price Warren paid per share, $5.44. This equates to a profit potential of $2.43 a share ($7.87 − $5.44 = $2.43).

He then multiplies his potential profit, $2.43, by the chances of success, expressed as a percentage. In this case the deal has been announced and approved by the Justice Department. There is little that can get in the way of its happening. This means that Warren can assign a 90% or better figure for the chances that the sale will take place. So if Warren multiples his profit potential, $2.43, by 90%, he would get $2.18, adjusted to the probability for success.

Warren has to figure in the amount that he would lose if the transaction didn't take place. If the sale got canceled, the per share price of the stock would probably fall back to the price it was before the sale was announced. If the sale doesn't happen, the per share price of Bayuk Cigar's stock would return to $4.50 a share, the price it was before the sale and liquidation were announced. This means that if Warren paid $5.44 a share and the price of the stock then dropped to $4.50 a share, Warren would lose $.94 a share.

But remember that Warren would also have to calculate in the chances of a loss occurring. This is done by subtracting the chances of success, 90%, from 100%, which would give Warren a 10% chance of the transaction not happening. Now the amount of the projected loss, $.94, is multiplied by 10%, which gives Warren a projected loss of $.09.

Warren then would have to figure in the length of time it would take for the transaction to take place. The company, in liquidating its assets, would have to distribute the proceeds within the fiscal year or there would be a capital gains tax. So Warren could figure that once the sale occurred, the proceeds would be paid out within the year. Warren assigned a holding period of one year for the sale and liquidation to occur.

Here is the Graham Arbitrage Formula applied to the Bayuk Cigar situation:

G = \$2.43, the expected gain in the event of success

L = \$.94, the expected loss in the event of failure

C = 90%, the expected chances of success, expressed as a percentage

Y = 1 year, the expected time of holding

P = \$5.44, the current price of the security.

$$\text{Annual return} = \frac{CG - L(100\% - C)}{YP}$$

or

$$\text{Annual Return} = \frac{\overset{C}{90\%} \times \overset{G}{\$2.43} - \overset{L}{\$.94}(100\% - \overset{C}{90\%})}{\underset{Y}{1} \times \underset{P}{\$5.44}}$$

or

$$\text{Annual Return} = \frac{\overset{CG}{\$2.18} - \overset{LC}{\$.09}}{\underset{Y}{1} \times \underset{P}{\$5.44}}$$

or

$$\text{Annual Return} = \frac{\$2.09}{\$5.44} = 38\%$$

Warren can figure that his annual rate of return will be 38% if the transaction and the liquidation of Bayuk Cigar occurs on schedule. Not a bad rate of return for a short-term commitment of capital.

Warren has played many different arbitrage opportunities. Besides the Bayuk Cigar and RJR deals, for arbitrage purposes he has owned shares in Texas National Petroleum, Allegis, Lear-Siegler, Chesebrough-Pond's, Kraft, Interco, Federated, Southland, and Marine Midland, to name a few. In a given year he may have up to twenty different arbitrage positions, or he may have none.

From a historical perspective, what Warren discovered is that in the field of arbitrage the realization of value problem that plagues value investing is solved by the certainty of the transaction date. The investment will reach its full value at a certain date. The investor merely has to calculate whether it affords a sufficient rate of return to merit a commitment of his capital.

But remember, as we said earlier, Warren will take arbitrage positions only *after the buyout or liquidation has been announced.*

44

Bringing It All Together: The Case Studies

The case studies that follow evaluate companies in which Warren has invested in the past. The format for each case study is the same, with slight variations in the mathematical portion of the price analysis and determination of the annual compounding rate of return. We do this to give some diversity to the analysis process and to show you some of the different applications and perspectives the mathematical tools can bring.

GANNETT CORPORATION, 1994

Warren's love affair with the newspaper business probably started when he was a boy living in Washington, D.C., where he had a *Washington Post* newspaper route. As we know, he later took a sizeable position in that company.

In the summer of 1994, Warren started buying large blocks of the Gannett Corporation, a newspaper holding company. He eventually spent $335,216,000 for 6,854,500 shares of Gannett's common stock, which equates to a purchase price of $48.90 a share. Let's look and see what he found so enticing.

DOING YOUR DETECTIVE WORK

The background work on this one is easy. All of us know *USA Today,* the newspaper that you can find on any newsstand in America. If you have read more than one of these gems of mass circulation, then a light may have gone off in your head that sparked the question: Who publishes this newspaper and is it is publicly traded? Well, Gannett publishes it, and the answer to the second question is yes.

A check of the *Value Line Investment Survey* tells us that the Gannett Corporation publishes 190 newspapers in thirty-eight states and U.S. territories. Its largest publications are the *Detroit News* (circulation 312,093) and *USA Today* (circulation 2.1 million). Gannett also owns thirteen radio stations and fifteen network-affiliated TV stations.

Once you have assembled the financial information, it's time to work through our questions.

1

Does the company have any *identifiable consumer monopolies or brand-name products,* or do they sell a commodity-type product? Newspapers and radio and TV stations, we know, are good businesses. As we know, usually a newspaper is a great business if it is the only game in town—less competition means bigger bucks to the owners. The majority of Gannett Corporation's newspapers, we found, are the only game in town. Nice.

2

Do you *understand how it works?* This is, yes, another of those cases that you, the consumer/investor, have intimate knowledge of, and experience with using the product. You're stuck in an out-of-town airport with nothing to do, so you go to the newsstand and buy a newspaper. Which one do you buy? The local paper? No. You have no interest in what is going on in local government. But, hey, there's *USA Today,* and it has national news!

3

Is the company *conservatively financed?* A check of the debt to equity indicates in 1994 Gannett had a total long-term debt of $767 million and a little over $1.8 billion in equity. Though it is not debt free, given the company's strong earnings in 1994 of $465 million, it is easy to see that Gannett could pay off its entire debt burden in just two years.

4

Are the *earnings* of the company *strong* and do they show an *upward trend?* Earnings in 1994 were estimated to be $3.20 a share. A check of Gannett's per share earnings indicates that they grew at an annual compounding rate of 8.6% for the period of 1984 to 1994, and at a rate of 5.3% for the period from 1989 to 1994.

Per share earnings can be considered very stable, increasing every year from 1984 to 1994 with the exception of 1990 and 1991, in which the entire publishing and media business was experiencing a recession due to weakening advertising rates. Remember, a *general* recession in an industry is often a buying opportunity.

A glance at the yearly per share earnings figures indicates that they are strong and show an upward trend, which is what we are looking for.

Year	Earnings
1983	$1.13
1984	1.40
1985	1.58
1986	1.71
1987	1.98
1988	2.26
1989	2.47
1990	2.36
1991	2.00
1992	2.40
1993	2.72
1994	3.20 (est.)

5

The company allocates capital only to those businesses within its realm of *expertise,* which in this case is the media industry.

6

Further investigation indicates that Gannett has been buying back its shares. It has bought back 21.2 million of its outstanding shares in the period from 1988 through 1994. This is a sign that management utilizes capital to increase shareholder value when it is possible.

7

The way management has spent the retained earnings of the company appears to have increased the per share earnings and, therefore, *shareholders' value.*

The company from 1984 to 1994 had retained earnings of

$11.64 a share. Per share earnings grew by $1.80 a share, from $1.40 a share at the end of 1984 to $3.20 by the end of 1994. Thus, we can argue that the retained earnings of $11.64 a share are projected to produce in 1994 an after-corporate-income-tax return of $1.80, which equates to a 15.5% rate of return.

8

The company's *return on equity is above average*. As we know, Warren considers it a good sign when a business can earn above-average returns on equity. An average return on equity for American corporations for the last thirty years is approximately 12%. The return on equity for Gannett for the last ten years looks like this:

YEAR	R.O.E
1983	17.6%
1984	19.6%
1985	19.9%
1986	19.3%
1987	19.8%
1988	20.4%
1989	19.9%
1990	18.3%
1991	19.6%
1992	21.9%
1993	20.8%
1994	24.5% (est.)

This gives Gannett an average annual rate of return on equity for the last ten years of 20.4%. But more important than averages is the fact that the company has earned consistently high returns on equity, which indicates management is doing an excellent job in profitably allocating retained earnings to new projects.

9

Is the company free to adjust prices to inflation? Newspapers used to cost a dime, now they cost fifty cents to a dollar. But newspapers and TV stations make their real money by selling advertising. If you own the only newspaper in town, you can charge really high advertising rates, and there is not much in the way of alternatives for people to switch to. As noted earlier, classified advertising, supermarkets, auto dealers, and entertainment, such as movie theaters, are reliant upon advertising in the local newspaper. As a whole, we can assume that Gannett can adjust its prices to inflation without running the risk of losing sales.

10

Do operations require large capital expenditures to constantly update the company's plant and equipment? As we discussed earlier, all the benefits of earning tons of money can be offset by a company constantly having to make large capital expenditures to stay competitive. Gannett's mainstay in business is its newspapers and broadcast stations. So once its initial infrastructure is in place and recently updated, there is not a lot needed down the road in the way of capital equipment. Printing operations run for years before they wear out, and TV and radio stations need only an occasional new transmitter.

This means that when Gannett makes money it doesn't have to go out and spend it on research and development or major costs for upgrading plant and equipment. Gannett can instead go out and buy more newspapers and radio stations or it can use the excess cash to buy back its own stock. This means that Gannett's shareholders get richer and richer.

Summary of Data

Since Warren gets positive responses to the above key questions, he concludes that Gannett Corporation is a company that he can fit in his "realm of confidence" and that its earnings can be predicted with a fair degree of certainty. But a positive response to these questions *does not* invoke an automatic buy response. Once a company is identified as *one of the kinds of businesses* we want to be in, we still have to calculate if the market price for the stock will allow a return equal to or better than our other options.

PRICE ANALYSIS

As we have said and will say again, *identify the company* and then *let the market price determine the buy decision.*

Initial Rate of Return and Relative Value to Government Bonds

In the case of Gannett, the per share earnings in 1994 were estimated to be $3.20 a share. Divide $3.20 by the long-term government bond interest rate for 1994, which was approximately 7%, and you get a relative value of $45.71 a share. This means that if you paid $45.71 for a share of Gannett, you would be getting a return equal to that of the government bonds. In 1994 you could have bought Gannett stock for $46.40 to $59 a share. As we said, Warren paid an average price of $48.90 a share.

Since the 1994 earnings are estimated to be $3.20 a share, if you paid, say, $48.90 a share you would be getting an estimated initial rate of return of 6.5%. A review of Gannett's per share earnings growth rate for the last ten years indicates that it has been growing at an annual compounding rate of 8.6%. Thus you can ask yourself this question: What would I rather own—$48.90 worth of a government bond with a static rate of return of 7%, or a Gannett Corporation equity/bond, with an initial rate of return of 6.5%, that has a coupon that is projected to grow at a rate of 8.6% a year?

Gannett Corporation's Stock As an Equity/Bond

From a return-on-equity standpoint, we can argue that in 1994 Gannett had a per share equity value of $13.04; if Gannett can maintain its average rate of return on equity of 20.4% over the next ten years and retain approximately 60% of that return, then per share equity value should grow at an annual rate of approximately 12.24%, to approximately $41.37 a share in Year 10—2004. On your calculator punch in $13.04 as the present value, PV; 10 for the number of years, N; 12.24 for the annual rate of interest, %i. Hit the CPT button and then the future value button, FV, and $41.37 will appear as your future value.

If per share equity value is $41.37 in Year 10, 2004, and Gannett is still earning a 20.4% return on equity, then Gannett should report per share earnings of $8.44 a share ($41.37 × 20.4% = $8.44). If Gannett is trading at its low P/E for the last ten years, which is 15, the stock should have a market price of approximately $126.60 a share ($8.44 × 15 = $126.60). If per share earnings are multiplied by the ten-year-high P/E of 23, you get a per share market price of $194.12 ($8.44 × 23 = $194.12). Add in the projected total dividend pool of $23.85 earned from 1994 to 2004, and you get a projected total pretax annual compounding rate of return for the ten years of somewhere between 11.89 and 16.12%.

Project an Annual Compounding Rate of Return Using the Historical Annual Per Share Earnings Growth Figure

Warren can figure that if per share earnings continue to grow at a rate of 8.6% annually and if Gannett continues to pay out dividends at a rate of 40% of per share earnings, then the following per share earnings and dividend disbursement picture will develop over the next ten years:

This means that in the year 2004 Warren can project that Gannett will have per share earnings of $7.48. If Gannett is trading at the lowest price-to-earnings ratio that it has had in the last ten years—15—then we can calculate that market price

YEAR	EARNINGS	DIVIDENDS
1995	$3.56	$1.42
1996	3.86	1.54
1997	4.20	1.68
1998	4.56	1.82
1999	4.95	1.98
2000	5.38	2.15
2001	5.84	2.33
2002	6.34	2.53
2003	6.89	2.75
2004	7.48	2.99
		$21.19

will be $112.20 ($7.48 × 15 = $112.20). Add in the pretax dividend pool of $21.19, and our total pretax return jumps to $133.39 a share ($112.20 + $21.19 = $133.39).

If it is trading at the highest P/E that it has had in the last ten years, 23, then we can calculate that the market price for the stock will be $172.04 in the year 2004. Add in the pretax dividend pool of $21.19 and our total pretax return becomes $193.23 ($172.04 + $21.19 = $193.23).

If you were Warren and you spent $48.90 a share for your Gannett stock in 1994, using this method, you could project that in ten years it would be worth with dividends somewhere between $133.39 and $193.23 a share. This equates to a pretax annual compounding rate of return of somewhere between 10.55 and 14.72%. (You can get these figures by taking out the calculator and punching in $48.90 for the present value, PV; 10 for the number of years, N; and either $133.39 or $193.23 for the future value, FV. Hit the CPT key followed by the interest key, i%. Presto, your annual compounding rate of return will appear—either 10.55% or 14.72%.)

In Summary

In the summer and fall of 1994 Warren bought approximately 6.854 million shares of Gannett Corporation common stock at $48.90 a share, for a total purchase price of $335,216,000. When Warren bought the stock he could argue that he just bought a Gannett equity/bond with a yield of 6.5% that had a coupon that is projected to grow at a rate of approximately 8.6% a year. He could also figure that if he held the stock for ten years, his projected pretax annual compounding rate of return would be between 10.55 and 16.12%.

This means in ten years' time his investment of $335,216,000 in Gannett Corporation will be worth in pretax terms somewhere between $913,936,654 and $1,494,166,165.

FEDERAL HOME LOAN MORTGAGE CORPORATION, 1992

Warren's involvement with the banking industry led him to the doorsteps of the Federal Home Loan Mortgage Corporation, popularly known as Freddie Mac. Freddie Mac is in the business of securitizing and guaranteeing mortgages. When you take out a mortgage with your local bank, the bank ends up selling that loan to Freddie Mac, which in turn packages it (with other mortgages that it has bought) into a large pool of mortgages. Freddie Mac then sells interests in that pool of mortgages to institutional investors. When you pay interest on your mortgage, your interest payment ends up in the hands of the investors who bought interests in that pool of mortgages. On Wall Street these securitized pools of mortgages are called *mortgage-backed bonds.*

In 1988, when Freddie Mac started to trade publicly, Berkshire acquired 4% of the company through a Berkshire subsidiary, Wesco Financial. In 1992, with Freddie Mac trading at or near its lifetime high, Warren increased Berkshire's holdings in Freddie Mac by 8,711,100 shares. He paid approximately $337 million, or $38.68 a share, for this increase in ownership. At the end of 1992, Berkshire owned 9% of Freddie Mac's outstanding shares.

The subject of our case study will be Berkshire's 1992 increase in its holdings of Freddie Mac stock. The focus of our inquiry is the nature of the business economics of Freddie Mac in 1992 that compelled Warren to add to his position.

DOING YOUR DETECTIVE WORK

Doing the background on this one *would not be* easy. Though it is a visible stock, it is unlikely that you will ever have anything to do with the company in real life.

Value Line covers the stock and it is followed by a number of investment houses. So you may have discovered it from one of those sources. A check of the business periodicals and a call to the company for annual reports and 10-Ks will supply you with sufficient information to work through our list of questions.

1

Does the company have any *identifiable consumer monopolies or brand-name products,* or is it a company that produces or sells a commodity-type of product? Though mortgages are a commodity-type product, Freddie Mac, along with a similar company called Fannie Mae, is essentially a government-sanctioned entity created by Congress to raise money to help people who want to buy home mortgages. In the process, Freddie Mac and Fannie Mae have developed a quasimonopoly on this segment of the market.

2

Is the company *conservatively financed?* No. However, Freddie Mac's liabilities are offset by corresponding assets that are highly liquid—mortgages. But since it does enjoy government agency status, any financial problems would draw immediate attention of the U.S. Congress—and they have a *big* checkbook, the American taxpayer, to help see their little brother through hard times. Still, if there were considerable defaults on the underlying mortgages in the pools, then it would be conceivable that Freddie Mac could find itself in trouble.

3

YEAR	EARNINGS
1986	$1.24
1987	1.51
1988	1.91
1989	2.19
1990	2.30
1991	3.08
1992	3.29

Are the *earnings* of the company *strong, with an upward trend?* A check of Freddie Mac's per share earnings indicates that they have been growing at a rate of 17.66% compounded annually from 1986 to 1992, a period of six years.

Yearly per share earnings are strong and show an upward trend, which is what we are looking for.

4

The company allocates capital only to those businesses that are within its *realm of expertise,* which in this case is the mortgage-backed securities industry.

5

Further investigation indicates that Freddie Mac has not been buying back its shares. Nor has it been issuing new shares for acquisitions. (*Please note:* In 1995 Feddie Mac started a stock buyback program.)

6

The way management has spent the retained earnings of the company appears to have increased the per share earnings and therefore shareholders' value.

The company from the end of 1986 to the end of 1992 had retained earnings of $11.00 a share. Per share earnings grew by $2.05 a share, from $1.24 a share at the end of 1986 to $3.29 by the end of 1992. Thus, we can argue that the retained earnings of $11.00 a share produced in 1992 an after-corporate-income-tax return of $2.05, which equates to an 18.6% rate of return.

7

The company's *return on equity is above average.* As we know, Warren considers it a good sign when a business can earn above-average returns on equity. An average return on equity for American corporations for the last thirty years is approximately 12%. The return on equity for Freddie Mac for the last six years looks like this:

This gives Freddie Mac an average return on equity for the last seven years of 22.3%. But more important than averages is the fact that the company has earned con-

Year	R.O.E.
1986	25.9%
1987	25.5%
1988	24.1%
1989	22.8%
1990	19.4%
1991	21.6%
1992	17.4%

sistently high returns on equity, which indicates management is doing an excellent job in allocating retained earnings and expanding the business.

8

Is the company free to adust prices to inflation? Inflation causes housing prices to rise. Increased housing prices mean bigger mortgages. Bigger mortgages mean that Freddie Mac gets a larger pie to cut from, which means increased profits. If you charge 6% to raise $100 million in mortgage money, you make $6 million. If prices double and the $100 million become $200 million and you charge 6%, you make $12 million.

9

Do the operations require large capital expenditures to constantly update the company's plant and equipment? As we discussed earlier, all the benefits of earning tons of money can be offset by a company constantly having to make large capital expenditures to stay competitive.

Freddie Mac is in the business of securitizing pooled mortgages, which requires very little in the way of capital equipment or research and development. It can expand operations at will with nominal plant expansion. Large capital expenditures are not needed to update the company's plant and equipment.

Summary of Data

Since Warren gets positive responses to the above key questions, he concludes that Freddie Mac is a company that he can fit in his *realm of confidence* and that its earnings can be predicted with a fair degree of certainty. But a positive response to these questions *does not* invoke an automatic buy response. Once a company is identified as *one of the kinds of businesses* we want to be in, we still have to calculate whether the market price for the stock will allow a return equal to or better than our other options.

PRICE ANALYSIS

As we have said and will say again, *Identify the company* and then *let the market price determine the buy decision.* We do it this way *because the price you pay determines your rate of return.*

Initial Rate of Return and Relative Value to Government Bonds

In the case of Freddie Mac, the per share earnings in 1992 were estimated to be $3.29 a share. Divide $3.29 by the long-term interest rate for 1992, which was 7.39%, and you get a relative value of $44.51 a share. In 1992 you could have bought Freddie Mac stock for between $33.80 and $49.30 a share.

In 1992 earnings were $3.29 a share. If you paid what Warren was paying, an average price of $38.68 a share, you would be getting an estimated initial rate of return of 8.5%.

A review of Freddie Mac's per share earnings growth rate for the last eight years indicates that it has been growing at an annual compounding rate of 17.66%. Thus, you can ask yourself this question: What would I rather own—$38.68 worth of a government bond with a static rate of return of 7.39%, or a Freddie Mac equity/bond, with an initial rate of return of 8.5%, that has a coupon that is increasing at an annual compounding rate of 17.66%?

Freddie Mac's Stock As an Equity/Bond

From a return-on-equity standpoint, we can argue that if Freddie Mac can maintain the average annual return on equity it earned over the last six years—22.3%—and over the next ten years it annually retains approximately 72% of that return, then per share equity value should grow from $19.67 a share in 1992 to approximately $87.19 a share by the year 2002.

If per share equity value is $87.19 in the year 2002 and Freddie Mac is still earning a 22.3% return on equity, then Freddie Mac should report per share earnings of $19.44 a share ($87.19 × .223 = $19.44). If Freddie Mac is trading at its historical low P/E of 9, this will equate to a market price of $174.96 a share. If per share earnings are multiplied by the historical high P/E of 12.8, you get a per share market price of $248.83. Add the dividend pool of approximately $30.47 and you get a total pretax return of somewhere between $205.43 and $279.30.

This means that Warren's investment of $38.68 a share in 1992 is projected to produce a pretax annual compounding rate of return of between 18.17 and 21.85%. ($100,000 compounding at annual rate of 21.85% would be worth $721,531 in ten years' time.)

Projecting an Annual Compounding Rate of Return Using the Historical Annual Per Share Earnings Growth Figure

Warren can figure that if per share earnings continue to grow at a rate of 17.66% annually, and if Freddie Mac continues to pay out dividends at a rate of 28% of per share earnings, then the following per share earnings and dividend disbursement picture will develop over the next ten years:

This means Warren can project that in the year 2002 Freddie Mac will have per share earnings of $16.72. If Freddie Mac is trading at the lowest price-to-earnings ratio that it has had since it started actively being traded in 1989—9—then we can calculate that market price for the stock in the year 2002 will be $150.48 ($16.72 × 9 = $150.48).

If it is trading at the highest P/E that it has had since 1989—12.8—then we can calculate that the market price for the stock will be $214.01 in the year 2004.

If you spent $38.68 for a share of Freddie Mac stock in 1992 and in ten years it was worth somewhere between $150.48 and $214.01 a share, then your pretax annual compounding rate of return will be somewhere between 14.55% and 18.65%. You can get these figures by taking out the calculator and punching in $38.68 for the present value, PV; 10 for the number of years, N; and either $150.48 or $214.01 for the future value, FV. Hit the CPT key followed by the interest key, i%, and, presto, your rate of return will appear.

If we add dividends, which total $25.03, our projected pretax return jumps to somewhere between $175.51 and $239.04, which equates to a pretax annual compounding rate of return between 16.32% and 19.97%.

In Summary

In 1992 Warren bought approximately 8,711,100 shares of Freddie Mac common stock at a price of approximately $38.68 a share, for a total purchase price of approximately $337 million. When Warren bought the stock he could argue that he just bought a Freddie Mac equity/bond with a rate of return of 8.5% that would grow at a rate of approximately 17.66% a year. He could also figure that if he held the stock for ten years, his pretax annual compounding rate of return would be between 16.32 and 21.85%.

McDONALD'S CORPORATION, 1996

Warren has long been fascinated with fast food, and he is particularly interested in restaurant chains, like McDonald's, that have taken a generic food like the hamburger and turned it into a brand-name product. During 1996 Berkshire Hathaway purchased 30,156,600 shares of McDonald's at an average cost of $41.95 a share. Let's see why Warren found McDonald's so attractive in 1996.

DOING YOUR DETECTIVE WORK

How the product works is easy. You eat it.

Go over to the library. Check out the *Value Line,* find the listing for McDonald's Corporation, and go next to the *Guide to Business Periodicals* and pull out a list of magazine articles on the company. Call the company (630-623-7428) and ask for an annual report. After you have assembled all of your information, you read on.

1

Does the company have an *identifiable consumer monopoly or brand name products,* or does it produce a commodity-type product? Ever eaten a McDonald's hamburger? In fact, you might be hard pressed to find anybody who hasn't. McDonald's is the world's largest restaurant chain. With over twenty thousand restaurants in more than one hundred countries around the world, Ronald McDonald is a hard guy to get away from. In fact, McDonald's has sold more hamburgers than there are people in the world. Quite a feat.

Yes, McDonald's has an identifiable consumer-monopoly brand-name product. (You should be aware that McDonald's has recently experienced an increase in competition on its home front. Will McDonald's rally the troops and protect its market share in America, or is this its first real setback in its domination of the world market for fast food? Warren already has placed his vote. What do *you* think?)

2

Is the company *conservatively financed?* A check of the long-term debt indicates the company has long-term debts that account for 35% of its capital structure, which is conservative, given its long history of strong earnings.

3

Are the *earnings* of the company *strong* and do they *show an upward trend?* A check of the McDonald's per share earnings indicates that they have been growing at a rate of 13.5% compounded annually for the period of 1986 to 1996, and at a rate of 13.37% for the last five years. Earnings can be considered very consistent, increasing every year for the last ten years.

Year	Earnings
1986	$ .62
1987	.72
1988	.86
1989	.98
1990	1.10
1991	1.18
1992	1.30
1993	1.45
1994	1.68
1995	1.97
1996	2.21

A fast look at the yearly per share earnings chart below indicates they are strong and have an upward trend, which is what we are looking for.

4

The company allocates capital only to those businesses within its *realm of expertise,* which in this case is expansion of its operations.

5

Further investigation indicates that McDonald's has been buying back its shares.

6

The way management has spent the retained earnings of McDonald's appears to have increased the per share earnings and therefore *shareholders' value.*

The company from 1986 to 1996 had retained earnings of

$11.48 a share. Per share earnings grew by $1.59 a share, from $.62 a share at the end of 1986 to $2.21 by the end of 1996. Thus, we can argue that the retained earnings of $11.48 a share produced in 1996 an after-corporate-income-tax return of $1.59 a share, which equates to a rate of return of 13.8%. This indicates that there has been a profitable allocation of retained earnings and, as we can see, a corresponding increase in per share earnings. This has caused a parallel increase in the market price for McDonald's stock, from approximately $10.00 a share in 1986 to approximately $47.00 in 1996.

7

The company's *return on equity is above average.* As we know, Warren considers it a good sign when a business can earn above-average returns on equity. An average return on equity for American corporations for the last thirty years is approximately 12%. The return on equity for the McDonald's Corporation for the last ten years looks like this:

This gives you an average annual rate of return on equity for the last ten years of 18.25%. More important than averages is the fact that the company has earned consistently high returns on equity. This indicates that McDonald's management does an excellent job of profitably allocating retained earnings.

Year	R.O.E.
1986	19.1%
1987	18.8%
1988	18.9%
1989	20.5%
1990	19.2%
1991	17.8%
1992	16.0%
1993	17.3%
1994	17.8%
1995	18.2%
1996	18.0%

8

Is the company free to adjust prices to inflation? This is an easy one, because many of us remember paying fifteen cents for a McDonald's hamburger, which now costs seventy-five cents. So we answer this question with a *yes.* Inflation will not affect the demand for McDonald's products, nor will it stop McDonald's from passing any increase in production costs on to the consumer.

9

McDonald's operations do not require large capital expenditures to constantly update the company's plant and equipment. There really isn't any research and development going on here, and the franchisees are responsible for the costs of building most of the restaurants. Nor does the company have to spend large amounts of money upgrading plant and equipment.

Summary of Data

Since Warren gets positive responses to the above key questions, he concludes that this is a company that he can fit in his realm of confidence and that its earnings can be predicted with a fair degree of certainty.

PRICE ANALYSIS

Initial Rate of Return
and Relative Value to Government Bonds

McDonald's had per share earnings in 1996 of $2.21 a share. Divide $2.21 by the interest rate on long-term government bonds in 1996, approximately 7%, and you get a relative value of $35.71 a share ($2.21 ÷ .07 = $31.57).

During 1996 you could have bought a share of McDonald's stock for as little as $41 a share and for as much as $54 a share. Since 1996 per share earnings were $2.21 a share, if you paid between $41 and $54 a share your initial rate of return would be between 4% and 5.3%. Warren's average cost for Berkshire's shares was $41.95, which equates to an initial rate of return of 5.2%.

A review of McDonald's per share earnings growth rate for the last ten years indicates that it has been growing at an annual compounding rate of 13.5%. So if you were Warren you could have asked yourself this question: What would I rather own—a government bond with a static rate of return of 7% or a McDonald's equity/bond with an initial rate of return of 5.2% that is increasing at an annual rate of 13.5%?

McDonald's Stock As an Equity/Bond

From a return-on-equity standpoint, we can argue that in 1996 McDonald's had a per share equity value of $12.35. If McDonald's can maintain its ten-year average rate of return on equity of 18.25% and retain approximately 84% of that return, with 16% being paid out as a dividend, then McDonald's per share equity value should grow at an annual compounding rate of 15.33% year (84% × 18.25% = 15.33%). If McDonald's per share equity value grows at a rate of 15.33% a year, it will grow to approximately $51.41 a share by Year 10, 2006.

If per share equity value is $51.41 in Year 10, 2006, and McDonald's is still earning an 18.25% return on equity, then McDonald's should report per share earnings of $9.38 a share ($51.41 × 18.25% = $9.38). If McDonald's is trading at the average price-to-earnings ratio that it has for the last ten years, a P/E of 16.7, then we can project that the market price for a share of McDonald's stock in the year 2006 will be $156.64 ($9.38 × 16.7 = $156.64). Add in the dividend pool of approximately $7.50 a share, and our total proceeds from the sale, plus dividends, jump to $164.14 a share. Total proceeds of $164.14 a share equates to a pretax annual compounding rate of return of 14.6%.

This means that if you, like Warren, paid $41.95 a share in 1996 and sold your investment in the year 2006, you could expect a pretax annual compounding rate of return of 14.6%.

Projecting an Annual Compounding Rate of Return Using the Historical Annual Per Share Earning's Growth Figure

Warren can figure that if McDonald's per share earnings were $2.21 in 1996, and if McDonald's per share earnings continue to grow at a rate of 13.5% annually, and if it continues to pay out dividends at a rate of 16% of per share earnings, then the per share earnings and dividend disbursement picture (shown in the chart on page 278) will develop over the next ten years.

This means that we can project that in the year 2006 McDonald's will have per share earnings of $7.81 a share. If McDonald's is trading at its average price-to-earnings ratio that it has for the

Year	Earnings	Dividends
1997	$2.50	$ .40
1998	2.83	.45
1999	3.22	.51
2000	3.65	.58
2001	4.14	.66
2002	4.70	.75
2003	5.34	.85
2004	6.06	.97
2005	6.88	1.10
2006	7.81	1.25
		$7.52

last ten years, a P/E of 16.7, then we can calculate that the market price for a share of McDonald's stock in the year 2006 will be $130.42 ($7.81 × 16.7 = $130.42).

If you spent, like Warren, $41.95 for a share of McDonald's stock in 1996, and in ten years it is worth approximately $130.42 a share, then your pretax annual compounding rate of return would be approximately 12.01%. You can get these figures by getting out the calculator and punching in $41.95 for the present value, PV; 10 for the number of years, N; and $130.42 for the future value, FV. Hit the CPT key followed by the interest key, i%, and, presto, your pretax compounding annual rate of return will appear—12.01%.

If we add in the dividends that McDonald's will have paid out, a total of $7.52, to the $130.42 projected 2006 share price, then our total proceeds from the sale increase to $137.94 a share, which gives us a projected pretax annual compounding rate of return of 12.6%.

In Summary

In 1996 Warren bought 30,156,600 shares of McDonald's Corporation common stock at a price of $41.95 a share, for a total purchase price of approximately $1.265 billion. When Warren bought the stock he could argue that he just bought a McDonald's equity/bond with an initial rate of return of 5.2% that would grow at a rate of approximately 13.5% a year. He could also figure that if he held the stock for ten years, his pretax annual compounding rate of return would be between 12.6% and 14.6%.

45

How Warren Got Started: The Investment Vehicle

Now that you are equipped with some Buffettology, you should be able to bring in an average return of, say, 15 to 25% compounded annually over the long term. This means that if you start with $1 million, in thirty years you will have, max, $807 million. What? No billion dollars! (I thought you said that this was a guide to becoming a billionaire.)

It is. It's just that there is still one trick to the game that you have to learn—in order to become a billionaire you have to get other people to give you their money to invest.

There are several avenues you could take, but since this is essentially a guide to making a billion dollars the Warren way, we will follow his lead and explain how Warren got other people's money to invest.

First of all, you must decide on the investment vehicle you will use. Warren had the choice of many, but the most simple and the most profitable is the limited partnership. That is what he chose when he first started to raise money on his own back in 1957.

I say it is simple because as long as you don't take on more than one hundred investors, you are exempt from SEC rules requiring registration for mutual funds. If you are a mutual fund you have to comply with more regulations than a private in the Marine Corps.

Another advantage of a limited partnership is that you can charge whatever fees you want. With a mutual fund you are limited by federal law.

In 1956, after Warren had apprenticed with Benjamin Graham in New York, he came back to Omaha. The vehicle with which he chose to raise money was the limited partnership. He set up Buffett Associates, Ltd., which had seven limited partners. Warren was the general partner. The limited partners contributed $105,000 in capital.

This is how the certificate of limited partnership looked:

CERTIFICATE OF LIMITED PARTNERSHIP

The undersigned hereby certified that they have this day entered into a limited partnership, and that:

I

The name of the partnership is
BUFFETT ASSOCIATES, LTD.

II

The character of the business to be carried on shall consist of the buying and selling, for the account of the partnership, of stocks, bonds and other securities, commodities and investments.

III

The location of the principal place of business shall be Omaha, Douglas County, Nebraska.

VI

The general partner is:
Warren E. Buffett
   Omaha, Nebraska

The limited partners are:
Charles E. Peterson, Jr.
   Omaha, Nebraska
Elisabeth B. Peterson
   Omaha, Nebraska
Doris B. Wood
   Omaha, Nebraska
Daniel J. Monen, Jr.
   Omaha, Nebraska
William H. Thompson
   Omaha, Nebraska

Alice R. Buffett
   Omaha, Nebraska
hereinafter called collectively the limited partners.

V

The term for which the partnership is to exist begins on May 1, 1956, and ends on April 30, 1976, unless sooner terminated, as provided in the Partnership Agreement or as provided under the laws of Nebraska.

VI

The amount of cash contributed by each limited partner is as follows:

Limited Partners:	Contributed Capital:
Charles E. Peterson, Jr.	$ 5,000.00
Elisabeth B. Peterson	25,000.00
Doris B. Wood	5,000.00
Truman S. Wood	5,000.00
Daniel J. Monen, Jr.	5,000.00
William H. Thompson	25,000.00
Alice R. Buffett	35,000.00

VII

The limited partners have not agreed to make any additional contributions.

VIII

No time has been agreed upon, short of the termination date of the partnership or the withdrawal of a limited partner from the partnership, for a return of the limited partners' contributions.

IX

The share of the profits or other compensation by way of income which each limited partner shall receive by reason of his contribution is as follows: Each limited partner shall be paid interest at the rate of 4% per annum on the balance of his capital account as of December 31 of the immediately preceding year as shown by the Federal Income Tax Return filed by the partnership applicable to said year's business, said interest payments to be charged as expenses of the partnership business. In lieu of a separate computation of interest for the period ending December 31, 1956, each limited partner shall be paid 2% of his original capital contribution, said payments to be charged as expenses of the partnership business for said period. In addition each of the limited partners shall share in the overall net profits of the partnership, that is, the net profits of the partnership from the date of its formation to any given point of time in proportions set opposite their respective names:

Charles E. Peterson, Jr.	1/42
Elisabeth B. Peterson	5/42
Doris B. Wood	1/42
Truman S. Wood	1/42
Daniel J. Monen, Jr.	1/42
William H. Thompson	5/42
Alice R. Buffett	7/42

X

A limited partner has no right to substitute an assignee as contributor in his place.

XI

No right is given the partners to admit additional limited partners.

XII

There is no priority among the limited partners.

XIII

No right is given the remaining partners to continue the partnership business on the death, retirement or insanity of the general partner.

XIV

No right is given a limited partner to demand and receive property other than cash in return for his contribution.

Dated this 1st day of May, 1956.

In the presence of:
(Signatures)
Warren E. Buffett
Charles E. Peterson, Jr.
Elisabeth B. Peterson
Doris B. Wood
Truman S. Wood
Daniel J. Monen, Jr.
William H. Thompson
Alice R. Buffett

That was simple wasn't it?

Warren didn't stop there. Between 1956 and 1962 he set up nine additional limited partnerships to manage the money of various people: Ann Investments, Ltd.; Buffett Fund Ltd.; Buffett-Holland, Ltd.; Buffett-TD, Ltd.; Dacee, Ltd.; Endee, Ltd.; Gaenoff, Ltd.; Mo-Buff Ltd.; and the Underwood Partnership, Ltd.

To keep things sane, in 1962 Warren merged all of these limited partnerships into Buffett Partnership, Ltd. By then he had gathered ninety-eight limited partners and $10.55 million in capital.

The terms of the Buffett Partnership, Ltd., were fairly simple. Warren was to receive 25% of the profits above the 6% the investors could earn in a savings account in any given year. He felt that his investors should not be charged a fee if they did not make at least what they could have earned if they kept their money in a savings account at the local bank. Additionally, he would offset any losses in any given year against profits from a preceding year, something he never had to do because he never had a down year.

An investment limited partnership agreement can be drafted by any attorney familiar with securities and partnership law, and under no condition should you try to put together an investment limited partnership without the help of an attorney. The SEC and state securities registration requirements, although easy to understand and often inexpensive to comply with, are draconian in their penalties for noncompliance. Hire a lawyer to help you! Besides, having a lawyer around will provide a professional environment.

FINDING INVESTORS

Charity begins at home, and home is the first place look for potential investors. Warren started with family and friends, and that is where anyone should start. After you have covered the home turf, you need to start approaching anybody you know, or don't know, who has money. Warren used to throw little investment get-togethers at his house. Susie, his wife, would put on a pot of chicken soup and invite people to hear the wisdom of the young investment genius espousing the wisdom of Benjamin Graham.

After Warren was in business for a few years, he started raising the amount required of potential investors to get into the partnership. Remember, you are limited to one hundred investors, so you want the wealthiest investors in town to be your limited partners and you especially want the people who are making money—like doctors!

Warren was famous for holding court with his doctor friends/investors at a little chicken-dinner place called Rose's Lodge. A plate of fried chicken, a few beers, a couple of words of Grahamian wisdom, and the checkbooks would come dancing out. Several of those early investors are now worth over $100 million. Actually, Laurence Tisch became a limited partner and made some big money after he caught wind of Warren from Howard Newman, who had been Graham's partner at Graham-Newman.

After a while, the investment environment changed and the market became overvalued. Warren, being price motivated, told his partners that things were too high. Instead of trying a different strategy with which he would be uncomfortable, he decided to close out the partnership. Several years later the market corrected itself in manic-depressive fashion by taking a nosedive. So there Warren sat with a pocketful of cash, and suddenly his favorite companies were selling for a fraction of their intrinsic value. Warren started buying.

Now, back in the old days when income taxes were 50% or better for high-income types, it was advantageous to invest through a corporation, which was taxed at a lower rate. The only catch was that you could not own more than 49% of the company or the IRS considered it a personal holding company and would tax you at personal-income-tax rates, which were, yes, 50% or better. (The problem with personal holding companies still exists. So watch out!)

So Warren went out and bought himself 48% of a textile company called Berkshire Hathaway, which he picked on the basis of a Grahamian bargain, which really turned out to be a Grahamian dog. The textile business, though once great, was a commodity business, and Berkshire's mill just couldn't compete. Warren, upon seeing this, did a very smart thing and started buying insurance companies with the working capital of Berkshire. In essence, money that at one time would have been put into new looms was spent buying the National Indemnity Insurance Company.

Why insurance companies? It's not that they are such a great buy. The economics of the business attracted Warren. You see, when you send your check to your insurance company for your car, house, life, and so forth, the insurance company puts that money into a pool of funds. If you crash your car, burn down your house, or die, and you or your spouse files a claim, the insurance company will pay you out of that pool of funds. But that claim may come years from now, and until then the insurance company gets to use your money. It is this pool of funds, known in the insurance business as the *float,* that Warren so coveted.

An insurance company makes money from the pool of funds, or float, by investing it. And what is Warren great at? Investing. In 1996 Berkshire's insurance business had acquired a float of $6.7 billion. This means that in 1996 Warren had the free use of $6.7 billion of other people's money—money that someday would go to pay claims, but till then was free for Warren to invest with.

The key to making a billion dollars in the investment game is to learn how to make an average compounded rate of return of 23% or better, start a limited investment partnership, inspire your investors, and after you get enough money, buy yourself 49% of an insurance company. (P.S. I almost forgot. You have to get your friends to buy the other 2% of the insurance company so you can effectively control 51% of the voting stock of the company, which means you get to control the board of directors, who in turn control the company.)

Sound easy? It was for Warren. And it might be for you, if you let business perspective investing guide the way.

46

Fifty-four Companies to Look At

There are literally thousands of companies that are publicly traded, and to go through all of them searching for that excellent business would be an ominous task. To save you an enormous amount of time, we have provided you with the following list of fifty-four companies that Warren has invested in in the past and that we believe he will continue to keep his eyes on. *Most of the companies listed are being named here for the first time as Buffett companies.*

Keep in mind that on some days the market will be wildly enthusiastic about some of these companies and price them high; on other days the market will be depressed about their prospects and price them low. We are interested in the days the market prices them low.

We have labeled each company either as a consumer monopoly, or as a toll bridge. Remember, a consumer monopoly is an excellent company that has a brand-name-type product like Coca-Cola; a toll bridge is an excellent company that provides services that other businesses *have* to use if they want to do business, for example, an advertising agency. Often there is a real blur between the two.

We have also provided you with the phone numbers of these businesses. You can call them to obtain a free annual report. As we noted earlier, you might also ask for a free 10-K, which is an information and financial document filed with the SEC. It usually contains more detailed information than the annual report. (References to *Value Line* and *S&P* refer to *Value Line Investment Survey* and *Standard and Poor's Stock Reports*.) We have included also the Internet addresses on the World Wide Web for those companies that have them.

Enjoy!

ADVO INC.
Toll Bridge

Advo Inc. is the largest direct-mail marketing company in the nation. You know all that junk mail you receive, trying to sell you something? Well, Advo Inc. probably sent it to you. If you are trying to mass-market anything through the mail today, this is the company you'll probably use. Yes, they even do political campaigns.

Think of this company in the same way you think of advertising firms. That is, if a business wants to advertise nationally or internationally, it has to use one of a handful of international advertising agencies. And if you want to do a major direct-mail campaign, you have to use Advo Inc. It's a kind of toll bridge spanning the waters of commerce. If you want to pitch your product through the mail, you have to either build your own bridge or pay Advo the toll.

Value Line follows it, and you can call the company at 203-285-6100. Remember, a great company is a great company, but the price you pay for the shares will determine your rate of return.

AMERICAN BRANDS
Consumer Monopoly

This company owns Gallaher Tobacco Limited, the market leader in the United Kingdom. They make Benson & Hedges cigarettes. American Brands sold its American tobacco operations in 1994 and said good-bye to all that bad press and possible expense associated with the cancer lawsuits. Cigarette products have great profit margins, which means big bucks. American Brands owns other things as well, but tobacco reaps the bountiful harvest. The tobacco operations are a classic consumer monopoly.

Value Line covers it, and you can get an annual report by calling 203-698-5000.

AMERICAN EXPRESS
Toll Bridge

American Express is a major financial services company that just about does it all. But its strength is travel-industry-related services for businesses, where they are king. Credit cards are a kind of toll bridge in Warren's world. Someone spends money using the American Express card for payment. American Express in turn charges the merchant a fee, and then it charges the card user a fee. Every time there is a transaction, AMEX benefits. A nice place to be.

In the early 1990s AMEX started to have problems; from September 1991 to September 1994, the company lost approximately 2.2 million individual card users and saw its share of the total credit card market drop from 22.5% in 1990 to 16.3% in 1995. This was caused in part by AMEX trying to become a one-stop shop for all your financial needs. In the process of diversifying into different financial products, they lost focus of their credit card operations—the bread and butter of their business. You should keep in mind that wonderful businesses sometimes have managements that, as a result of diversification, end up ignoring the wonderful underlying business that made the company great to begin with. In AMEX's case Harvey Golub rode to the rescue as the company's new CEO and Warren jumped on Golub's wagon and started buying the stock. Remember you invest not only in the company but also in the people that run it. It takes two to tango.

Value Line and *S&P* follow it, and if you call 212-640-2000 you can get an annual report. Internet: http://www.americanexpress.com.

AMERICAN HOME PRODUCTS
Consumer Monopoly

This is another drug company. It is a leading manufacturer of prescription drugs, but also owns some wonderful over-the-counter brand names such as Advil, Anacin, Lodine, and Robitussin. The return on equity for the last ten years has always been over 30%. Per share earnings growth has been at 7.9%. At the right price, it's a great buy worth holding forever. People have a habit of getting sick, and I don't see that changing in the near future.

Value Line follows it, and you can get an annual report by calling 201-660-5000.

AMERICAN SAFETY RAZOR
Consumer Monopoly

This is a competitor to Gillette. It makes dozens of brand-name products and is king of the private-label and value-brand shaving blades. The company is over one hundred years old. It used to belong to Philip Morris and it was taken private in the seventies. It came public again in 1993 and has just started to make acquisitions.

S&P follows it, and you can get an annual report by calling 504-248-8000.

ANHEUSER-BUSCH
Consumer Monopoly

It isn't Coca-Cola, but a lot of people drink beer. Anheuser-Busch is the *world's largest* brewing organization, and America's second-largest producer of baked goods. These people really like yeast. This is what Warren calls a consumer monopoly: you order your beer by brand name.

Value Line follows it, and if you want an annual report, call 314-577-2000.

BHC COMMUNICATIONS
Consumer Monopoly and Toll Bridge

BHC Communications operates eight television stations and is one of the largest broadcasting companies in America in terms of households reached. Its signals reach 20% of the U.S. population. In early 1995 it launched United Paramount Network. At the right price, it's a buy.

Value Line and *S&P* follow this company, and you can get an annual report by dialing 212-421-0200.

BEAR STEARNS
Toll Bridge

This is an investment bank and brokerage house. It raises money for companies and earns transaction fees for being the middleman on security sales. It posted returns on equity of 20% or more in five of the last ten years. In the other five years it posted returns on equity of between 11.3 and 18%. What makes the company interesting is that it occasionally sells at below book value. Since its assets are highly liquid (they can easily be turned into cash), you are essentially buying a company that has great returns for less than its net asset value.

Value Line and *S&P* follow it, and you can get an annual report by calling 212-272-2000.

BRISTOL-MYERS SQUIBB COMPANY
Consumer Monopoly

They sell about $11 billion in drugs and health and beauty products a year. Some of the key brand names are Ban, Bufferin, and Clairol. The company's return on equity for the last ten years has been over 20% a share, and for the last five years it has been over 30% a share. Per share earnings have been growing at an average annual compounding rate of 10% for the last ten years.

Check it out and run the numbers. For an annual report, call 212-546-4000.

CAMPBELL SOUP
Consumer Monopoly

We all know these soups from our growing-up years. But did you know Campbell Soup also owns Franco-American, V8, Swanson, Pepperidge Farm, Vlasic, Mrs. Paul's, Prego (which means "thank you" in Italian), and dozens of other brand names that you might find in your grocery basket?

Value Line follows it, and you can get an annual report by calling 609-342-4800.

CIRCUIT CITY STORES
Toll Bridge

Superstores like Circuit City (and Wal-Mart) are in such a powerful buying position that they can force the manufacturers to lower prices. Computers—which are Circuit City's business—allow for centralized warehousing, and in some cases these stores can actually shift the warehousing onto the manufacturer.

Consumer electronics such as computers have become a commodity item, with all the manufactures competing via price. Circuit City is in a great position. It can offer lower prices because it is a huge buyer. Its return on equity for the last ten years has fluctuated between 15.4 and 25.4%, which is very respectable. Per share earnings have been growing for the last ten years at an annual rate of 23%, which is real nice.

Value Line follows it, and an annual report can be had by calling 804-527-4000.

COCA-COLA CO.
Consumer Monopoly

You know this one by now! At the right price, it is still a buy. Don't miss it when Chicken Little once again dances down Wall Street screaming the sky is falling.

Warren also owns interests in a lot of Coca-Cola bottling companies. Coca-Cola when it was expanding years ago sold rights to use its products. These companies now have *very* lucrative businesses. Check out Coca-Cola Bottling Company Consolidated, Coca-Coca Enterprises, Panamerican Beverages, and Coca-Cola Femsa SA.

Value Line follows Coca-Cola. For an annual report call 404-676-2121.

COCA-COLA BOTTLING COMPANY CONSOLIDATED
Consumer Monopoly

Coca-Cola Bottling Company Consolidated bottles Coca-Cola in eleven states.

S&P follows it, and an annual report can be had by dialing 704-551-4400.

COCA-COLA ENTERPRISES
Consumer Monopoly

This is the world's largest bottler of Coca-Cola. It distributes approximately 55% of all of Coca-Cola's products consumed in the United States.

For an annual report for Coca-Cola Enterprises call 770-989-3796. (P.S. My former brother-in-law, Howard Buffett, now sits on the board of directors of Coca-Cola Enterprises.)

COCA-COLA FEMSA
Consumer Monopoly

Coca-Cola FEMSA is a joint venture between Coca-Cola Company and FEMSA. It produces and markets Coca-Cola in Mexico City and Buenos Aires.

S&P follows it, and an annual report can be yours by dialing (5) 209-09-09.

COX COMMUNICATIONS
Toll Bridge

A major provider of cable TV.

No services follow this company. For an annual report call 404-834-5000.

DEAN WITTER, DISCOVER & CO.
Toll Bridge

This is an investment bank with a retail brokerage and credit card operation. It is what they call a diversified financial services company. This one has $67 billion under management, which makes it as big as most money-center banks. The return on equity has fluctuated between 15.25 and 17.45% for the last five years. Per share earnings have been growing at an annual rate of around 23% for the last four. Please note: This company recently merged with Morgan Stanley Group to form Morgan Stanley, Dean Witter, Discover & Co.

Value Line follows it, and if you want an annual report call 212-392-2000.

THE WALT DISNEY COMPANY
Consumer Monopoly

They own Mickey Mouse and now they own Capital Cities/ABC. Warren always loved this company and has owned stock in it since the sixties. Now he owns even more of the company since the merger, and you can count on him keeping it. Warren doesn't like to sell a good business. The return on equity has been over 20% in six of the last ten years, and between 13.7 and 18.9% for the other four. Per share earnings have been growing at an annual rate of 18.9% for the last ten years.

Value Line and *S&P* follow it, and Mickey will send you an annual report if you call the Magic Kingdom at 818-560-1000.

FEDERAL HOME LOAN MORTGAGE CORPORATION
A Strange Type of Toll Bridge

As noted, Wall Street refers to this fantastic business as Freddie Mac. We have already done a case study on this company. Just remember, if a bank wants to sell your mortgage, these are the people they have to go see. Yes, Warren owns a ton of this stock and would probably buy more whenever the price gets low enough.

Value Line follows it, and an annual report can be had by calling 703-903-2000.

GABELLI EQUITY TRUST

That's right, Warren owns a little of Gabelli Equity Trust. It is managed by one of the great investors of all time—Mario Gabelli. If you own a little of this stock the trust sends you an annual report that lists its investments. In the investment game you can get good ideas from reports like this. Care to find out what Mario is up to? Call 800-422-3554 and ask for an annual report.

GANNETT CORPORATION
Consumer-Monopoly-Type Toll Bridge

These people publish 134 newspapers and *USA Today*. We worked up a case study on this one. Yes, Warren owns a lot of this company.

Value Line follows it, and you can get an annual report by calling 703-284-6000.

GENERAL ELECTRIC
Monopoly Capital

Originally GE had a lockdown on the electrification of the planet. For most people electricity is a fact of life, but a mere hundred years ago it wasn't. One company provided the knowledge and equipment to wire up the planet, and that company was GE. And it made a fortune. Today GE is one of the largest and most diversified industrial giants on earth. With this position it has the financial power to play in any game that is happening.

The return on equity for the last ten years has fluctuated between 16.5 and 23%, which is great. The per share earnings have been growing at an annual compounding rate of 11.6%, which is also electrifying.

Value Line follows it, and an annual report can be had by dialing 203-373-2211.

GILLETTE
Consumer Monopoly

Every day roughly half the population shave its face, and frequently the other half of the population shaves its legs. What products do they use to accomplish this task? Gillette. These people really know how to make money. For the last ten years the return on equity has been consistently above 30%, and in some years more than 40%. Per share earnings over the last ten years have grown at an annual rate of 19%.

Warren loves this company.

Value Line follows it, and an annual report can be had by phoning 617-421-7000.

HERSHEY FOODS
Consumer Monopoly

The largest producer of *chocolate* in America. The majority of the voting stock for the company is held in trust for the benefit of the Milton Hershey School for Orphans. The company's founder, Milton Hershey, in the end left the majority of his wealth to benefit the children who made him rich. What this means to you, the investor, is that there is one very large shareholder—the trust for the orphanage—which can wield an incredible amount of weight.

Value Line follows it, and you can get an annual report by calling 717-534-6799.

INTERNATIONAL FLAVORS & FRAGRANCES
Toll Bridge and Consumer Monopoly

This company creates and manufactures flavors and fragrances that are found in perfumes, soaps, cosmetics, soaps, detergents, prepared foods, beverages, dairy foods, pharmaceuticals, confectionery, and tobacco. Last year it sold about $1.5 billion of its products. These people are in your life in a big way and you didn't even know it.

The financials on this company are superb! The return on equity for the last ten years has been consistently about 16% and more recently above 20%. The per share earnings have been growing at an annual rate of 14% for the last ten years.

Value Line follows it, and an annual report can be had by calling 212-765-5500.

INTERPUBLIC
Toll Bridge

Interpublic is an international advertising agency. Advertising agencies, according to Warren, earn a royalty on the growth of others. When manufacturers want to take their product to market, they have to advertise, so they use an agency. Agencies produce and place ads in the media, and are paid a percentage of what the advertiser spends for these services. Agencies are almost inflationproof. Inflation causes advertisers to spend more for the same amount of work, and the more advertisers spend, the more the agencies make.

Agencies are service businesses, so they spend only modestly on capital equipment, which means that profits don't have to be designated to replace worn-out plants and equipment.

Plus, only 4% of U.S. advertisers change hands every year! This means that despite the public assumption to the contrary, big accounts often do stay in place. Many of the large agencies that dominated the marketplace years ago still dominate the market place today. Seven of the top ten are in their *fifth or sixth generation of management.*

The numbers on Interpublic are great. For the last ten years it has earned an annual return on equity of 15% or better. In the last three years the annual return on equity has been over 20%. Per share earnings for the last ten years have been growing at an annual rate of 13.8%.

Check it out.

Value Line follows the company, and you can get an annual report by calling 212-399-8000.

KNIGHT-RIDDER
Consumer Monopoly

This is a newspaper publishing company. It owns thirty-two daily newspapers in fifteen states. Warren likes newspapers.

S&P follows it, and you can get to read its annual report if you call 305-376-3838.

LEUCADIA NATIONAL
Toll Bridge

This is a property-casualty insurance company that gets above-average returns on equity and could have been bought for below book value from about 1985 to 1992.

S&P follows it and an annual report can be yours by dialing 212-460-1900.

LOEWS CORPORATION
Consumer Monopoly

Laurence Tisch has control of this company, and he has been friends with Warren since the 1960s. Tisch knows how to make money. Loews used to own 23% of CBS, which it sold to Westinghouse for $890 million. The company also owns CNA Financial Corp. and Lorillard Inc., the fourth-largest tobacco producer in the U.S.A..

Value Line and *S&P* follow it, and you can call Tisch at 212-545-2000 and he will send you an annual report.

MBIA INC.
Toll Bridge

This is the insurance company that insures the timely payment of principal and interest on municipal bonds. Municipalities, like your local county, issue municipal bonds to pay for such things as hospitals and airports. If they cover the bonds with insurance from MBIA, they get to pay a lower rate of interest because the investors believe that insured municipal bonds are safer than those that aren't insured.

The company went public in 1987. Its annual return on equity is in the 13% to 15% range for the last five years. Per share earnings for the last five years have been growing at an annual rate of 11.7%.

Value Line follows it, and you can get an annual report by calling 914-273-4545.

McDONALD'S CORP.
Consumer Monopoly

With 9 zillion sold, the majority of the world has probably consumed a few McDonald's hamburgers. Alone, I have probably consumed one thousand of them! Warren loves this company. They have made the hamburger into a brand-name product, not an easy feat.

The company over the last ten years has had a yearly return on equity of between 16 and 20%, which is delicious. And its per share earnings have been growing at an annual rate of 13.4%.

Value Line follows it, and you can call Ronald McDonald for an annual report at 630-623-7428. Internet: http//www.mcdonalds.com.

MEDIA GENERAL INC.
Toll Bridge and Consumer Monopoly

Media General is a major newspaper publisher and owner of TV and cable systems. A group led by that genius of value investing Mario Gabelli has a ton of the stock.

S&P follows it, and you can get an annual report by calling 804-649-6000.

Internet: http//www.mediageneral.com.

MERCURY GENERAL CORP.
Toll Bridge

Mercury is the largest agency writer of passenger auto insurance in California, and in case you don't know, California has a lot of cars. It gets great returns on equity.

S&P follows it, and dialing 213-937-1060 will get you an annual report.

MERRILL LYNCH & COMPANY, INC.
Toll Bridge

A diversified financial services company that has a huge retail brokerage operation working in its favor. Occasionally you can buy it for less than its book value. Check it out.

Value Line follows it, and you can get an annual report by stampeding to the phone and dialing 212-449-1000.

MORGAN STANLEY GROUP
Toll Bridge

Another diversified financial services company that consistently earns above-average returns on equity; this company can sometimes be bought at discount to its book value. (As we already noted, Morgan Stanley Group recently merged with Dean Witter, Discover & Co. to form Morgan Stanley, Dean Witter, Discover & Co. Now you have two reasons to keep an eye on this company.)

Value Line and *S&P* follow it, and you can get an annual report by calling 212-703-4000.

NESTLE SA
Consumer Monopoly

This is a Swiss holding company. Its subsidiaries produce and sell drinks, cereals, powdered milk, culinary products, frozen food, chocolate, ready-to-eat dishes, pet foods, pharmaceuticals, and cosmetics. *Nestle has 494 production facilities in approximately seventy-one countries!*

It is traded in America as an ADR. You can get an annual report by making an international call to 41-21924-2111.

NEW YORK TIMES
Toll Bridge and Consumer Monopoly

This company owns the *New York Times* and the *Boston Globe*. It also owns six network TV stations and two radio stations.

Value Line and *S&P* follow it, and you can get annual report by dialing 212-556-3660.

PANAMERICAN BEVERAGES
Toll Bridge

This Mexican company is the largest bottler of Coca-Cola outside the United States. Its operations are mainly in Mexico, Brazil, and Columbia.

S&P follows it, and you can get an annual report by calling 212-687-8080.

PEPSICO, INC.
Consumer Monopoly

Before Warren started drinking three or four Cherry Coca-Colas a day, he was a Pepsi man. There may be a cola war, but they both charge the same price and very few people complain if they get a Pepsi instead of a Coca-Cola, and vice versa. If Coca-Cola's stock is a little pricey, try Pepsi.

PepsiCo is a fantastic company with an annual return on equity for the last ten years of over 20% and per share earnings growing at an annual rate of 16.9%. If you can't beat them, join them.

Value Line follows it, and you can get an annual report by calling 914-253-2000.

PHILIP MORRIS
Consumer Monopoly Extraordinaire

They manufacture the number-one-selling cigarette in the world, Marlboro, and literally hundreds of brand-name foods that you find every day in your local supermarket.

Value Line covers it, and you can get an annual report by phoning 212-880-5000.

PREMIER INDUSTRIAL CORPORATION
Dozens of Toll Bridges

It distributes and manufactures electronic components, maintenance products, and firefighting products. Returns on equity for the last eight years have been 20% or better.

S&P follows it, and an annual report is yours by dialing 216-391-8300.

PROPERTY CAPITAL TRUST
Liquidation

This is a liquidation. The company decided to liquidate by selling its assets and sending its shareholders the money. Warren paid $4.80 a share in 1993 and over the next six years he could figure that the company will pay out $11.50, which would give him an annual rate of return of 15%.

S&P follows it, and if you call 617-451-2499 you can get an annual report.

PROGRESSIVE CORP.
Consumer Monopoly of Sorts

Progressive is an insurance company that specializes in high-risk insurance. It is a niche player. It has great underwriting margins and its annual return on equity is consistently over 20%, which doesn't happen much in the insurance business. Per share earnings, though somewhat erratic, have grown at an annual rate of 22% over the last ten years.

Value Line covers it and an annual report can be had by dialing 301-986-3000.

RALSTON PURINA GROUP
Consumer Monopoly

Ralston Purina Group is the world's largest producer of dry cat and dog food and dry cell batteries. Talk about things that get eaten or wear out fast. Its annual return on equity for the last five years has been consistently over 40%.

Value Line covers it, and if you call 314-982-2161 you can get an annual report.

SEAGRAM CO.
Consumer Monopoly

If you buy a bottle of imported wine in a restaurant, the chances are good that it was imported by Seagram. The company produces and markets some 225 brands of distilled spirits and some 210 brands of wines and champagnes—all with brand names. It also is a leading producer of branded fruit juices and owns Tropicana Products. Think of it as an adult beverage company. It owns an 80% interest in the entertainment company MCA.

Value Line and *S&P* follow it and you can get an annual report by phoning 514-849-5271.

SUNTRUST BANKS
Owner of a Big Chunk of Coca-Cola

Warren likes this stock, and I suspect it is because it owns several billion dollars' worth of Coca-Cola stock, which it carries on its balance sheet at its initial cost of $110 million. It also earns above-average returns on equity.

S&P follows it, and you can get an annual report by calling 404-588-7711.

THOMSON CORP.
Toll Bridge

Thomson Corp. is in the business of publishing, which includes newspapers. The numbers for this company don't look really good currently, because of the recession in advertising that hurt all the newspaper companies. Just look at the figures for the *New York Times*.

Value Line covers it, and if you want an annual report you can call 416-360-8700.

TIFFANY & CO.
Consumer Monopoly

Tiffany is a jewelry store—*the* jewelry store! It has a consumer monopoly. It has the capacity to earn high returns on equity and recessions offer us a great opportunity to buy in. Face it. It was *the* class act thirty years ago and it still is.

S&P follows it, and an annual report can be yours by calling 212-755-8000.

TIMES MIRROR
Consumer Monopoly and Toll Bridge

This the newspaper company that owns the *Los Angeles Times*. The advertising recession hurt it, but it is capable of earning high return on equity.

Value Line and *S&P* follow it, and you can get an annual report by calling 213-237-3700.

TORCHMARK CORP.
Toll Bridge

This is an insurance and financial services company. It consistently earns a return on equity in excess of 19%. Its per share earnings have been growing at an annual rate of 10.9% for the last ten years. Over the last couple of years there have been occasions to buy it at an attractive price.

Value Line and *S&P* follow it, and you can get an annual report by calling 205-325-4200.

UST INC.
Consumer Monopoly

It makes smokeless tobacco and it makes a ton of money.

Value Line covers it, and you can get an annual report by calling 203-661-1100.

WAL-MART STORES
Toll bridge

Wal-Mart can outbuy the competition, which means it can give its customers a better buy on just about anything. Thus, everybody shops there. More shoppers mean more volume, which means more money. How much money? Wal-Mart's annual return on equity for the last ten years has always been over 20%. Its per share earnings have been growing at an annual rate of 24%. It is, after all, the world's largest retailer.

Value Line follows it, and if you call 501-273-4000 they will send you an annual report.

WARNER-LAMBERT COMPANY
Consumer Monopoly

This is a pharmaceutical, consumer health care, and gums and mints company. It has such brand name products as Listerine, Bromo-Seltzer, Halls cough tablets, Rolaids antacid, Schick, and Wilkinson Sword razors and blades. Its gums and mints division owns Dentyne, Trident, Freshen-up, Bubblicious, Mondo, Cinn-a-Burst, Clorets, and Certs. The return on equity is consistently above 30%, and per share earnings have been growing at an annual rate of 11% for the last ten years.

Value Line and *S&P* follow it, and you can get an annual report by calling 201-540-2000.

WASHINGTON POST
Consumer Monopoly and Toll Bridge

The Washington Post includes the newspaper, *Newsweek* magazine, six TV stations, and fifty-three cable TV systems in fifteen states. Warren has owned this company for a long time.

Value Line and *S&P* follow it, and you can call 202-334-6000 for an annual report.

WELLS FARGO
Toll Bridge

Warren loves this bank. He bought at a cheap price, $63 a share, and it has since traded at over $250 a share. It may never be cheap again. But if it is, you could be there waiting.

Value Line and *S&P* follow it, and you can have an annual report by dialing 415-396-3606.

47

Waiting for the Perfect Pitch

There are many ways to make and lose money on Wall Street. Some stock is always shooting to the moon, and around every corner one of the chosen has fallen from grace. As Graham loved to say, quoting Horace, "Many shall be restored that now are fallen and many shall fall that now are in favor." Most people, and that includes investment managers, jump from one strategy to another and in the process lose course and end up clinging to fear and greed as their guide through the turbulent seas of finance.

Warren found religion in Graham. Graham gave Warren the conviction to weather the storms of doubt, which a falling market can foster even among the most courageous of Wall Street warriors. The realization that good things come to those who wait and who know what they are doing may seem a bit biblical, but Warren found that in Graham's philosophy of investing strictly from a business perspective. And Warren has followed that particular strategy with all the zeal of a Muslim on his way to Mecca. During those times in which the strategy offers no opportunities, when it cannot be applied, Warren just kicks back and waits. What do you mean, he waits? That's right, he just sits back and waits. And sure enough, he has never had to wait very long before the market offers up to him a perfect opportunity to practice his particular brand of business perspective investing.

Warren equates his strategy to waiting for the perfect pitch in a ball game in which the only way to strike out is to swing at the ball. Warren stands at bat carefully waiting for the perfect pitch and only on the perfect pitch will he swing his business perspective bat.

Sure enough, after thousands of pitches and sometimes a year or two of waiting for the perfect pitch, a consumer monopoly with excellent management and a fantastic price comes sliding gently across the plate, and Warren slams it into the bleachers. A home run for Warren and another $1 billion for the Berkshire Hathaway team.

Are you that patient? I don't know many people who are. Instead, the money is burning a hole in your pocket and you want that investment opportunity right now. Let's say that you just inherited $1 million. One of the first questions that should come to your mind is, How should this money be invested? But if I told you to sit on it until something comes up at an attractive price, you would look at me like I was crazy. If you phoned a stockbroker, more than likely he would have all kinds of ideas, because if he didn't have a lot of ideas, you would go find one that did.

Fund managers and individual investors all have a difficult time sitting patiently, waiting for the perfect pitch. Sure, they may know what a perfect pitch looks like, but waiting is something you do in an airport. After a while their impatience sends them wandering off, conjuring new images of the perfect pitch. Before they know it they have jettisoned the old and eloped with the newest trend.

If people chose their spouses as they do their stocks, no marriage would last a week. Can you imagine listing all the attributes you would find desirable in a spouse and giving yourself only one week to come up with a candidate you want? You wouldn't do it. And you would tell anybody who suggested it that they were crazy. Yet this is what happens all the time in the investment game. You know this is true because if I gave you $1 million tomorrow you would immediately be out trying to invest it, be it in a certificate of deposit down at the local bank or by a visit to your broker, who would be more than happy to suggest numerous ways for you to profit from his wisdom. Every day you would read in the *Wall Street Journal* about some stock that doubled in the last six months, and you'd be wondering why you were not on that ticket. It takes only one, you know. Got to keep that money working.

But changing investment strategies in midstream is a lot like trying to change careers in midstream. Let's say you are training to be a doctor and after four years of school you read about some lawyer who made $1 million and you decide that lawyers make more money and that you want to be a lawyer. So you drop out of medical school and enroll in law school and after a year or two you discover that MBAs on Wall Street are making a huge amount of money and you decide to become an MBA instead of a lawyer and drop out of law school and enroll in business school. The scenario could go on forever, and the result would be that you would end up with nothing, whereas if you had stayed in medical school, you would now be a doctor making good money. The same applies in the business world. You don't see Ford Motor Company trying to build computers and you don't see IBM trying to build cars. Each has its own way of doing things and each has its own products and each spent years learning its businesses.

Berkshire Hathaway owns two distinctly different businesses that are only a few miles apart and are run by families related to one another. One family runs one of the largest jewelry stores in the United States, Borsheim's, and the other owns the largest furniture store in the country, Nebraska Furniture Mart. Because each business is so specialized, the management of one would be lost trying to run the other, and vice versa. Acquiring the necessary acumen to run the business would be enormously expensive and would probably severely damage both businesses.

The same applies to investment strategies. It takes a long time to learn the subtleties of what you are doing and to be able to distinguish investment situations that are truly opportunities from those that invite folly. Are you a market timer, arbitrage player, day trader, emerging-growth strategist, old-school Grahamian, or new-school Buffettologist? Each strategy has its rules, and jumping from one to another is like constantly repeating the first grade.

Warren so subscribes to this theory of waiting for the perfect pitch that in 1971, when the market was really high, he folded up his investment fund, telling his investors that the strategy he had been using was no longer applicable to the market with which they were dealing. Instead of going forward with another strategy, one he was not comfortable with, he closed up shop and returned the money to his investors.

For two more years the market stayed high and many people made tons of money on what was a wild ride. But Warren just sat there on the sidelines, waiting. Then one day it happened. The market bombed and stocks sank like bricks, and who was waiting at the bottom of that pit of fear but Warren, "loaded for bear." And as he has said, suddenly Wall Street was giving things away, and his business perspective investment strategy told him to start swinging his money bat at what were some unbelievable pitches. Probably the greatest pitch he swung at during this time was the *Washington Post.*

The bottom line of all this is that you must stay with the strategy and not waver from it if you are to stand strong when all the doubting Thomases are shouting "Fire" and jumping ship. It also means that when the whole world is seeing gold under every rock you let sound *business perspective judgment* dictate your buy decision, and not the mad enthusiasm of the crowd.

So, be patient and wait for that screaming buy pitch. It will come. And remember that it is stock market pessimism, not optimism, that throws the most profitable pitches.

EPILOGUE

Well, you made it to the end of the book. Hopefully we have done our job and have given you a new understanding of the history and tools that go into being a Buffettologist.

For those of you that want to know more, we recommend the popular Internet BuffettWatch Web site, which does an excellent job covering all things Buffett and can be found at http://www.BuffettWatch.com on the World Wide Web.

We leave you with this final bit of advice. If you really want to learn business perspective investing, you probably will have to read this book more than once. Business perspective investing is not difficult to learn, but it does take some effort to master—as does any strategy that works. But once mastered, it can be very rewarding.

Good luck in all your investment endeavors.

M.B. & D.C.

INDEX